Eating and Drinking

AN ANTHOLOGY FOR EPICURES

Sit down and feed,
   welcome to our table.
WILLIAM SHAKESPEARE,
      As You Like It

Eating and Drinking

AN ANTHOLOGY FOR EPICURES

Compiled by Peter Hunt

WITH AN INTRODUCTION BY

André L. Simon

Ebury Press

© Rainbird, McLean Ltd 1961
Designed and produced for the Ebury Press
30 Grosvenor Gardens, London SW1
by Rainbird, McLean Ltd, 11 Charlotte Street, London W1
Printed by The Alcuin Press, Welwyn Garden City
Hertfordshire

Contents

COLOUR PLATES

Frontispiece: The Oyster Luncheon by de Troy (1679–1752).
Musée Condé, Chantilly.
The Young Bacchus: Caravaggio *facing page* 32
Back from the Market: Chardin *facing page* 193
The Gourmet: Picasso *facing page* 224

Acknowledgments

The publishers and compiler of this anthology wish to thank the following individuals and firms for permission to quote material from the sources given: Mrs Montagu Allwood, *English Countryside and Gardens* by Montagu C. Allwood; Edward Arnold Ltd, *A Passage to India* by E. M. Forster; Benson & Campbell Thomson Ltd, *Corvette Command* by Nicholas Monsarrat; Peter Black, *The Daily Mail*; The Bodley Head Ltd, *Winnowed Wisdom* by Stephen Leacock, *The Chronicles of Clovis* by "Saki", and one of "Two Prose Fancies" by Richard Le Gallienne, originally in *The Yellow Book*, VIII, January 1896, and reproduced in *The Yellow Book; a Selection*, published by them in 1949; Jonathan Cape Ltd, *Eastern Approaches* by Fitzroy MacLean; Cassell & Co. Ltd, *Kitchen Fugue* by Sheila Kaye-Smith, and *Trumpet Voluntary* by G. B. Stern; Gordon Catling, "No Pie for Me, Please"; Chatto & Windus, *Swann's Way* by Marcel Proust, *Alone* and *Almanac*, both by Norman Douglas, and *Five Months at the Ice Station* by August Courtauld from *Northern Lights* – the official account of the British Arctic Air-Route Expedition, 1930–31; Dr F. T. Cheng and Hutchinson & Co. Ltd, *Musings of a Chinese Gourmet*; Constable & Co. Ltd, *Viniana* by Charles Walter Berry; Cresset Press, *Springtime in Paris* by Elliot Paul; J. M. Dent & Sons Ltd, *Lovely is the Lee* by Robert Gibbings, and J. S. Chartres' translation of *Salammbô* by Gustave Flaubert; Gerald Duckworth & Co. Ltd, *When the Going was Good* by Evelyn Waugh; Duell, Sloane & Pearce Inc., *Artists Say the Silliest Things* by Guy Pène du Bois; Faber & Faber Ltd, *Nuts in the Rookery* by Mathena Blomfield, *Hasta La Vista* by Christopher Morley, and *Notes Towards the Definition of Culture* by T. S. Eliot; Rosita Forbes, *The Secret of the Sahara: Kufara*; M. Maurice Goudeket and Hachette, Paris, *Prisons et Paradis* by Colette; Hamish Hamilton, London, *The Snow Mountain* by Ludwig Bemelmans; Rupert Hart-Davis Ltd, *Trumpets from the Steep* by Diana Cooper, and *The Journal of William Beckford in Portugal and Spain, 1787–8*, edited by Boyd Alexander; Messrs William Heinemann Ltd, *Crazy Like a Fox* by S. J. Perelman, *South* by Ernest Shackleton, and *Venus in the Kitchen* by Pilaf Bey, edited by Norman Douglas; Hodder & Stoughton Ltd, *The Gobi Desert* by Mildred Cable and Francesca French, and *The Ascent of Everest*, based on the original dispatches from Brigadier Sir John Hunt and other members of the Everest Expedition to *The Times*; Hurst & Blackett Ltd, *Memoirs of William Hickey*, Vol. IV, edited by Alfred Spencer; Michael Joseph Ltd, *The Commodore* by C. S. Forester; T. Werner Laurie Ltd, Marjorie Laurie's translation of *Madame Husson's Rose-king* by Guy de Maupassant; Laurie Lee and the Hogarth Press Ltd, *Cider with Rosie*; Liveright, Publishers, N.Y., *Aphrodite* by Pierre Louys; Sir Robert Bruce Lockhart, *Memoirs of a British Agent*; Longmans, Green & Co. Ltd, *Cold Comfort Farm* by Stella Gibbons, *South Latitude* by F. D. Ommanney, *Grave and Gay* by H. Cholmondeley-Pennell; Macmillan & Co. Ltd and Sir Raglan Squire, "Ballade of Soporific Absorption" by Sir John Squire; Macmillan & Co. Ltd, "Sing High! Sing Low!" from *Collected Poems* of Sir Osbert Sitwell, and "Ferdinando and Elvira" from *The Bab Ballads* by Sir W. S. Gilbert; Don Marquis and Faber & Faber Ltd, "subtle wit" from *archy and mehitabel*;

6

ACKNOWLEDGMENTS

Methuen & Co. Ltd, *What the World Showed Me* by Per Høst; Robert J. Misch, "Death of a Gourmet"; John Murray Ltd, *A Pattern of Islands* by Sir Arthur Grimble, *Raggle Taggle* by Walter Starkie, and *Travels among the Great Andes of the Equator* by Edward Whymper; Sir Harold Nicolson and Constable & Co., *Journey to Java*; Oxford University Press, Tolstoy's *War and Peace* translated by Louise and Aylmer Maude; Putnam & Co. Ltd, *Alone* by Admiral Richard Byrd; Executors of the late George Saintsbury, *Notes on a Cellar-Book* by George Saintsbury; The Society of Authors and the Literary Trustees of Walter de la Mare, "Buttons"; Nancy Spain, "In Defence of Drinking"; Walter Starkie and Christy & Moore Ltd, *Don Gypsy*; the Trustees of the Estate of Sir Arthur Conan Doyle and John Murray Ltd, *The Memoirs of Sherlock Holmes* by Sir Arthur Conan Doyle; Univ. of Oklahoma Press, *Tombs, Temples, and Ancient Art* by Joseph Lindon Smith; the Owner of the Copyright and Chatto & Windus, *Grand Babylon Hotel* by Arnold Bennett; the Trustees of Christopher Morley, *Travels in Philadelphia*.

They would also like to thank the Wine and Food Society for the use of articles from their journals, by G. B. Stern, Ernest Oldmeadow, Betty P. Metcalfe, Louis Golding, George Slocombe, Samuel E. Morison, Christopher Dilke, John Dismukes Green, Sir Francis Colchester-Wemyss K.B.E., Baron de Belabre, Frank W. Lane, Martin Armstrong, Rosemary Bazley, Helen Morris, Pierce Synnott, André L. Simon and Ifan Kyrle Fletcher. (The issues in which these articles originally appeared are given in the text.)

Although every effort has been made to trace the owners of copyrights, it may be that their rights have been unwittingly infringed. To them apologies are offered in advance.

Thanks are due to the following, for permission to reproduce pictures: Bodley Head Ltd, for Aubrey Beardsley's illustration from *The Yellow Book*; W. and A. Gilbey Ltd, for two cartoons by Smilby from *The Compleat Imbiber, I*; Kingleo Studios and *What's On* for the Larry cartoon on page 57; the Mansell Collection, for illustrations on pages 164 and 242; George Newnes Ltd, for the Sidney Paget illustration on page 109; the New Yorker Magazine Inc., for the James Thurber cartoon (copyright 1937); *Punch*, for cartoons by Call, Larry, Sillince, Sprod and H. F. Wiles; Mr Ronald Searle; Frederick Warne and Co. Ltd, for two illustrations by L. Leslie Brooke to Edward Lear's *Nonsense Songs*.

The frontispiece and the colour plate opposite page 193 are reproduced from transparencies provided by Giraudon, Paris; that opposite page 32 by Scala, Milan; and that opposite page 224 by the National Gallery of Art, Washington.

NOTES ON ILLUSTRATIONS

The illustrations on pages 13, 21, 45, 70, 73, 119, 135, 143, 154, 169, 219, 245, 279 and 319 are reproduced from Bertall's illustrations to *Physiologie du Goût* by Brillat-Savarin, 1850 (?); on pages 27, 201, 205 and 211 by John Leech, from R. S. Surtees' *Handley Cross*, Methuen, 1854; on pages 116, 249, 276, by the same artist, from *Pictures of Life and Character from Punch*, 1842–64; on page 29, by George Cruickshank, from his pamphlet *The Glass and the New Crystal Palace*, 1853; on pages 48, 54, 60 and 64 from *Facts about Port* by Henry Vizetelly, 1880; on pages 87 (detail) and 223 by George du Maurier, *Punch*, 1879, 1881; on pages 157 and 179 from *Bibliographie Gastronomique*, 1890; on page 77 from Caxton's edition of Chaucer's *Canterbury Tales*, late 15th century; on page 107, by Phiz, from Dickens' *David Copperfield*, 1849; on pages 90, 112, and 266 by Dickie Doyle, *Punch*, 1849; on page 98 from *Cris de Paris* by Jean le Clerc, about 1600; on page 214 from Chambers' *Book of Days*, 1863; Edward Lear's illustrations to his limericks are from the original *Book of Nonsense*, 1846.

The design on the binding is based on Dickie Doyle's picture on page 90.

Preface

It seems a pity that the lover of wine and good food should have to read so many books to find descriptions of the objects of his devotions. I have attempted, therefore, to bring together some of the best of these descriptions of wine and food, of meals and their consumption. I have cast my net as widely as possible in time and place and although some of the passages I have quoted are well known, there are others, I hope, which will come fresh to many readers.

Compiling an anthology can be a pleasant occupation. For months all one's major reading seems to centre around the chosen subject, and even when reading for other purposes one marks possible passages for inclusion. Soon the library shelves begin to present a somewhat odd appearance, for scores, then perhaps two or three hundred of the books sprout slips of paper.

When I first started to collect the material for this anthology, I echoed Spenser's words in *The Faerie Queene*, "Oh what an endless work have I in hand". But soon I found myself digging more and more deeply into the literary references to eating and drinking and found it an absorbing task. A half-remembered passage in a book read long ago would lead to a search, desultory at first, then frantic, until the quotation was run to earth. Books not on my own shelves were sought in the libraries of friends where I found other possible quotations. Books long out of print and difficult to obtain were found for me by the London Library and Kent County Library, to whose Librarians and staff I am very grateful.

My thanks are due also to Major and Mrs Marcel Godfrey for the loan of books and for suggestions, to Mr and Mrs Arthur Hodson for the loan of books and illustration material, to Miss Diana Watson for suggestions (and for typing many of the extracts), to Miss Mary Judge for much help with the typing, and last, but not least, to my wife for various suggestions, particularly in connection with the illustrations.

PETER HUNT

Introduction

Woman in space! Wonderful! She was no cook: she might as well be in orbit, but we cannot afford to let any of our cooks, male or female, go into outer space. We have none to spare. Cooks are the pillars of Gastronomy, the master and the servant – the friends of Gaster-the-Belly; Gastronomy, the hall-mark and the more rewarding achievement of our Western civilization. Sheer self gratification is all that the gluttons and hedonists care for: not so the gastronomes. They are the fortunate people who were granted at birth the use of all their senses and the rarer gift of common sense to use them rightly, all of them, the senses of taste and smell as much as sight and hearing. Some of us, we know, are born blind and others are born deaf; and there are those who are born tone-deaf or colour-blind, and they never can be artists nor singers: likewise those who do not happen to be born with normal senses of taste and smell can never be gastronomes, but this does not mean that they never will be famous. The great Duke of Wellington, for instance, could never tell beef from mutton: he had no taste-buds, in spite of which he certainly did quite well in life; he did miss a great deal, nevertheless, as all must who take no interest in their daily meals. Gastronomes do take an interest, an intelligent and pleasurable interest, in their meals. Food is not just fuel to them, but fun as well. Their senses of taste and smell have been trained by constant practice and they have become highly sensitive, which means that they will readily appreciate and inwardly enjoy the right balance and pleasing harmony of well-cooked food partnered with suitable wines; but, naturally, it also means that they may only too often be made painfully aware of gastronomical heresies or shortcomings which do not offend others, just as anybody with an ear for music winces at a flat note which goes unnoticed by others. Practice makes perfect, and the pianist who is a gastronome as well as a good musician, as Mark Hambourg was and as most pianists are, does not grudge the time he has to spend every day at practice, and still less the time which he spends at table, and not by himself this time.

Gastronomes may be greedy up to a point, but they never are gluttons: they know too well that there never can be any real appreciation where there is excess, and that without self-control the golden rule of moderation in all things has no meaning.

Gastronomes do not make a god of their belly: they make it their servant, a servant well deserving of every consideration, since it is responsible for the "good conduct" of all the inner works upon which their bodily health and good temper depend to such an extent.

In Gastronomy, as in all arts, the amateur can be as good as the professional; and, like all artists, gastronomes can make others share their experiences by recounting in the right manner either pleasurable occasions or lamentable disappointments in the field of Gastronomy A number of gastronomes among gifted writers of all times and many nations have recorded their views on most matters of gastronomic interest, and the selection of their writings which has been assembled in these pages will be enjoyed by all who appreciate good writing as well as good fare and good wine.

ANDRÉ L. SIMON,
President of the Wine and Food Society

HINTS FOR EPICURES

Man is an Epicure

I became aware that I was eating something particularly delicious, soft-boiled eggs embedded in a layer of meat jelly, seasoned with herbs, and discreetly iced. To please Marambot I smacked my lips.

"First-rate, this."

He smiled.

"The two essential ingredients are good jelly, which is not easily procured, and good eggs. How rare they are, really good eggs, with reddish yolks, and the proper flavour. I keep two poultry yards, one for eggs and one for fowls for the table. I have a special method of feeding my layers. I have my own ideas on the subject. In an egg, just as in chicken, beef, mutton or milk, you recover, and you should be able to taste, the extract, the quintessence of all the food that the animal has consumed. How much better people would fare if they paid more attention to that point."

"I see you are an epicure," I laughed.

"I should think so. So is everyone who isn't an idiot. Man is an epicure just as he is an artist, a scholar, a poet. The palate, my dear fellow, is as delicate and susceptible of training as the eye or ear, and equally deserving of respect. To be without a sense of taste is to be deficient in an exquisite faculty, that of appreciating the quality of comestibles, just as a person may lack the faculty of appreciating the quality of a book or a work of art. It is to want a vital sense, one of the elements of human superiority.

"It consigns a man to one of the innumerable categories of cripples, degenerates and fools, of which our race is composed. In a word, it implies an alimentary stupidity, precisely on a footing with mental deficiency. A man who cannot tell a crayfish from a lobster, or a herring, that admirable fish which comprises all the different flavours and essences of the sea, from a mackerel or a whiting, or a William pear from a Duchess, may be compared to a man who cannot distinguish Balzac from Eugène Sue, a Beethoven symphony from a military march by a regimental bandmaster, the Apollo Belvedere from the statue of Général de Blanmont."

GUY DE MAUPASSANT,
Madame Husson's Rose-king

The Reason Why

Those predisposed to epicurism are for the most part of middling height. They are broad-faced and have bright eyes, small forehead, short nose, fleshy lips and rounded chin. The women are plump, chubby, pretty rather than beautiful, with a slight tendency to fulness of figure.

It is under such an exterior that we must look for agreeable guests. They accept all that is offered to them, eat without hurry, and taste with discrimination. They never make any haste to get away from houses where they have been well treated, but stay for the evening, because they know all the games and other after-dinner amusements.

Those, on the contrary, to whom nature has denied an aptitude for the enjoyments of taste, are long-faced, long-nosed, and long-eyed: whatever their stature, they have something lanky about them. They have dark, lanky hair, and are never in good condition. It was one of them who invented trousers.

BRILLAT-SAVARIN,
Gastronomy as a Fine Art (1826)

The Ideal Cuisine

The ideal cuisine should display an individual character; it should offer a menu judiciously chosen from the kitchen-workshops of the most diverse lands and peoples – a menu reflecting the master's alert and fastidious taste.

NORMAN DOUGLAS,
An Almanac

Domestic food is wholesome, though 'tis homely,
And foreign dainties poisonous, though tasteful.

SIR WALTER SCOTT

Sleevice

"*. . . and just as it comes to the boil you add a teaspoonful of salt.*"

Culture and Cuisine

If we take culture seriously, we see that a people does not merely have enough food to eat but a proper and particular *cuisine*: one symptom of the decline of culture in Britain is indifference to the art of preparing food. Culture may even be described simply as "that which makes life worth living".

T. S. ELIOT,
Notes Towards the Definition of Culture

Vegetable Ifs

If Leekes you like, but do their smelle dislike, eat Onyons, and you shall not smell the Leeke. If you of Onyons would the scente expelle, eat Garlicke that shall drowne the Onyon's smell.

Philosophers' Banquet (1633)

Eating and Old Age

A series of strictly exact observations has demonstrated that a succulent, delicate and choice diet delays for a long time and keeps aloof the external appearances of old age. It gives more brilliancy to the eye, more fresh- ness to the skin, more support to the muscles; and as it is certain in physiology that it is the depression of the muscles that causes wrinkles, these formidable enemies of beauty (to which may be added "flabbiness" and "fleshiness"), it is equally true that, all things being equal, those who know how to eat are comparatively ten years younger than those ignor- ant of that science.

BRILLAT-SAVARIN,
Gastronomy as a Fine Art (1826)

The Wholesome Dyet

The wholesome dyet that breeds good sanguine juyce, such as pullets, capons, sucking veal, beef not above three years Old, a draught of morning milk fasting from the cow; grapes, raysons, and figs be good before meat; Rice with Almond Milk, birds of the Field, Feasants and Partridges, and fishes of stony rivers, Hen eggs potcht, and such like.

NICHOLAS BRETON,
Fantasticks, Serving for a Perpetual Prognostication (1626)

Importance of Minding One's Belly

Some people have a foolish way of not minding, or of pretending not to mind, what they eat. For my part, I mind my belly very studiously and very carefully; for I look upon it that he who does not mind his belly will hardly mind anything else.

SAMUEL JOHNSON

In eating, a third of the stomach should be filled with food, a third with drink and the rest left empty.

The Talmud

Tell me what kind of food you eat, and I will tell you what kind of man you are.

BRILLAT-SAVARIN

Nature in the Raw

Raw flesh has only one inconvenience: it sticks to the teeth; otherwise, it is not at all unpleasant to taste. Seasoned with a little salt, it is easily digested, and must be at least as nourishing as any other.

Dining with a captain of Croats in 1815, "Gads," said he, "there's no need of so much fuss in order to have a good dinner! When we are on scout duty and feel hungry, we shoot down the first beast that comes in our way, and cutting out a good thick slice, we sprinkle some salt over it, place it between the saddle and the horse's back, set off at the gallop for a sufficient time, and" (working his jaws like a man eating large mouthfuls) "*gniaw, gniaw, gniaw*, we have a dinner fit for a prince."

Similarly, when sportsmen in Dauphiné go out shooting in September, they are provided with pepper and salt, and if one kills a fig-pecker, he plucks and seasons it, carries it for some time in his cap, and then eats it. They declare that these birds, when so dressed, eat better than if roasted.

BRILLAT-SAVARIN
Gastronomy as a Fine Art (1826)

No one does not eat and drink; but few can appreciate [the nicety of] taste.

CONFUCIUS

There was an Old Person of Sparta,
Who had twenty-five sons and one daughter;
    He fed them on snails,
    And weighed them in scales,
That wonderful Person of Sparta.

EDWARD LEAR

Choosing Wine

Choose your wine after this sort; it must be fragrant and redolent, having a good odour and flavour in the nose; it must sprinkle in the cup when it is drawn or put out of the pot into the cup; it must be cold and pleasant in the mouth; and it must be strong and subtle of substance. And then moderately drunken it doth quicken a man's wits, it doth comfort the heart, it doth scour the liver; specially, if it be white wine, it doth rejoice all the powers of man, and doth nourish them; it doth engender good blood, it doth comfort and doth nourish the brain and all the body, and it resolveth fleume; it engendereth heat, and it is good against heaviness and pensifulness; it is full of agility; wherefore it is medicinable, specially white wine, for it doth mundify and cleanse wounds and sores.

ANDREW BOORDE,
Dyetary (1562)

"It's a naïve domestic Burgundy without any breeding, but I think you'll be amused by its presumption."

(*Drawing by James Thurber;* © *1937, New Yorker Magazine Inc.*)

TO INDULGE OR
NOT TO INDULGE

The Euphoria Remains

I should not be dealing candidly with my reader, if I did not warn him that Pussyfoot scientists call the state of perceived well-being and capability for well-doing, which alcohol induces, "toxic euphoria". Toxic euphoria as a phrase is good; it is even better than "mobled queen"; it is delicious. It brings a fresh pang at the approaching *dys*thanasia of its language which some people (including pretty surely the Pussyfoot scientists themselves) are trying to bring about. But as they use it, it carries a vain and fallacious meaning, fondly if not fraudulently invented. As real men of science (who cannot be too carefully distinguished from "scientists") have pointed out before now alcohol is auto-antidotic, its narcotic quality tending to dispel its other tendency, as Mr Gargery so delicately put it, to "over-stim*i*late". The toxicity, as all bad things unfortunately do not *yet* do, whatever Apocatastasis may bring about (if they want Greek they can have plenty) vanishes; the euphoria, as all good things do, and always will do, remains.

GEORGE SAINTSBURY,
Notes on a Cellar-Book

Part of the secret of success in life is to eat what you like and let the food fight it out inside.

MARK TWAIN

Digestion is the great secret of life.

SYDNEY SMITH

Those persons who suffer from indigestion, or who become drunk, are utterly ignorant of the true principles of eating and drinking.

BRILLAT-SAVARIN

A Visitation Dinner

As the man in black takes every opportunity of introducing me to such company as may serve to indulge my speculative temper, or gratify my curiosity, I was by his influence lately invited to a *visitation* dinner. To understand this term, you must know that it was formerly the custom here for the principal priests to go about the country once a year, and examine upon the spot whether those of subordinate orders did their duty, or were qualified for the task; whether their temples were kept in proper repair, or the laity pleased with their administration . . . .

The thoughts of being introduced into a company of philosophers and learned men (for such I conceived them) gave me no small pleasure. I expected our entertainment would resemble those sentimental banquets so finely described by Xenophon and Plato. I was hoping some Socrates would be brought in from the door, in order to harangue upon divine love; but as for eating and drinking I had prepared myself to be disappointed in that particular. I was apprised that fasting and temperance were tenets strongly recommended to the professors of Christianity; and I had seen the frugality and mortification of the priests of the East; so that I expected an entertainment where we should have much reasoning, and little meat.

Upon being introduced I confess I found no great signs of mortification in the faces or persons of the company. However, I imputed their florid looks to temperance, and their corpulency to a sedentary way of living. I saw several preparations indeed for dinner, but none for philosophy. The company seemed to gaze upon the table with silent expectation; but this I easily excused. Men of wisdom, thought I, are ever slow of speech; they deliver nothing unadvisedly. "Silence," says Confucius, "is a friend that will never betray." They are now probably inventing maxims, or hard sayings, for their mutual instruction, when some one shall think proper to begin.

My curiosity was now wrought up to the highest pitch. I impatiently looked round to see if any were going to interrupt the mighty pause; when, at last, one of the company declared, that there was a sow in his neighbourhood that farrowed fifteen pigs at a litter. This I thought a very preposterous beginning: but just as another was going to second the remark, dinner was served, which interrupted the conversation for that time.

The appearance of dinner, which consisted of a variety of dishes, seemed to diffuse new cheerfulness upon every face; so that I now expected the philosophical conversation to begin, as they improved in good humour. The principal priest, however, opened his mouth, with only observing, that the venison had not been kept enough, though he had given strict orders for having it killed ten days before. "I fear," continued he, "it will be found to want the true heathy flavour: you will find nothing of the original wildness in it." A priest, who sat next him, having smelt it and wiped his nose: "Ah, my good lord," cries he, "you are too modest, it is perfectly fine; everybody knows that nobody understands keeping venison with your lordship." "Ay, and partridges too," interrupted another; "I never find them right anywhere else." His lordship was going to reply, when a third took off the attention of the company, by recommending the pig as inimitable. "I fancy, my lord," continues he, "it has been smothered in its own blood." "If it has been smothered in its blood," cried a facetious member, helping himself, "we'll now smother it in egg sauce." This poignant piece of humour produced a long loud laugh, which the facetious brother observing, and now that he was in luck, willing to second his blow, assured the company he would tell them a good story about that: "As good a story," cries he, bursting into a violent fit of laughter himself, "as ever you heard in your lives. There was a farmer of my parish, who used to sup upon wild ducks and flummery; so this farmer – " "Doctor Marrowfat," cries his lordship, interrupting him, "give me leave to drink your health" – "So being fond of wild ducks and flummery" – "Doctor," adds a gentleman who sat next him, "let me advise to a wing of this turkey" – "So this farmer being fond" – "Hob nob, Doctor, which do you choose, white or red?" – "So being fond of wild ducks and flummery" – "take care of your band, sir, it may dip in the gravey." The doctor, now looking round, found not a single *eye* disposed to listen; wherefore calling for a glass of wine, he gulped down the disappointment and the tale in a bumper.

The conversation now began to be little more than a rhapsody of exclamations; as each had pretty well satisfied his own appetite, he now found sufficient time to press others. "Excellent, the very thing; let me recommend the pig; do but taste the bacon; never eat a better thing in my life; exquisite, delicious." This edifying discourse continued through three courses, which lasted as many hours, till every one of the company was unable to swallow or utter any thing more.

OLIVER GOLDSMITH,
The Citizen of the World

The order of food is from the most substantial to the lightest.

BRILLAT-SAVARIN

The Cause of Drunkenness

Wine, the divine liquor of the grape, finding itself in a golden richly chased cup upon Mahomet's table, after being transported with pride at such an honour, was suddenly assailed by a contrary feeling, and said to itself: "What am I doing? What is it that I am rejoicing at? Cannot I see that I am near to my death, in that I am about to leave my golden dwelling in this cup and enter into the foul and fetid caverns of the human body, to be there transformed from a sweet fragrant nectar to a foul and disgusting fluid?" It cried to heaven demanding vengeance for such injury and that an end might be put to such an insult, so that since that part of the country produced the most beautiful and finest grapes in the whole world these at least should not be turned into wine. Then Jove caused the wine which Mahomet drank to rise in spirit up to the brain, and to infect this to such a degree as to make him mad; and he committed so many follies that when he came to his senses he made a decree that no Asiatic should drink wine; and thus the wine and its fruits were left at liberty.

As soon as the wine has entered into the stomach it commences to swell up and boil over; and then the spirit of that man commences to abandon his body, and rising as though towards the sky it reaches the brain, which causes it to become divided from the body; and so it begins to infect him and to cause him to rave like a madman; and so he perpetrates irreparable crimes, killing his own friends.

LEONARDO DA VINCI

24

Wine a Cause of Melancholy

All black wines, over-hot, compound, strong thick drinks, as Muscadine, Malmsey, Alicant, Rumney, Brownbastard, Metheglen, and the like, of which they have thirty several kinds in Muscovy, all such made drinks are hurtful in this case, to such as are hot, or of a sanguine choleric complexion, young or inclined to head-melancholy. For many times the drinking of wine alone causeth it. Arculanus, *c. 16. in 9. Rhasis,* puts in wine for a great cause, especially if it be immoderately used. Guianerius, *tract. 15. c. 2.* tells a story of two Dutchmen, to whom he gave entertainment in his house, "that in one month's space were both melancholy by drinking of wine, one did nought but sing, the other sigh."

ROBERT BURTON,
The Anatomy of Melancholy (1621)

An Alternative to Eating and Drinking

It is a frequent solemnity still used with us, when friends meet, to go to the alehouse or tavern, they are not sociable otherwise: and if they visit one another's houses, they must both eat and drink. I reprehend it not, moderately used; but to some men nothing can be more offensive; they had better, I speak it with Saint Ambrose, pour so much water in their shoes.

Ibid.

Before Drinking

Drinke first a good large draught of Sallet Oyle, for that will floate vpon the wine which you shall drinke, and suppresse the spirites from ascending into the braine. Also what quantitie soeuer of newe milke you drinke first you may well drinke thrise as much wine after, without daunger of being drunke. But howe sicke you shall bee with this preuention, I will not heere determine, neither woulde I haue set downe this experiment, but openly for the helpe of such modest drinkers as sometimes in companie are drawne, or rather forced to pledge in full bolles such quaffing companions as they would be loth to offend, and will require reason at their hands as they terme it.

SIR HUGH PLAT,
The Jewell House of Art and Nature (1594)

The Bedroom Companion

The wines were chiefly port, sherry and hock; claret and even Burgundy being then designated "poor, thin, washy stuff". A perpetual thirst seemed to come over people, both men and women, as soon as they had tasted their soup; as, from that moment, everybody was taking wine with everybody else till the close of the dinner; and such wine as produced that class of cordiality which frequently wanders into stupefaction. How all this sort of eating and drinking ended was obvious, from the prevalence of gout, and the necessity of everyone making the pill box their constant bedroom companion.

CAPTAIN R. H. GRONOW

Say, then, physicians of each kind,
Who cure the body and the mind.
What harm in drinking can there be,
Since punch and life so well agree?

SAMUEL JOHNSON

Inscribed on a Pint-pot

There are several reasons for drinking
And one has just entered my head;
If a man cannot drink when he's living
How the Hell can he drink when he's dead.
Anon.

26

An Eighteenth-century Cure by Claret

Sir John Royds was indebted to claret for his very unexpected recovery; during the last week of the disease they poured down his throat from three to four bottles of that generous beverage every four-and-twenty hours, and with extraordinary effect.

The Memoirs of William Hickey

The Cure

Let, then, every man who has drunk too deeply from the cup of pleasure, every man who has devoted to work a considerable part of the time due to sleep, every man of wit who feels that he has temporarily become stupid, every man who finds the air damp, the weather unendurable, or time hanging heavy on his hands, every man tormented with some fixed idea which deprives him of the liberty of thinking – let all such people, we say, prescribe to themselves a good pint of chocolate mixed with amber in the proportion of from sixty to seventy grains to the pound, and they will see wonders.

BRILLAT-SAVARIN,
Gastronomy as a Fine Art (1826)

After Drinking Cure for the Heid-ake

Take green Hemlock that is tender, and put it in your Socks, so that it may lie thinly between them and the Soles of your Feet; shift the Herbs once a Day.

THE HON. ROBERT BOYLE,
Medical Experiments (1692–94)

Dealing with the After Effects

Surfeit-water

Take Centaury, Marigold-flowers, Mint, Rosemary, Mugwort, Scordium, Rue, Carduus, Balm, Dragons, St. John's wort, each two handfuls; roots of Angelica, Butter-bur, Piony, Scorzonera, each seven ounces; Calamus Aromaticus, Galingal, Angelica-seeds, Caraways each ten drachms, Ginger six drachms, red Poppy-flowers three handfuls; proof-spirits three gallons; water one gallon and a half; macerate, distil and dulcify with fine Sugar, one pound and a half for use.

Virtues of White Surfeit-water

This water is compounded of cephalic, neurotic, hysteric, alexipharmic, carminative and stomachic ingredients, whose virtues being conjoined and designed to strengthen the most principal organs and viscera, must needs be very effectual against crapula's, indigestions, crudities and rawness at the Stomach, vomiting, and other symptoms thence arising. It is used successfully against cholicks, gripings in the stomach and bowels, flatulencies and vapours, all of which it discusses by its carminative virtue; it attenuates the humours, and helps perspiration, and is therefore good in all epidemical and contagious distempers. It resists putrefaction and expels the malignity from the center to the circumference, which it discharges by a gentle dew upon the surface of the cuticle; and this it effects by the efficiency of the alexipharmic ingredients, wherewith this compound water is well stored.

GEORGE SMITH,
A Compleat Body of Distilling, Explaining the Mysteries of that Science, in most easy and familiar Manner, etc. (1738)

A Hymne to Bacchus

Bacchus, let me drink no more:
Wild are the seas, that want a shore.
When our drinking has no stint,
There is no one pleasure in't.
I have drank up for to please
Thee, that great cup Hercules:
Urge no more; and there shall be
Daffadills g'en up to thee.
ROBERT HERRICK

28

By Any Other Name

When the bill against spirituous liquors was past, the people "at Norwich, Bristol and other places, as well as at London, made themselves merry on the death of madam gin, and some of both sexes got soundly drunk at her funeral, for which the mob made a formal procession, but committed no outrages. Riots were apprehended in the metropolis, so that 'a double guard for some days mounted at Kensington: the guard at St James's and the Horse Guards at Whitehall were reinforced, and a detachment of the Life Guards and Horse Grenadiers paraded Covent Garden, etc.' But there was no disturbance. To evade the Act the brandy shops in High Holborn, St Giles's, Tothill Street, Rosemary Lane, Shore Ditch, the Mint, Kent Street, etc; sold drams under the names of Sangree, Tow-row, Cuckold's Comfort, Parliament Gin, Bob, Make Shift, the Last Shift, the Ladies Delight, the Balk, King Theodore of Corsica, Cholic, and Grape Waters, etc."

The London Magazine, October, 1736

A Surgeon and apothecary in Turnmill Street, and a chemist in Shoreditch were fined 100l. each for retailing spirituous liquors contrary to the Act.

Ibid.

By the first week of January in the next year after the Act past, forty-seven persons were convicted of this offence, of whom twenty-eight paid the fine, the rest had moved off their goods; eleven more were convicted on the 11th of the month, and several afterwards.

Ibid.

A Little Drunkenness Discreetly Used

To unbosom myself frankly and freely to your Grace, I always looked upon Drunkenness to be an unpardonable Crime in a young Fellow, who, without any of the foreign Helps, has Fire enough in his Veins to do Justice to *Coelia* whenever she demands a Tribute from him. In a middle-age Man, I consider the Bottle as only subservient to the nobler Pleasure of Love; and he that would suffer himself to be so far infatuated by it, as to neglect the Pursuit of a more agreeable Game, I think deserves no Quarter from the Ladies. In old Age, indeed, when it is convenient to forget and steal from ourselves, I am of opinion that a little Drunkenness, discreetly used, may as well contribute to our Health of Body as Tranquility of Soul.

SIR GEORGE ETHEREGE,
Letter to the Duke of Buckingham, 12 November, 1688

There was a mad fashion among riotous drinkers about 1792, of eating the wine glass, – biting a piece out, grinding it with the teeth, and actually swallowing; – the enjoyment being to see how an aspirant cut his mouth! I never saw this, but R.L. *has done it*. Mortimer the artist did it, and is said never to have recovered from the consequences.

ROBERT SOUTHEY,
Common-place Book (1849–51)

There was an Old Person of Hurst,
Who drank when he was not athirst;
    When they said, "You'll grow fatter,"
    He answered, "What matter?"
That globular Person of Hurst.

EDWARD LEAR

The Use and Abuse of Coffee

It is beyond doubt that coffee acts upon the functions of the brain as an excitant. Every one who drinks it for the first time is certain to be deprived of part of his sleep; and many never drink it without that excitation, though in general it is modified by use.

Voltaire and Buffon drank a deal of coffee, to which habit some would ascribe the wonderful clearness in everything the former wrote, as well as the harmony and warmth which pervade the style of the latter; several of whose pages on man, on the dog, the tiger, the lion, and the horse, were evidently written in a state of unusual cerebral excitement.

Sleeplessness caused by coffee is not painful. One has the mental perception very clear, and there is no desire for sleep; that is all. There is not the agitated, unhappy feeling which proceeds from other forms of sleeplessness, yet the artificial excitement may in the long run become very hurtful. A man of good constitution can drink two bottles of wine a-day throughout a long lifetime; but he would not stand the same quantity of coffee so long. He would become an idiot, or die of consumption.

In Leicester Square, London, I have seen a man whom the immoderate use of coffee had reduced to the state of a helpless cripple. He no longer suffered any pain, but had become accustomed to the state, and limited himself to five or six glasses a-day.

BRILLAT-SAVARIN,
Gastronomy as a Fine Art (1826)

Patience

Patience has never been a quality of mine. Since it is wiser for me to say it first, I shall admit that my head can easily go into Jesuitical somersaults and with no qualms of conscience whatever, displace justice with logic. The end is certainly greater than the means. Perhaps we bother too much about the latter – think more of the manner of holding the fork than of the food picked up by it. Little men do in any case. They are the grammarians who can halt the flow of a great epic with a quibble about its diction. They mince in perfected steps a little minuet which, besides being meaningless, is going nowhere. American escapists, numbered in legions, have invented a language which can, though shorn of nimbleness and wit, snake through life's most twisted alleys without touching or being touched by them. It must be that their revulsions, affected by their forefathers, have now become natural to them, as natural as the unconscious reflexes of flesh. They need no longer watch out for the dogmatists who will dry them up, for they have already been got by them – really got by them, for instead of being impure men they are very pure mannikins.

It is quite possible that I owe the unreasonable impatience which they arouse in me to my Uncle George. A wine merchant in New York City for a great many years, he was constantly irritated by what he considered the thinness and ignorance of American tastes in wines and food. One of his explosions stands out in my mind above all the others. He had, on his way home, met a man who was delighted that the main course of his dinner that night would consist of fried corn-meal mush. "He was looking forward to it!" my uncle gasped in breathless fury. "He was really and truly, I give you my word, looking forward to it." Of course, one never left my uncle's table in a very comfortable state. One certainly paid a penalty for its pleasures. But when that had passed, bringing the return of ease, memories flowed. A soup or an entrée or a wine stood forth, like any experience for which one has had to pay and paid, in its full glory. It is impossible to say as much for the unpunishing purities of the escapist.

GUY PÈNE DU BOIS,
Artists Say the Silliest Things

Academic Questions

Now, whether it were not best to conform unto the simple diet of our forefathers; whether pure and simple waters were not more healthful than fermented liquors; whether there be not an ample sufficiency with all flesh, in the food of honey, oil, and the several parts of milk; in the variety of grains, pulses, and all sorts of fruit, since either bread or beverage may be made almost of all; whether nations have rightly confined unto several meats; or whether the common food of one country be not more agreeable unto another; how indistinctly all tempers apply unto the same, and how the diet of youth and old age is confounded; were considerations much concerning health, and might prolong our days, but not this discourse.

SIR THOMAS BROWNE,
Urne-Buriall (1658)

Facing: The Young Bacchus by Caravaggio (1573-1610). *Uffizi.*

In Defence of Drinking

What do they know of Heaven, Sir, who only know the stars?
  We, too, can reach these heights, my friend, who sit in public bars,
On gin and on martini, yes, and with lager beer,
  We, too, can wander Heavenwards, our feet in sawdust here.
Add to these, moreover, the bright lights and the song,
  The joy of all the ancient soaks who suddenly feel strong,
Who feel young blood run through their veins, who suddenly feel fine.
  Do not condemn these blessings, Sir, when you condemn our wine.

Some think the world twirls on its stem, because of love, young love.
  But some of us have been through that – and found the going rough.
So whether (lads) we loved and lost, or if we loved and won –
  We still thought all the world was ours when we were twenty-one.
Love warms the cockles of the heart – and that's its great design,
  But so can good old alcohol, God bless its swinging sign,
Since when we've been through everything, from war to What's My Line,
  So think upon these horrors, Sir, ere you condemn our wine.

NANCY SPAIN

Athol Brose

Charm'd with a drink which Highlanders compose,
  A German traveller exclaim'd with glee, –
Potztausend! sare, if dis is Athol Brose,
  How goot dere Athol Boetry must be!

THOMAS HOOD

The Five Reasons

If all be true that I do think,
There are *Five Reasons* we should drink;
Good Wine, a Friend, or being Dry,
Or lest we should be by and by;
Or any other Reason why.

DEAN HENRY ALDRICH

To Live Merrily, and
to Trust to Good Verse

Now is the time for mirth,
    Nor cheek, or tongue be dumbe:
For with the flowrie earth,
    The golden pomp is come.

The golden pomp is come;
    For now each tree do's weare,
Made of her pap and gum
    Rich beads of amber here.

Now raignes the rose, and now
    Th' Arabian dew besmears
My uncontrolled brow,
    And my retorted haires.

Homer, this health to thee,
    In sack of such a kind,
That it wo'd make thee see,
    Though thou wert ne'r so blind.

Next Virgil, Ile call forth,
    To pledge his second health
In wine, whose each cup's worth
    An Indian common-wealth.

A goblet next Ile drink
    To Ovid; and suppose,
Made he the pledge, he'd think
    The world had all one nose.

Then this immensive cup
    Of aromatike wine,
Catullus, I quaffe up
    To that terce muse of thine.

Wild I am now with heat;
    O Bacchus! coole thy raies!
Or frantick I shall eate
    Thy thyrse, and bite the bayes.

34

Round, round, the roof do's run;
   And being ravisht thus,
Come, I will drink a tun
   To my Propertius.

Now, to Tibullus, next
   This flood I drink to thee:
But stay; I see a text,
   That this presents to me.

Behold, Tibullus lies
   Here burnt, whose smal return
Of ashes, scarce suffice
   To fill a little urne.

Trust to good verses then;
   They onely will aspire,
When pyramids, as men,
   Are lost, i' th' funerall fire.

And when all bodies meet
   In Lethe to be drown'd
Then onely numbers sweet
   With endless life are crown'd.

ROBERT HERRICK

Upon drinking in a Bowl

Vulcan contrive me such a cup
   As Nestor us'd of old:
Shew all thy skill to trim it up;
   Damask it round with gold.

Make it so large, that, fill'd with sack
   Up to the swelling brim,
Vast toasts, on the delicious lake,
   Like ships at sea, may swim.

Engrave not battle on his cheek;
   With war I've nought to do:
I'm none of those that took Mastrick,
   Nor Yarmouth Leaguer knew.

Let it no name of planets tell,
    Fixed stars, or constellations:
For I am no Sir Sidrophel,
    Nor none of his relations.

But carve thereon a spreading vine;
    Then add two lovely boys;
Their limbs in amorous folds intwine,
    The type of future joys.

Cupid and Bacchus my saints are;
    May drink and love still reign
With wine I wash away my cares,
    And then to love again.

JOHN WILMOT, EARL OF ROCHESTER

Drinking

The thirsty earth soaks up the rain,
And drinks, and gapes for drink again.
The plants suck in the earth, and are
With constant drinking fresh and fair;
The sea itself – which one would think
Should have but little need of drink –
Drinks ten thousand rivers up,
So filled that they o'er flow the cup.
The busy sun – and one would guess
By's drunken fiery face no less –
Drinks up the sea, and when he's done,
The moon and stars drink up the sun:
They drink and dance by their own light,
They drink and revel all the night.
Nothing in Nature's sober found,
But an eternal health goes round.
Fill up the bowl then, fill it high,
Fill up the glasses there; for why
Should every creature drink but I:
Why, man of morals, tell me why?

ABRAHAM COWLEY

36

Ballade of Soporific Absorption

Ho! Ho! Yes! Yes! it's very all well,
  You may drunk I am think, but I'll tell you I'm not,
I'm as sound as a fiddle and fit as a bell,
  And stable quite ill to see what's what.
  I under *do* stand you surprise a got
When I headed my smear with gooseberry jam:
  And I've swallowed, I grant, a beer of a lot –
But I'm not so think as you drunk I am.

Can I liquor my stand? Why, yes, like hell!
  I care not how many a tossed I've pot,
I shall stralk quite weight and not yutter an ell,
  My feet will not spalter the least little jot:
  If you knownly had own! – well I gave him a dot,
And I said to him "Sergeant, I'll come like a lamb –
  The floor it seems like a storm in a yacht,
But I'm not so think as you drunk I am."

For example to prove it I'll tale you a tell –
  I once knew a fellow named Apricot –
I'm sorry, I just chair over a fell –
  A trifle – this chap, on a very day hot –
  If I hadn't consumed that last whisky of tot! –
As I said now, this fellow called Abraham –
  Ah? One more? Since it's you! Just a do me will spot –
But I'm not so think as you drunk I am.

Envoi

  So, Prince, you suggest I've bolted my shot?
Well, like what you say, and soul your damn!
  I'm an upple litset by the talk you rot –
But I'm not so think as you drunk I am.

SIR J. C. SQUIRE

To Youth

Drink wine, and live here blithefull, while ye may:
The morrowes life too late is, live to-day.

ROBERT HERRICK

37

Trials of a Dyspeptic

"Lunch Sir? Yes-ser, pickled salmon,
Cutlets, Kidneys, Greens, and" – Gammon!
Have you got no wholesome meat, sir?
Flesh or fowl that one can eat, sir?
"Eat, sir? Yes-ser, on the dresser
Pork, sir?" Pork, sir, I detest, sir –
"Lobsters?" Are to me unblest sir –
"Duck and peas?" I can't digest sir –
"Puff, sir?" Stuff sir! "Fish, sir?" Pish sir!
"Sausage?" Sooner eat the dish sir –
"Shrimps, sir? prawns, sir? crawfish? winkle?
Scallops ready in a twinkle?
    Wilks and cockles, crabs to follow!"
    Heav'ns, *nothing* I can swallow! ...
      WAITAR!
     "YES – SAR."
    Bread for twenty –
    I shall starve in midst of plenty!

                  H. CHOLMONDELEY-PENNELL

There was an Old Man of the South,
Who had an immoderate mouth;
    But in swallowing a dish,
    That was quite full of fish,
He was choked, that Old Man of the South.

                  EDWARD LEAR

Spectator ab Extra

As I sat at the Café I said to myself,
  They may talk as they please about what they call pelf,
They may sneer as they like about eating and drinking,
But help it I cannot, I cannot help thinking
    How pleasant it is to have money, heigh-ho!
    How pleasant it is to have money.

I sit at my table *en grand seigneur*,
And when I have done, throw a crust to the poor;
Not only the pleasure itself of good living,
But also the pleasure of now and then giving:
    So pleasant it is to have money, heigh-ho!
    So pleasant it is to have money.

They talk as they please about what they call pelf,
And how one ought never to think of one's self,
How pleasures of thought surpass eating and drinking, –
My pleasure of thought is the pleasure of thinking
    How pleasant it is to have money, heigh-ho!
    How pleasant it is to have money.

Le Dîner

Come along, 'tis the time, ten or more minutes past,
And he who came first had to wait for the last;
The oysters ere this had been in and been out;
Whilst I have been sitting and thinking about
    How pleasant it is to have money, heigh-ho!
    How pleasant it is to have money.

A clear soup with eggs; *voilà tout*; of the fish
The *filets de sole* are a moderate dish
A la Orly, but you're for red mullet, you say:
By the gods of good fare, who can question to-day
    How pleasant it is to have money, heigh-ho!
    How pleasant it is to have money.

39

After oysters, sauterne; then sherry, champagne,
Ere one bottle goes, comes another again;
Fly up, thou bold cork, to the ceiling above,
And tell to our ears in the sound that they love
    How pleasant it is to have money, heigh-ho!
    How pleasant it is to have money.

I've the simplest of palates; absurd it may be,
But I almost could dine on a *poulet-au-riz*,
Fish and soup and omelette and that – but the deuce –
There were to be woodcocks, and not *Charlotte Russe*!
    So pleasant it is to have money, heigh-ho!
    So pleasant it is to have money.

Your Chablis is acid, away with the Hock,
Give me the pure juice of the purple Médoc:
St Peray is exquisite; but if you please,
Some Burgundy just before tasting the cheese.
    So pleasant it is to have money, heigh-ho!
    So pleasant it is to have money.

As for that, pass the bottle, and d – n the expense,
I've seen it observed by a writer of sense,
That the labouring classes could scarce live a day,
If people like us didn't eat, drink, and pay.
    So useful it is to have money, heigh-ho!
    So useful it is to have money.

One ought to be grateful, I quite apprehend,
Having dinner and supper and plenty to spend,
And so suppose now, while the things go away,
By way of a grace we all stand up and say:
    How pleasant it is to have money, heigh-ho!
    How pleasant it is to have money.

ARTHUR HUGH CLOUGH

Moderation in All Things

We now have made in one design
The Utile and Dulce join,
And taught the poor and men of wealth
To reconcile their tastes to health.

Restrain each forward appetite
To dine with prudence and delight,
And, careful all our rules to follow,
To masticate before they swallow.
'Tis thus Hygeia guides our pen
To warn the greedy sons of men
To moderate their wine and meat
And eat to live, not live to eat.

DR WILLIAM KITCHINER,
Apicius Redivivus or The Cook's Oracle (1817)

Plaint of a Perverse Palate

I have dined too long off delicate food:
I am now in far too coarse a mood:
Bring me a thick beefsteak *saignant*,
A mountain cheese and an onion,
Garlic soup and a smoking mess
Of fish unknown to *bouillabaisse*!
My palate is perversely off
Dinde truffé, sauce Strogonoff,
Suprême and Mornay and Cardinal,
Dubarry and Hollandaise *et al*,
Give me coarse black bread and boeuf tartare,
I am sick to death of Caviare.

I have drunk too deep of delicate wine
To broach a bottle of Rieselstein,
Hospices de Beaune or Gruaud Larose,
Nuits-St-Georges or any château's
Ancient and throat caressing *cru*:
I thirst for some far stronger brew.
The fierce and brutal joys I seek
Of Planter's rum from Martinique,
Grappa and vodka and arrack,
Eau de vie and applejack.
I am bored with cocktails at the Ritz:
Bring me a bottle of slivovitz.

GEORGE SLOCOMBE,
Wine and Food, 14

Drinking in Wartime

The smell of food the Preobrazhénskis were eating and a sense of hunger recalled him from these reflections; he had to get something to eat before going away. He went to an hotel he had noticed that morning. There he found so many people, among them officers who like himself had come in civilian clothes, that he had difficulty in getting a dinner. Two officers of his own division joined him. The conversation naturally turned on the peace. The officers, his comrades, like most of the army, were dissatisfied with the peace concluded after the battle of Friedland. They said that had we held out a little longer Napoleon would have been done for, as his troops had neither provisions nor ammunition. Nicholas ate and drank (chiefly the latter) in silence. He finished a couple of bottles of wine by himself. The process in his mind went on tormenting him without reaching a conclusion. He feared to give way to his thoughts yet could not get rid of them. Suddenly, on one of the officers saying that it was humiliating to look at the French, Rostov began shouting with un-called-for warmth, and therefore much to the surprise of the officers:

"How can you judge what's best?" he cried, the blood suddenly rushing to his face. "How can you judge the Emperor's actions? What right have we to argue? We cannot comprehend either the Emperor's aims or his actions!"

"But I never said a word about the Emperor!" said the officer, justifying himself, and unable to understand Rostov's outburst except on the supposition that he was drunk.

But Rostov did not listen to him.

"We are not diplomatic officials, we are soldiers and nothing more," he went on. "If we are ordered to die, we must die. If we're punished, it means that we have deserved it, it's not for us to judge. If the Emperor pleases to recognize Bonaparte as Emperor and to conclude an alliance with him, it means that that is the right thing to do. If once we begin judging and arguing about everything, nothing sacred will be left! That way we shall be saying there is no God – nothing!" shouted Nicholas banging the table – very little to the point as it seemed to his listeners, but quite relevantly to the course of his own thoughts.

"Our business is to do our duty, to fight and not to think! That's all . . ." said he.

"And to drink," said one of the officers, not wishing to quarrel.

"Yes, and to drink," assented Nicholas. "Hullo there! Another bottle!" he shouted.

LEO TOLSTOY,
War and Peace

GRAPES AND BOTTLES

Keats on Claret

I like claret . . . For really 'tis so fine – it fills one's mouth with a gushing freshness – then goes down cool and feverless – then you do not feel it quarrelling with your liver – no, it is rather a Peacemaker, and lies as quiet as it did in the grape; then it is as fragrant as the Queen Bee, and the more ethereal part of it mounts into the Brain, not assaulting the cerebral apartments like a bully in a badhouse looking for his trull, and hurrying from door to door bouncing against the wainscot, but rather walks like Aladdin about his enchanted palace so gently that you do not feel his step.

Letter to George and Georgiana Keats in America, 18 February, 1819

The Lucky Hour of Great Wines

I was very well brought up. As convincing proof of such a categorical assertion, let me say that when I was barely three years of age my father, who believed in gentle and progressive methods, gave me a full liqueur glass of a reddish-brown wine sent to him from his native Southern France; the Muscat Wine of Frontignan.

It was like a sun-stroke, or love at first sight, or the sudden realization of a nervous system; this consecration rendered me a worthy disciple of Wine for ever afterwards. A little later, I learnt to quaff my glass of mulled wine, aromatic, with cinnamon and lemon, to a dinner of boiled chestnuts. At the age when one can barely read I was spelling out, drop by drop, red Burgundies, old and light, and dazzling Yquems. Champagne passed in its turn, a murmur of foam, leaping pearls of air, across birthday dinners and first communion festivities: with it came grey

Puisaye truffles. . . . A fine lesson from which I acquired familiar and discreet knowledge of wine, not swallowed greedily, but measured out into narrow glasses, absorbed in mouthfuls with long spaces in between, and carefully reflected upon.

It was between my eleventh and my fifteenth years that this beautiful educational programme was completed. My mother feared that, as I grew older, I should become anaemic. One by one, she unearthed from their dry sand some bottles which were ageing beneath our house in a cellar – it is, thank Heavens! still intact – carved out of the granite itself. Whenever I think about it, I envy the little brat who was so privileged. To accompany my modest provisions on my return to school – a cutlet, the drumstick of a chicken, or one of those hard cheeses that are matured beneath wood-cinders and which one breaks into splinters with a blow from one's fist like a pane of glass – I had Château-Larose, Château-Lafite, Chambertin and Corton which had escaped the Prussians in 1860. Certain of the wines had perished and were pale and smelt faintly of dead roses; they rested in a bed of tannin which dyed the bottles deeply; but most of them kept their fine fire, strength and vigour. What delightful times those were! I drained the cream of the paternal cellar, glass by glass, delicately. . . . My mother recorked the open bottles and contemplated the glory of the French vintages on my colouring cheeks.

How lucky are the children who do not distend their stomachs with great draughts of artificially reddened wine at meals! How well advised are the parents who dole out to their offspring an inch of pure wine – meaning "pure" in the highest sense of the word – and teach them that: "When it is not mealtime, you have the pump, the tap, the springs and filters. Water is for thirst! Wine is, according to its quality and its flavour, a necessary tonic, a luxury or a tribute paid to food."

Is it not also a nourishment? What lovely times those were when the natives of my village in Lower Burgundy would gather around a bottle clad in dust and silky cobwebs and kiss their fingers in the air to it, exclaiming – even before tasting it – "Nectar!" Do you not admit, then, that in telling you about wine here I am speaking about what I know? It is not a little thing to have learnt contempt, at an early age, both for those who drink no wine and those who drink too much.

The Vineyard and Wine are great mysteries. Alone in the vegetable kingdom, the vine gives us a true understanding of the savour of the earth. And how faithfully it is translated! It partakes of, and reveals, all the secrets of the soil. Through it we realize that even flint can be living, yielding, nourishing. Even the unemotional chalk weeps in wine, golden tears. If you transplant a vine to a distant country, it struggles to retain its personality and sometimes triumphs over powerful mineral chemicals.

Gathered near Algiers, the white wines remember perfectly, for many years, the noble Bordeaux scion which sweetened them just sufficiently, softened them and gave them gaiety. It is Madeira that colours and warms the heavy dry wine which ripens at Château-Chalon, on the ridge of a narrow rocky plateau.

From the grapes flourishing on the twisted vine-plant, heavy, of a transparent dull agate colour, or blue and powdered with silver, the eye falls to the bare wood, like a wooden snake, wedged in between two boulders; with what, then, does this southern land feed itself, where there is no rain and which is only kept together by a network of roots? The dews of the night and the sunshine of the day are enough for it – the fire of a star, the life-sweat of another star – marvels.

What single cloudless day, what soft late rainfall decide that a vintage shall be great among the others? Human care can do almost nothing towards it; it is all celestial wizardry, the orbits of planets, sunspots.

Follow with your finger, my fair readers, on the map, beneath the eye of Nectar, the honours-list of the "years". Learn your vintage chronology and the litanies of Saints Estéphe, Julien, Emilion . . . Fashion would have it so. If – still in the name of Fashion – you do not eat enough, at any rate you have lately learnt how to drink. You lack discernment and preference, and in this these charts will help you. It is sweet, merely by uttering the names of our provinces and our towns to sing the praises of the venerated vineyards. It is profitable both to the mind and to the body – believe me – to taste wine in its home, in the country which gave it all it possesses. What surprises has not a carefully thought out pilgrimage in store for you! Young wine, tried in the dim light of the wine-cellar – virgin Angevin wine, uncorked beneath a dusty bower beside a high road on a stormy summer afternoon – or exciting odds and ends discovered in an old cellar which either does not know its wealth or has forgotten it. . . . From such a cellar, in Franche-Comté, I once fled as though I had robbed a museum. . . . Some crazy furniture, sold by auction in a little village square included, between the dressing table, an iron bedstead and some empty bottles, six full bottles; it was there that I made, whilst yet a young girl, the acquaintance of a Prince, fiery, imperious and treacherous as are all great seducers: Jurançon. These six bottles made me more interested in their country of origin than any professor could have done. I admit that at such a price geography lessons are not at everyone's beck and call. And we drank this glorious wine, one day, in the low-ceilinged parlour of an inn, so dark that we never even knew the colour of the wine. Its memory is like that which a lady traveller retains of a nocturnal adventure, of the Unknown whose face she does not see, and who reveals himself only in his kisses.

47

Gastronomic snobbishness has given rise to a collection of Inns, such as never used to be seen. It reverences Wine. Will wisdom be reborn of an ill-enlightened faith, confessed by mouths armour-plated by a hundred cocktails, poisonous aperitifs, withering spirits? Let us hope so. With the dawn of old age I can offer, for my small part, the example of a stomach that has no remorse or damage, a friendly liver and a sensitive palate, preserved by honest wine. Fill then, Nectar, this glass which I hold out to you. A fine and simple wine as you yourself love it, you who know, giving a light bubble in which play the ruddy fires of a great Burgundian ancestor, the topaz of Yquem, the balas ruby, sometimes tinged with mauve, or violet-perfumed Bordeaux. . . .

And may your slim chef of a bronzed cellarer understand me when I clink your dainty glass against a thick-sided goblet; you know well – there comes a time in life when one worships youth – that on a southern shore there is being kept for me a chaplet of wickered demijohns. One vintage fills them, the next finds them empty and fills them in its turn. Do not disdain, you who lay down fine bottles, these short-lived wines; they are clear, dry, varied, they flow evenly from the throat to the paunch and do not tarry on their way. So long as the temperament of the wine be warm, we do not care, down there, if the day be sultry, but drink great draughts of wine which refreshes us and leaves behind it a double taste of muscat and of cedarwood.

COLETTE

A Taste of Sherry

In the town of Sherry there exists a firm of wine merchants that has had a great and noble history. It was in 1730 that the founder, Pedro Domecq, established his *bodegas* in the city and soon became famous all over Europe for his wine.

When in 1928, I was the guest of the late Marques de Almocaden, the head of the house of Domecq, I had the opportunity of looking through the records of the company's history. The names of George IV, Pitt, Fox, Wellington, Napoleon appear in many documents. In the old *bodega* dating back to 1730, dark and grimy with age, are the casks of priceless wine. In one corner I saw some inscribed with the names of Wellington and Napoleon; on another I saw the royal arms of Ferdinand VII of Spain, and near it two casks with the names of Alfonso XIII and Victoria Eugenia, signed by them in chalk. Outside the city lie acre after acre of lands containing the white grape from which the wine is made. The earth, which is white, brittle and full of lime, is cultivated three times a year by workmen with the hoe. On the hills stand large farmhouses where the work is carried on and where stand the pressing troughs.

Round the enormous central hearth in these houses are numerous straw mats, on which the workmen sleep. But when the vintage time comes round there is very little time for sleep, for the people spend most of the night singing *soleares* and dancing *bulerias* and *tangos*. For Jerez is a frontier city also for folk-song and folk-dance. At one moment its singers are sentimental in their *canas* and *soleares*; at another they let themselves go in their *bulerias* and *tangos* when the grape-pressing brings out the spirit of *jaleo*, which the ancient Greeks called ἀλαλη and late moderns "whoopee". No wonder that Jerez de la Frontera was the cradle of the greatest singers of *Cante Flamenco* and *Cante Jondo*. It was the spirit of the wine-troughs that created the peerless Antonio Chacon, Manuel Toree and many other singers famed in the annals of Andalusian folksong.

When a guest arrives in Jerez de la Frontera for the first time he finds that wellnigh every hour of his day and night is taken up. That was my experience with the hospitable firm of Domecq. In the morning I was taken to the famous *bodegas* to taste the various types of ancient sherry. First of all I was given some of the wine over a hundred and fifty years old, which is dark in colour and most fragrant to smell. It is too concentrated for a palate unaccustomed to its age, and gives a slight impression of bitterness. The finest wine of all is about ninety years old. When drinking it the fragrance is so penetrating that it seems to echo down my palate like a resonant note played on a violin string. Another quality of sherry is its cleanness; it never clings to the tongue like other thicker wines. Sherry should never become monotonous, for there are four distinct types. In Spain, what is called *Fino* is popular in clubs, instead of our cocktails. It is pale in colour, and has a light bouquet. One of the authorities told me that if the *Fino* is allowed to get old it will become an *amontillado* wine, which is peerless for fragrance and subtlety. The name *amontillado*, by the way, is derived from Montilla in the province of Cordoba.

I was very interested to hear that Ruskin had connection with the Domecq firm. His father was the agent of the firm in England, and it is said that the wealth thus acquired enabled the celebrated son to take up with ease the career of art and literature. A few years after that first visit to the *bodegas* of Domecq I again came across the name of Ruskin in strange circumstances. During a visit to the United States I stayed as guest of an old lady called Mrs Carl Stockel in Norfolk, Connecticut. It was during the gloomy days of Prohibition, when even the most optimistic European became suspicious when he was offered liquor. My hostess, seeing that I lacked animation, sent her butler off to the cellars to fetch me a bottle of wine. When the bottle came I noticed that it was covered with cobwebs and dust.

"My husband," said the old lady, "liked wine and laid down great cellars, but I have not touched a drop of wine since his death years ago."

I took up the bottle and scraped away the grime and cobwebs. To my amazement I read the magic name Ruskin and the date 1848.

"Give me a golden goblet to drink your health in this wine," said I to the old lady. But she, good soul, would not touch a drop, and so I was left to finish the whole bottle by myself and thank my stars that I had remembered in time the full significance of the label "Ruskin 1848".

WALTER STARKIE,
Don Gypsy

There was an Old Man with an Owl,
Who continued to bother and howl;
    He sate on a rail,
    And imbibed bitter ale,
Which refreshed that Old Man and his Owl.

EDWARD LEAR

A Jug of Wine

Granny Wallon's wines were famous in the village and she spent a large part of her year preparing them. The gathering of the ingredients was the first of the mysteries. At the beginning of April she would go off with her baskets and work round the fields and hedges, and every fine day till the end of summer would find her somewhere out in the valley. One saw her come hobbling home in the evening, bearing her cargoes of crusted flowers, till she had buckets of cowslips, dandelions, elder-blossom crammed into every corner of the house. The elder-flowers, drying on her kitchen floor, seemed to cover it with a rancid carpet, a crumbling rime of grey-green blossom fading fast in a dust of summer. Later the tiny grape-cluster of the elderberry itself would be seething in purple vats, with daisies and orchids thrown in to join it, even strands of the dog-rose bush.

What seasons fermented in Granny Wallon's kitchen, what summers were brought to the boil, with limp flower-heads piled around the floor holding fast to their clotted juices – the sharp spiced honey of those cowslips first, then the coppery reeking dandelion, the bitter poppy's whiff of powder, the cat's breath, death-green elder. Gleanings of days and a dozen pastures, strippings of lanes and hedges – she bore them home to her flag-tiled kitchen, sorted them each from each, built up her fires and loaded her pots, and added her sugar and yeast. The vats boiled daily in suds of sugar, revolving petals in throbbing water, while the air aromatic, steamy, embalmed, distilled the hot dews and flowery soups and ran the wine down the dripping walls.

And not only flower-heads went into these brews; the old lady used parsnips, too, potatoes, sloes, crab-apples, quinces, in fact anything she could lay her hands on. Granny Wallon made wine as though demented, out of anything at all; and no doubt, if given enough sugar and yeast, could have made a drink out of a box of old matches.

She never hurried or hoarded her wines, but led them gently through their natural stages. After the boiling they were allowed to settle and to work in the cool of the vats. For several months, using pieces of toast, she scooped off their yeasty sediments. Then she bottled and labelled each liquor in turn and put them away for a year.

At last one was ready, then came the day of distribution. A squeak and a rattle would shake our window, and we'd see the old lady, wispily grinning, waving a large white jug in her hand.

"Hey there, missus! Try this'n, then. It's the first of my last year's cowslip."

Through the kitchen window she'd fill up our cups and watch us, head cocked, while we drank. The wine in the cups was still and golden, transparent as a pale spring morning. It smelt of ripe grass in some far-away field and its taste was as delicate as air. It seemed so innocent, we would swig away happily and even the youngest guzzled it down. Then a curious rocking would seize the head; tides rose from our feet like a fever, the kitchen walls began to shudder and shift, and we all fell in love with each other.

Very soon we'd be wedged, tight-crammed, in the window, waving our cups for more, while our Mother, bright-eyed, would be mumbling gaily:

"Lord bless you, Granny. Fancy cowsnips and parsney. You must give me the receipt, my dear."

Granny Wallon would empty the jug in our cups, shake out the last drops on the flowers, then trot off tittering down the garden path, leaving us hugging ourselves in the window.

LAURIE LEE,
Cider with Rosie

Mischiefs Attributed to the Introduction of Spanish Wines

Though I am not old in comparison of other ancient men, I can remember Spanish wine rarely to be found in this kingdom. Then hot burning fevers were not known in England, and men lived many more years. But since the Spanish sacks have been common in our taverns, which (for conservation) is mingled with lime in its making, our nation complaineth of calenturas, of the stone, the dropsy, and infinite other diseases, not heard of before this wine came in frequent use, or but very seldom. To confirm which my belief, I have heard one of our learnedest physicians affirm, that he thought there died more persons in England of drinking wine, and using hot spices in their meats and drinks, than of all other diseases. Besides there is no year in which it wasteth not two millions of crowns of our substance, by conveyance into foreign countries; which, in so well a governed commonwealth as ours is acknowledged to be through the whole world, in all other constitutions, in this only remaineth to be looked into and remedied. Doubtless, whosoever should be the author of this reformation, would gain with God an ever-lasting reward, and of his country a statue of gold, for a perpetual memory of so meritorious a work.

SIR RICHARD HAWKINS,
Observations in his Voiage into the South Sea, A.D. 1593 (1622)

The Virtues of Red Wine

When we others arrived at the second camp, we ourselves were in good condition – which was to be expected, as we had ridden most of the way; but in about an hour I found myself lying on my back along with both the Carrels, placed *hors de combat*, and incapable of making the least exertion. We knew that the enemy was upon us, and that we were experiencing our first attack of mountain-sickness.

We were feverish, had intense headaches, and were unable to satisfy our desire for air, except by breathing with open mouths. This naturally parched the throat, and produced a craving for drink, which we were unable to satisfy – partly from the difficulty in obtaining it, and partly from trouble in swallowing it. When we got enough, we could only sip, and not to save our lives could we have taken a quarter of a pint at a draught. Before a mouthful was down, we were obliged to breathe and gasp again, until our throats were as dry as ever. Besides having our normal rate of breathing largely accelerated, we found it impossible to sustain life without every now and then giving spasmodic gulps, just like fishes when taken out of water. Of course there was no inclination to eat; but we wished to smoke, and found that our pipes almost refused to burn, for they, like ourselves, wanted more oxygen.

This condition of affairs lasted all night, and all the next day, and I then managed to pluck up spirit enough to get out some chlorate of potash, which by the advice of Dr W. Marcet, had been brought in case of need. Chlorate of potash was, I believe, first used in mountain travel by Dr Henderson, in the Karakorum range, and it was subsequently employed on Sir Douglas Forsyth's Mission to Yarkund in 1873–4, apparently with good effect. Before my departure, Dr Marcet (with whom I had been in communication) urged me to experiment, with a view of confirming these experiences. Ten grains to a wine glass of water was the proportion he recommended – the dose to be repeated every two or three hours, if necessary. It appeared to me to operate beneficially, though it must be admitted that it was not easy to determine, as one *might* have recovered just as well without taking it at all. At all events, after taking it, the intensity of the symptoms diminished, there were fewer gaspings, and in some degree a feeling of relief.

Louis Carrel also submitted himself to experiment, and seemed to derive benefit; but Jean-Antoine sturdily refused to take any "doctor's stuff", which he regarded as an insult to intelligence. For all human ills, for every complaint, from dysentery to want of air, there was, in his opinion, but one remedy; and that was Wine; most efficacious always if taken hot, more especially if a little spice and sugar were added to it.

The stories that he related respecting the virtues of Red wine would be enough to fill a book. The wine must be Red – "White wine" he used to say dogmatically, "is bad, it cuts the legs." Most of these legends I cannot remember, but there was one which it was impossible to forget, commencing thus. "Red wine when heated and beaten up with raw egg is good for many complaints – particularly at the Eve of St John, when the moon is at the full, for women who are in the family way; provided it is drunk whilst looking over the left shoulder, and" – I never heard the end of that story, because I laughed too soon. EDWARD WHYMPER,
Travels Amongst the Great Andes of the Equator

Wine of Capri

The wine of Capri used to be famed throughout Italy. It has now become a noisome sulphur-and-vinegar compound that will etch the bottom out of a copper cauldron; and although the natives still drink it by the gallon – what older travellers tell us of the sobriety of the Capriotes is hard to believe – yet, in the interests of public health, it would be better if the manufacturers of *vero vino di Capri* were confined to the distillers of the relatively harmless Neapolitan preparation which goes by that name. Montesquieu lodged with the Carthusians on Capri and praises their wine in his journal. This shows that the exigencies of French politeness are not necessarily at variance with truthfulness; no man of the world will sniff at monks' liquor. But the amiable monarch Ferdinand, whom the Capriote Arcucci used to entertain for weeks at his house with "Tears of Tiberius", a self-coined and self-manufactured native wine of noble pedigree, hit upon a more original way of showing gratitude for he hanged his good host in 1799 – hanged him, that is, after the Christian Bourbon fashion, when white-haired patriots and delicately nurtured women and mere lads of sixteen were attached by the neck to tall gibbets, and while one fiend in human shape, called *tira-piedi*, clung to their feet, the executioner climbed up from behind and seated himself firmly, like the Old Man of the Sea, upon their shoulders, where he was swayed to and fro by the victim's convulsions till at last the vertebrae were broken – all this, amid the shrieks of ten thousand ruffians, applauding the wit and wisdom of their lazzarone-king. It is well to bear these things in mind when one hears so much, even at Naples, of the good old times. Murat, the royal *tartarin*, had a finer conception of humanity; instead of murdering his benefactors, he planted French champagne grapes upon the heights beyond Naples, out of which they still extract a drinkable stuff called Asprigno. Try it, when you have the chance.

NORMAN DOUGLAS,
Siren Land

It Couldn't Have Been the Wine

That night Prince Aribert dined with his august nephew in the superb dining-room of the Royal apartments. Hans served, the dishes being brought to the door by other servants. Aribert found his nephew despondent and taciturn. On the previous day, when, after the futile interview with Sampson Levi, Prince Eugen had despairingly threatened to commit suicide, in such a manner as to make it "look like an accident", Aribert had compelled him to give his word of honour not to do so.

"What wine will your Royal Highness take?" asked old Hans in his soothing tones, when the soup was served.

"Sherry," was Prince Eugen's curt order.

"And Romanée-Conti afterwards?" said Hans. Aribert looked up quickly.

"No, not to-night. I'll try Sillery to-night," said Prince Eugen.

"I think I'll have Romanée-Conti, Hans, after all," he said, "It suits me better than champagne."

The famous and unsurpassable Burgundy was served with the roast. Old Hans brought it tenderly in its wicker cradle, inserted the corkscrew with mathematical precision, and drew the cork, which he offered for his master's inspection. Eugen nodded, and told him to put it down. Aribert watched with intense interest. He could not for an instant believe that Hans was not the very soul of fidelity, and yet, despite himself, Racksole's words had caused him a certain uneasiness. At that moment Prince Eugen murmured across the table:

"Aribert, I withdraw my promise. Observe that, I withdraw it."

Aribert shook his head emphatically, without removing his gaze from Hans. The white-haired servant perfunctorily dusted his napkin round the neck of the bottle of Romanée-Conti, and poured out a glass. Aribert trembled from head to foot.

Eugen took up the glass and held it to the light.

"Don't drink it," said Aribert very quietly. "It is poisoned."

"Poisoned!" exclaimed Prince Eugen.

"Poisoned, sire!" exclaimed old Hans, with an air of profound amazement and concern, and he seized the glass. "Impossible, sire, I myself opened the bottle. No one else has touched it, and the cork was perfect."

"I tell you it is poisoned," Aribert repeated.

"Your Highness will pardon an old man," said Hans, "but to say that this wine is poison is to say that I am a murderer. I will prove to you that it is not poisoned. I will drink it."

And he raised the glass to his trembling lips. In that moment Aribert saw that old Hans, at any rate, was not an accomplice of Jules. Springing up from his seat, he knocked the glass from the aged servitor's hands, and the fragments of it fell with a light tinkling crash partly on the table and partly on the floor. The Prince and the servant gazed at one another in a distressing and terrible silence. There was a slight noise, and Aribert looked aside. He saw that Eugen's body had slipped forward limply over the left arm of his chair. The Prince's arms hung straight and lifeless; his eyes were closed; he was unconscious.

"Hans!" murmured Aribert. "Hans! What is this?"

ARNOLD BENNETT,
The Grand Babylon Hotel

The Year of the Comet

He then rang the bell, and having ordered two fresh glasses to be brought, he went out and presently returned with a small pint bottle, which he uncorked with his own hand; then sitting down he said, "The wine that I bring here is port of eighteen hundred and eleven, the year of the comet, the best vintage on record; the wine which we have been drinking," he added, "is good, but not to be compared with this, which

I never sell, and which I am chary of. When you have drunk some of it, I think you will own that I have conferred an obligation upon you", he then filled the glasses, the wine which he poured out diffusing an aroma through the room; then motioning me to drink, he raised his own glass to his lips, saying, "Come, friend, I drink to your success at Horncastle."

GEORGE BORROW,
The Romany Rye (1857)

"For heaven's sake say it's all right this time."

Mistaken Identity

Did you ever taste Imperial Tokay? Your brother gave me some of the best ever tasted, I am told; and what do you think I said?

"Why, this cannot be Tokay!"

"Did you ever taste Tokay before?" said he.

"O yes, very often; but this is not Tokay."

"Be pleased to tell me what it is then," quoth Lestock.

"I don't know; but not Tokay, or a different sort from what I ever tasted, for that was sour and always drunk in green glasses."

Suddenly I recollected that I meant Hock!

MARIA EDGEWORTH,
Letter to Mrs Edgeworth, 2 January, 1841

Comfort for the Heart

Water is not wholesome sole by itself for an Englishman. Good wine moderately drunken doth actuate and doth quicken a man's wits; it doth comfort his heart; it doth scour the liver; it doth engender good blood; it doth comfort and nourish the brain, wherefore it is medicinal.

I myself, which am a physician, cannot away with water, wherefore I do leave all water, and do take myself to good ale, and otherwhile for ale I do take good Gascon wine, but I will not drink strong wines. Mean wines, as wines of Gascony, French wines is good with meats, specially claret wine. All sweet wines and grass wines doth make a man fat.

ANDREW BOORDE,
Dyetary (1562)

Careful Now!

To improve English Brandy, and make it appear like French.

	l.	s.	d.
20 Gallons of fine *English* Brandy, at 4s. and 6d.	04	10	00
2 Ounces of Tinctura Japonica	00	01	00
6 Ounces of spirit of *Nitre Dulcis*, at 4s. *per* Pound	00	01	06
	04	12	06

For sale,

	l.	s.	d.
20 Gallons of Brandy, at 8 or 9s. *per* Gallon	08	10	00

The chief and principal ingredient which operates most in improving *English* Brandy, and giving it the flavour of *French* goods, is the Tinctura Japonica; not made by Chymists after the manner that is fit for that purpose, without particular directions, and a very great charge to them to be just in the composition thereof, and then they not much to be depended on in the Composition of it; therefore I have here inserted the true receipt as it ought to be made for this Intention: And it is to be observed that it must be made so strong, as to make a strong reflection, or to hang upon the glass or phial in which it is put and kept for uses: at the same time you must have 1 pound or 2 pounds of spirit of Nitre Dulcis which is 4s. *per* pound, and mix 2 ounces of Tinctura Japonica with six ounces of spirit Nitre Dulcis, (as directed) very well incorporated together, and put to your Brandy and stirr'd or well romag'd therein, and you may sell it as soon as it is settled.

GEORGE SMITH,
A Compleat Body of Distilling, Explaining the Mysteries of that Science, in most easy and familiar Manner, etc. (1738)

Wine Lover's Odyssey

It is possible that someone, not a hopeless *bo*bolitionist may say, "Mr Saintsbury appears to have spent a great deal of money on mere luxuries." If I meet this "by anticipation" (as some people say when they want to save themselves the trouble of a letter of thanks, having previously tormented others with one of request) it is not out of pusillanimity or a guilty conscience. But I would request readers to observe in the first place that the outlay here implied or acknowledged was spread over rather more than half a century; and secondly, that, as I have more fully explained in the little book itself, I very rarely bought more at a time than a single dozen of each wine named, nay, half a dozen or even odd bottles by way of experiment. In wine, as in books and other things, I have tried to be a (very minor) Ulysses, steering ever from the known to the unknown. Thirdly, for nearly twenty years of the time I was a journalist and in other ways a working man of letters—a state of life to which Thackeray's ejaculation, "Grudge myself good wine? as soon grudge my horse corn", doth more particularly and specially apply; while for full another twenty I occupied a position in which, as one received much hospitality, it was not merely a pleasure, but a duty to show some. But I offer these as explanations, not excuses. There is no money, among that which I have spent since I began to earn my living, of the expenditure of which I am less ashamed, or which gave me better value in return, than the price of the liquids chronicled in this booklet. When they were good they pleased my senses, cheered my spirits, improved my moral and intellectual powers, besides enabling me to confer the same benefits on other people. And whether they were bad or good, the grapes that had yielded them were fruits of that Tree of Knowledge which, as theologians too commonly forget to expound, it became not merely lawful but incumbent on us to use, with discernment, when our First Mother had paid the price for it, and handed it on to us to pay for likewise.

GEORGE SAINTSBURY,
Notes on a Cellar-Book

Imperial Tokay

The Gypsies told me that it was the national hero, Rakoczi, Prince of Transylvania, who gave fame to this golden wine which is known in Hungary as the wine of kings and the king of wines. It is right that we should take our Tokay with the sweets, for it is not a dinner wine like claret or Burgundy. To me it seemed sacrilege to drink the golden liquid while seated at the table. It should be drunk when wandering beneath trees listening to the music; so that the sense of taste should linger like long-drawn double notes vibrated on the violin. In Tokay there is a bouquet that is as subtle to the tongue as Oloroso Sherry and when you have quaffed it the fragrance seems to possess overtones that resound like a note echoing on the piano-strings through all their harmonies. Legends are told of a monastery in Hungary containing a cave where Tokay was stored and such was its reputation that no one was allowed to approach save in Court dress bearing a silver candlestick. It is also said that Pope Pius IV at the Council of Trent was presented with a barrel of the wine by a Bishop as the most priceless gift that could be given, and the Pontiff exclaimed after tasting it – "Summum Pontificem talia vina decent": such wines are fit for his Holiness. I am sure that it was Tokay that Pope Leo X used to drink when Raphael came to tell him stories, and after the hunting expeditions the Papal servants would draw out the golden beakers full of nectar.

Tokay is the wine of Hungary and symbolizes the generosity of the Magyar race. Like the people it is sincere and no artificial doctoring clogs its taste. It is the wine to drink when the Tzigan tunes his fiddle and the dark girl by your side waits for the rhythmic impulse of the csárdás. It is the wine which leads us to the magic *Mulatni* when all the cares of the world fall away from us.

WALTER STARKIE,
Raggle-Taggle

An Occasional Glass of Wine

MR CRANIUM. Pardon me: it is here. – (*As he said these words, he produced a skull from his pocket, and placed it on the table, to the great surprise of the company.*) – This was the skull of Sir Christopher Wren. You observe this protuberance – (*The skull was handed round the table.*)

MR ESCOT. I contend that the original unsophisticated man was by no means constructive. He lived in the open air, under a tree.

THE REVEREND DOCTOR GASTER. The tree of life. Unquestionably. Till he had tasted the forbidden fruit.

MR JENKISON. At which period, probably, the organ of constructiveness was added to his anatomy, as a punishment for his transgression.

MR ESCOT. There could not have been a more severe one, since the propensity which has led him to building cities has proved the greatest curse of his existence.

SQUIRE HEADLONG – (*taking the skull.*) *Memento mori.* Come, a bumper of Burgundy.

MR NIGHTSHADE. A very classical application, Squire Headlong. The Romans were in the practice of adhibiting skulls at their banquets, and sometimes little skeletons of silver, as a silent admonition to the guests to enjoy life while it lasted.

THE REVEREND DOCTOR GASTER. Sound doctrine, Mr Nightshade.

MR ESCOT. I question its soundness. The use of vinous spirit has a tremendous influence in the deterioration of the human race.

MR FOSTER. I fear, indeed, it operates as a considerable check to the progress of the species towards moral and intellectual perfection. Yet many great men have been of opinion that it exalts the imagination, fires the genius, accelerates the flow of ideas, and imparts to dispositions naturally cold and deliberative that enthusiastic sublimation which is the source of greatness and energy. . . .

MR JENKISON. I conceive the use of wine to be always pernicious in excess, but often useful in moderation: it certainly kills some, but it saves the lives of others: I find that an occasional glass, taken with judgment and caution, has a very salutary effect in maintaining that equilibrium of the system, which it is always my aim to preserve. . .

THOMAS LOVE PEACOCK,
Headlong Hall

I think wealth has lost much of its value, if it have not wine.

RALPH WALDO EMERSON

The Right Temperature

The *Pergola* tavern deserves its name, the courtyard being overhung with green vines and swelling clusters of grapes. The host is a canny old boy, up to any joke and any devilry, I should say. He had already taken a fancy to me on my first visit, for I cured his daughter, Vanda, of a raging toothache by the application of glycerine and carbolic acid. We went into his cellar, a dim tunnel excavated out of the soft tufa, from whose darkest and chilliest recesses he drew forth a bottle of excellent wine – it might have lain on a glacier, so cold it was. How thoughtful of Providence to deposit this volcanic stuff within a stone's throw of your dining-table! Nobody need ice his wine at the *Pergola*.

NORMAN DOUGLAS,
Alone

A Magnum of Double-diamond

"David," said brother Ned.

"Sir," replied the butler.

"A magnum of the double-diamond, David, to drink the health of Mr Linkinwater."

Instantly, by a feat of dexterity, which was the admiration of all the company, and had been, annually, for some years past, the apoplectic butler, bringing his left hand from behind the small of his back, produced the bottle with the corkscrew already inserted; uncorked it at a jerk; and placed the magnum and the cork before his master with the dignity of conscious cleverness.

"Ha!" said brother Ned, first examining the cork and afterwards filling his glass, while the old butler looked complacently and amiably on, as if it were all his own property, but the company were quite welcome to make free with it, "this looks well, David."

"It ought to, sir," replied David. "You'd be troubled to find such a glass of wine as is our double-diamond and that Mr Linkinwater knows very well. That was laid down, when Mr Linkinwater first come, that wine was, gentlemen."

"Nay, David, nay," interposed brother Charles.

"I wrote the entry in the cellar-book myself, sir, *if* you please," said David, in the tone of a man quite confident in the strength of his facts. "Mr Linkinwater had only been here twenty year, sir, when that pipe of double-diamond was laid down."

"David is quite right, brother Charles," said Ned: "are the people here, David?"

"Outside the door, sir," replied the butler.

"Show 'em in, David, show 'em in."

At this bidding, the old butler placed before his master a small tray of clean glasses, and opening the door admitted the jolly porters and warehousemen whom Nicholas had seen below. They were four in all. As they came in, bowing and grinning, and blushing, the housekeeper, and cook, and housemaid, brought up the rear.

CHARLES DICKENS,
Nicholas Nickleby

Just Another Bottle

The wine circulated languidly, and Mr Jorrocks in vain tried to get up a conversation on hunting. The Professor always started his stones or Mr Muleygrubs his law, varied by an occasional snore from Mr Slowman, who had to be nudged by Jones every time the bottle went round. Thus they battled on for about an hour.

"Would *you* like any more wine?" at length inquired Mr Muleygrubs, with a motion of rising.

"Not any more I'm obleged to you," replied the obsequious Mr Jacob Jones, who was angling for the chaplaincy of Mr Marmaduke's approaching shrievalty.

"*Just another bottle!*" rejoined Mr Jorrocks encouragingly.

"Take a glass of claret," replied Mr Muleygrubs, handing the jug to our master.

"Rayther not, thank ye," replied Mr Jorrocks, "not the stuff for me. By the way now, I should think," continued Mr Jorrocks, with an air of sudden enlightenment, "that some of those old ancient ancestors o' yours have been fond o' claret."

"Why so?" replied Mr Muleygrubs pertly.

"Doesn't know," replied Mr Jorrocks, musingly, "but I never hears your name mentioned without thinking o' small claret. But come, let's have another bottle o' black strap – *it's good strap* – sound and strong – got wot I calls a good grib o' the gob."

"Well," said Mr Muleygrubs, getting up and ringing the bell, "if you must, you must, but I should think you have had enough."

"PORT WINE!" exclaimed he, with the air of a man with a dozen set out, to his figure footman, as he answered the bell.

ROBERT SMITH SURTEES,
Handley Cross

Rare Vintages and Vin Ordinaire

These are the children of long years of peace,
The high nobility of Earth's increase,
    Superbly useless, set apart.
A symbol and epitome of art.
Not theirs the genial office to assuage
The labourer's thirst, but solely to engage
Sophisticated palates and invite
To feasts of intellectual delight.
In famous vineyards of the white or red
Meticulously tended, pruned and fed,
Gathered and pressed and to the vats conveyed
They wait in comfortable darkness laid
    (Potential riches held in trust)
The gradual fermentation of the must,
Till, in due season grown authentic wine
By process scientific and divine,
Locked in their glassy cells they shall begin
The long novitiate of the Château bin.
Raised to the priesthood each, an anchoret
Cloistered in crystal, lies imprisoned yet,
For not to such as these shall come the call
Till robed and hatted as a Cardinal.
But these are matters more than half divine.

Now let us praise the wine
That quenched the thirst of Chaucer, Rabelais,
Ronsard and Shakespeare, wine of every day
That warms the blood and strengthens talk and cheer
with wholesome draughts born of no boasted year,
Pressed in no vaunted vineyard, with no name
To catch the eye and set the thoughts aflame;
   Of mere generic stock
   Yet potent to unlock
The wagging tongue of Falstaff and entrance
The Spanish Knight of doleful countenance,
   And wash the monstrous drought away
   Of Patriarch Grangousier.
Let none of us contemptuously rebuff
   Wine that was good enough
For men like these, but gladly sit and share
Our honest, rough, refreshing Ordinaire.

MARTIN ARMSTRONG, *Wine and Food*, 36

Ten Little Bottle Boys

Ten little bottle boys
Setting out to dine,
One had a faulty cork,
Then there were nine.

Nine little bottle boys
Looking so sedate,
One had a broken crust,
Then there were eight.

Eight little bottle boys,
Cherubim from Heav'n,
One couldn't stand upright,
Then there were seven.

Seven little bottle boys
Always in a fix,
A Cloete swallowed one,
Then there were six.

Six little bottle boys,
Very much alive,
One decanted all alone,
Then there were five.

Five little bottle boys
Out of half a score,
One caught the weevil bad,
Then there were four.

Four little bottle boys
From the cellar free,
One ullaged by himself,
Then there were three.

Three little bottle boys
Wond'ring what to do,
One enticed the butler,
Then there were two.

Two little bottle boys
When the day was done,
One was taken up to bed,
Then there was one.

One little bottle boy
Standing all alone,
Winked at his Master there,
Then there was none.

CHARLES WALTER BERRY,
Viniana

How He Would Drinke His Wine

Fill me my wine in christall; thus, and thus
I see't in's *puris naturalibus:*
Unmixt. I love to have it smirke and shine,
'Tis sin I know 'tis sin to throtle wine.
What mad-man's he, that when it sparkles so,
Will coole his flames, or quench his fires with snow?

ROBERT HERRICK

66

Welcome to Sack

Where hast thou been so long from my embraces,
Poore pittyed exile? Tell me, did thy graces
Flie discontented hence, and for a time
Did rather choose to blesse another clime?
Or went'st thou to this end the more to move me,
By thy short absence, to desire and love thee?
Why frowns my sweet? Why won't my saint confer
Favours on me, her fierce idolater?
Why are those looks, those looks the which have been
Time-past so fragrant, sickly now drawn in
Like a dull twi-light? Tell me; and the fault
Ile expiate with sulphur, haire, and salt:
And with the christal humour of the spring,
Purge hence the guilt, and kill this quarrelling.
Wo't thou not smile, or tell me what's amisse?
Have I been cold to hug thee, too remisse,
Too tem'prate in embracing? Tell me, ha's desire
To thee-ward dy'd i'th'embers, and no fire
Left in this rak't-up ash-heap, as a mark
To testifie the glowing of a spark?
Have I divorc't thee onely to combine
In hot adult'ry with another wine?
True, I confesse I left thee, and appeale
'Twas done by me, more to confirme my seale,
And double my affection on thee; as doe those,
Whose love growes more enflam'd, by being foes.
But to forsake thee ever, co'd there be
A thought of such like possibilitie?
When thou thy selfe dar'st say, thy iles shall lack
Grapes, before Herrick leaves canarie sack.
Thou mak'st me ayrie, active to be born,
Like Iphyclus, upon the tops of corn.
Thou mak'st me nimble, as the winged howers,
To dance and caper on the heads of flowers,
And ride the sun-beams. Can there be a thing
Under the heavenly Isis, that can bring
More love unto my life, or can present
My genius with a fuller blandishment?

Illustrious idoll! co'd th' Ægyptians seek,
Help from the garlick, onyon, and the leek,
And pay no vowes to thee? who wast their best
God, and far more transcendant then the rest?
Had Cassius, that weak water-drinker, known
Thee in thy vine, or had but tasted one
Small chalice of thy frantick liquor; he
As the wise Cato had approv'd of thee.
Had not Joves son, that brave Tyrinthian swain,
(Invited to the Thesbian banquet) ta'ne
Full goblets of thy gen'rous blood; his spright
Ne'r had kept heat for fifty maids that night.
Come, come and kisse me; love and lust commends
Thee, and thy beauties; kisse, we will be friends
Too strong for fate to break us: look upon
Me, with that full pride of complexion,
As queenes meet queenes; or come thou unto me,
As Cleopatra came to Anthonie;
When her high carriage did at once present
To the Triumvir, love and wonderment.
Swell up my nerves with spirit; let my blood
Run through my veines, like to a hasty flood.
Fill each part full of fire, active to doe
What thy commanding soule shall put it to.
And till I turne apostate to thy love,
Which here I vow to serve, doe not remove
Thy fiers from me; but Apollo's curse
Blast these-like actions, or a thing that's worse;
When these circumstants shall but live to see
The time that I prevaricate from thee.
Call me the sonne of beere, and then confine
Me to the tap, the tost, the turfe; let wine
Ne'r shine upon me; may my numbers all
Run to a sudden death, and funerall.
And last, when thee, deare spouse, I disavow,
Ne'r may prophetique Daphne crown my brow.

ROBERT HERRICK,
The Welcome to Sack

68

Bottle Doggerel

Try counting bottles
Instead of counting sheep,
And the right kind of bottles
Will send you to sleep.

High bottles, low bottles,
Heady have-a-go bottles,
Cannot-say-no bottles,
Row upon row;
Slim-hopped Shandy bottles,
Thin-lipped dandy bottles,
Rip-roaring Brandy bottles,
Every one aglow;
Well-worn Whisky bottles,
Bilious Bay of Biscay bottles,
Russian very risky bottles,
Peppermint or Port:
Wasp-waist loose bottles,
Stiff-necked puce bottles,
Lurid Lemon juice bottles,
Any shape or sort;
Lightly-coloured red bottles,
Slightly swollen-head bottles,
Carry-you-to-bed bottles,
Try them for yourself;
Cloudy bottles, clear bottles,
Greasy, queasy, queer bottles,
Better bitter Beer bottles,
All along the shelf;

Try counting bottles
Instead of counting sheep,
For the right kind of bottles
Will send you to sleep.

ROSEMARY BAZLEY,
Wine and Food, 93

Anacreontick Verse

Brisk methinks I am, and fine,
When I drink my capring wine:
Then to love I do encline,
When I drinke my wanton wine:
And I wish all maidens mine,
When I drinke my sprightly wine:
Well I sup, and well I dine,
When I drinke my frolick wine:
But I languish, lowre, and pine,
When I want my fragrant wine.

ROBERT HERRICK

What's in a Name?

I trow there shall be an honest fellowship, save first shall they of ale have
new backbones. With strong ale brewed in vats and tuns; Ping, Dran-
gollie, and the Draget fine, Mead, Mattebru, and the Metheling. Red
wine, the claret and the white, with Tent and Alicant, in whom I delight.
Wine of Languedoc and of Orleans thereto; Single beer, and other that
is double: Spruce beer, and the beer of Hamburgh: Malmsey, Tires, and
Romany.

Colin Blobol's Testament (fifteenth century)

GENIAL HOSTS,
GRACIOUS GUESTS

How to Eat Peas

When the ducks and green peas came, we looked at each other in dismay;
we had only two-pronged, black handled forks. It is true, the steel was
as bright as silver; but what were we to do? Miss Matty picked up her
peas, one by one, on the point of the prongs, much as Amine ate her
grains of rice after her previous feast with the Ghoul. Miss Pole sighed
over her delicate young peas as she left them on one side of her plate
untasted; for they *would* drop between the prongs. I looked at my host;
the peas were going wholesale into his capacious mouth, shovelled up
by his large round-ended knife. I saw, I imitated, I survived! My friends,
in spite of my precedent, could not muster up courage enough to do an
ungenteel thing; and, if Mr Holbrook had not been so heartily hungry,
he would probably have seen that the good peas went away almost
untouched.

After dinner, a clay pipe was brought in, and a spittoon; and, asking
us to retire to another room, where he would soon join us, if we disliked
tobacco-smoke, he presented his pipe to Miss Matty, and requested her
to fill the bowl. This was a compliment to a lady in his youth; but it was
rather inappropriate to propose it as an honour to Miss Matty, who had
been trained by her sister to hold smoking of every kind in utter abhorrence. But if it was a shock to her refinement, it was also a gratification
to her feelings to be thus selected; so she daintily stuffed the strong
tobacco into the pipe; and then we withdrew.

"It is very pleasant dining with a bachelor", said Miss Matty, softly,
as we settled ourselves in the counting-house, "I only hope it is not
improper; so many pleasant things are!"

ELIZABETH GASKELL,
Cranford

Dining at Length

The exhibition or play lasted for three hours, and then we left the theatre and retired into another room. While we were there the servants were busily employed in re-arranging the theatre, which was now to be converted into a dining-room.

When all was ready we were led in with great ceremony, and placed in the principal seats of honour. We had now an opportunity of seeing the extent to which the Chinese carry their ceremony and politeness amongst themselves when they are about to be seated at table. Our host and his friends were nearly a quarter of an hour before the whole of them were seated. Each one was pressing the most honourable seat upon his neighbour, who, in his turn, could not think of occupying such a distinguished place at the board. However, after a great deal of bowing and flattery, all was apparently arranged satisfactorily and dinner commenced.

The tables were now covered with a profusion of small dishes, which contained all the finest fruits and vegetables of the season, besides many of the most expensive kinds of soups, such as the celebrated bird's-nest and others, many of which were excellent even to the palate of an Englishman. The servants were continually employed in removing the centre dishes and replacing them by others of a different kind, until at last every one seemed perfectly satisfied. Still, however, the ceremony of bringing in new dishes went on, and these were merely looked at and removed. Our maiden efforts with the chop-sticks must have been a source of great amusement to our Chinese friends, but they were polite enough not to laugh at us, and did every thing in their power to assist us. The play was resumed again as soon as the dinner commenced, and continued as briskly as ever. The "lady actors" at intervals came down from the platform and supplied the guests with different kinds of wines. During the entertainment, a piece of money was handed to each of the guests, which they were desired to leave as a present for the actors at the conclusion of the piece. When this was given them, the whole of the *corps dramatique* came round and each made a most polite bow of acknowledgement and withdrew. Still, however, the dinner ceremonial went on; hundreds of fresh dishes were brought in, and as many in their turn removed. The Chinese guests were sometimes smoking, sometimes eating, just as it seemed good to them, and uniformly praising every thing which made its appearance on the table.

We had now been three or four hours at table and although the whole affair had been very amusing, we had had enough of it, and were beginning to tire. "How long shall the dinner last?" said I to a linguist who was placed next me, and who had most politely explained every thing which had occurred during the entertainment. "Oh," said he, "it will last for three or four hours longer, but if you want to go away, you may do so now." We were very glad to find that Chinese etiquette permitted us to withdraw, and ordered our chairs, which were waiting in the court-yard to receive us. Our host and his friends lighted us out with lanterns, and we took our departure in the same style in which we came. So ended my first Chinese dinner. Since then such things have been no rarity, either in the palaces of the rich or in the cottages of the poor, and they have been even more frequent in the temples with the priests.

ROBERT FORTUNE,
Wanderings in China (1847)

Carving, Siberian Style

When dinner was announced, Mr Gryll took in Miss Ilex. Miss Gryll, of course, took the arm of Lord Curryfin. Mr Falconer took in one of the young ladies and placed her on the left hand of the host. The Reverend Doctor Opimian took in another, and was consequently seated between her and Miss Ilex. Mr Falconer was thus as far removed as possible from the young lady of the house, and was consequently, though he struggled as much as possible against it, frequently *distrait*, unconsciously and unwillingly observing Miss Gryll and Lord Curryfin, and making occasional observations very wide of the mark to the fair damsels on his right and left, who set him down in their minds for a very odd young man. The soup and fish were discussed in comparative silence; the entrées not much otherwise; but suddenly a jubilant expression from Mr MacBorrowdale hailed the disclosure of a large sirloin of beef which figured before Mr Gryll.

MR MACBORROWDALE. You are a man of taste, Mr Gryll. That is a handsomer ornament of a dinner-table than clusters of nosegays, and all sorts of uneatable decorations. I detest and abominate the idea of a Siberian dinner, where you just look on fiddle-faddles, while your dinner is behind a screen, and you are served with rations like a pauper.

THE REVEREND DOCTOR OPIMIAN. I quite agree with Mr MacBorrowdale. I like to see my dinner. And herein I rejoice to have Addison on my side; for I remember a paper, in which he objects to having roast beef placed on a sideboard. Even in his day it had been displaced to make way for some incomprehensible French dishes, among which he could find nothing to eat. I do not know what he would have said to its being placed altogether out of sight. Still there is something to be said on the other side. There is hardly one gentleman in twenty who knows how to carve; and as to ladies, though they did know once on a time, they do not now. What can be more pitiable than the right-hand man of the lady of the house, awkward enough in himself, with the dish twisted round to him in the most awkward possible position, digging in unutterable mortification for a joint which he cannot find, and wishing the unanatomisable *volaille* behind a Russian screen with the footmen?

MR MACBORROWDALE. I still like to see the *volaille*. It might be put on table with its joints divided.

MR GRYLL. As that turkey-poult is, Mr MacBorrowdale; which gives my niece no trouble; but the precaution is not necessary with such a right-hand man as Lord Curryfin, who carves to perfection.

MR MACBORROWDALE. Your arrangements are perfect. At the last of these Siberian dinners at which I had the misfortune to be present, I had offered me, for two of my rations, the tail of a mullet and the drum-stick of a fowl. Men who carve behind screens ought to pass a competitive examination before a jury of gastronomers. Men who carve at a table are drilled by degrees into something like tolerable operators by the mere shame of the public process.

MR GRYLL. I will guarantee you against a Siberian dinner, whenever you dine with me.

THE REVEREND DOCTOR OPIMIAN. Mr Gryll is a true conservative in dining.

MR GRYLL. A true conservative, I hope. Not what a *soi-disant* conservative is practically: a man who sails under national colours, hauls them down, and hoists the enemy's. I like old customs, I like a glass of wine with a friend.

THOMAS LOVE PEACOCK,
Gryll Grange

Rule for Carving

Set never on fyshe, flesche, beest, ne fowle, more than two fyngers and a thombe.

WYNKYN DE WORDE,
Boke of Kervyng (1508)

Upon Shewbread

Last night thou didst invite me home to eate;
And shew'st me there much plate, but little meate.
Prithee, when next thou do'st invite, barre state,
And give me meate, or give me else thy plate.

ROBERT HERRICK

Keeping Open House

An householdere, and a gret, was he,
Seynt Julian he was in his countré,
His breed, his ale, was alway after oon;
A bettre envyned man was nowhere noon.
Without bake mete was never his hous,
Of fleissch and fissch, and that so plentyvous,
It snewed in his hous of mete and drynke,
Of alle deyntees that men cowde thynke.
Aftur the sondry sesouns of the yeer,
He chaunged hem at mete and at soper.
Ful many a fat partrich had he in mewe,
And many a brem, and many a luce in stewe,
Woo was his cook, but if his sauce were
Poynant and scharp, and redy al his gere;
His table dormant in his halle alway
Stood redy covered al the longe day.

GEOFFREY CHAUCER,
Description of the franklin in the Prologue to
The Canterbury Tales

A Harpooneer at Breakfast

They say that men who have seen the world, thereby become quite at ease in manner, quite self-possessed in company. Not always, though: Ledyard, the great New England traveller, and Mungo Park, the Scotch one; of all men, they possessed the least assurance in the parlour. But perhaps the mere crossing of Siberia in a sledge drawn by dogs as Ledyard did, or the taking a long solitary walk on an empty stomach, in the negro heart of Africa, which was the sum of poor Mungo's performances – this kind of travel, I say, may not be the very best mode of attaining a high social polish. Still, for the most part, that sort of thing is to be had anywhere.

These reflections just here are occasioned by the circumstance that after we were all seated at the table, and I was preparing to hear some good stories about whaling; to my no small surprise nearly every man maintained a profound silence. And not only that, but they looked embarrassed. Yes, here were a set of sea-dogs, many of whom without the slightest bashfulness had boarded great whales on the high seas – entire strangers to them – and duelled them dead without winking; and yet, here they sat at a social breakfast table – all of the same calling, all of kindred tastes – looking round as sheepishly at each other as though they had never been out of sight of some sheepfold among the Green Mountains. A curious sight; these bashful bears, these timid warrior whalemen!

But as for Queequeg – why, Queequeg sat there among them – at the head of the table, too, it so chanced; as cool as an icicle. To be sure I cannot say much for his breeding. His greatest admirer could not have cordially justified his bringing his harpoon into breakfast with him, and using it there without ceremony; reaching over the table with it, to the imminent jeopardy of many heads, and grappling the beefsteaks towards him. But *that* was certainly very coolly done by him, and every one knows that in most people's estimation, to do anything coolly is to do it genteelly.

We will not speak of all Queequeg's peculiarities here; how he eschewed coffee and hot rolls, and applied his undivided attention to beefsteaks, done rare. Enough, that when breakfast was over he withdrew like the rest into the public room, lighted his tomahawk-pipe, and was sitting there quietly digesting and smoking with his inseparable hat on, when I sallied out for a stroll.

HERMAN MELVILLE,
Moby Dick

Dining Ceremoniously

China being an ancient country with the dawn of her civilization at an early date, ceremony – a mark of culture – also plays a part. In pre-Republican days, such ceremony was very elaborate, but interesting enough to be recounted.

1. The host stands on the west side of the hall a few yards from the dinner table.

2. The "Master of Ceremony" bows to the guest of honour and conducts him to a place on the east side of the hall not far from but opposite to where the host is standing.

3. The host bows to the guest, who bows in return.

4. The host ascends the hall up to the dinner table and bows to the empty chair on which the guest is to sit. The guest, now facing the host bows in return.

5. The host walks to the chair and, with both sleeves, touches the cushion of the chair as a symbol of dusting it. After this he bows to the chair and the guest bows in return.

6. The host, with a bow, raises the wine cup to be used by the guest, who bows in return.

8. The host returns to the place where he stood and bows to the guest, who bows in return.

9. The guest leaves and is conducted to his seat. During this ceremony a solemn but cheerful music is played, while the eyes of all, in dead silence, are concentrated on the performance and try to catch a glimpse of the guest of honour. Though consisting of a few bows, the sight is full of meaning, dignified and beautiful. If negotiation of a treaty, for instance, were to take place after a meal clothed with such formality, it is inconceivable that the negotiators would use such unceremonial language as sometimes employed by certain diplomats in international conferences in recent time. They may, indeed, disagree, but they would agree to disagree.

F. T. CHENG,
Musings of a Chinese Gourmet

Crime and Punishment

Why streams the life-blood from that female throat?
She sprinkled gravy on a guest's new coat.

American anti-slavery poet (unknown)

Sugar-plums for My Lady

I had the honour to dine twice with the Duke [the Duke of Mecklenburg Strelitz] during my short stay in his territories. At table, surrounded by his little court, composed of young and agreeable individuals of both sexes, he amused me by recounting some particulars of the English who had from time to time been his guests. The Earl and Countess of Effingham were among the number. "They were always seated," said he, "opposite each other at dinner; and no sooner was the dessert placed before us than my Lord, ordering his lady to open her mouth, threw dragées (sugar-plums) into it across the table with surprising dexterity."

Memoirs of Sir Nathaniel William Wraxall (1815)

"Just sits there toying with her food."

Getting Ready

Of the Oeconomy of a Table

We have learned many little Arts of the French, and 'tis pity we do not a little more carefully follow them in this. The best Dinner in the World will have an ill Aspect if the Dishes are not properly disposed on the Table, and in this we are very deficient. We have a John Trot Method, in which we go on with perfect Sameness; they have a great Variety. We acknowledge that we have learned a great deal of the Art of Cookery from them; why should not we be as much obliged to them for this finishing Article, the Arrangement of the Dishes upon the Table. We seem to look upon it as a Trifle, but it is no more so than much of the Art beside. To please the Palate is one Design of this Branch of Study, and to please the Eye is the other. We shall give the Reader in this Chapter some general Idea of the Taste of the English, and that of the French on this Head, and lead him toward the improving the common Method by a proper and reasonable Imitation.

It is the Custom here to eat off square or long square Tables; the French in general eat on round or oval. We shall here find one of the first Occasions of our Deficiency in this Respect. It is true that we sit more conveniently, but the French have vastly the Advantage in the disposing and placing their Entertainment.

As great Entertainments are given more for Show than from any other Consideration, something should be considered for the Appearance as well for Convenience; we should therefore imitate them in this Respect, especially in grand Feasts, and we may from following the same Train of Thought, improve a great deal in our common Tables.

A great Painter has lately wrote to prove that there cannot be Beauty in strait Lines: The Tables we use are composed of such, and the Example was never more fully illustrated. The Form of the Table compels us to set the Dishes in the same Manner, that People may have room for their Plates, and thus all becomes ungraceful. But something may be done to avoid the necessity, even in this Case, of setting Things in Rows, tho' it has not yet been thought of.

Of Placing the Dishes

We shall first lay down the common Method of placing Dishes upon the Table in England, and this for two Reasons, as it will give the Housekeeper a general Direction for doing it to Satisfaction; and as it will lead her better to understand the Improvements we propose on this Head.

For two Dishes, the best shaped Table is a pretty long Square, such as will hold one at each End and two on each Side; and the Dishes are placed one near the Top, and the other near the Bottom, with Room for Plates between, as at the Sides, only less.

For three Dishes, the Table should be a broader Square, but still oblong; and one Dish is placed at the Top, and two Side by Side at the Bottom; this is a very awkward Method: But three is an odd Number; two upon the Table at once, and one of them removed, does better.

A Dinner of four Dishes is set upon the Table thus; there is one at the Top, one at the Bottom, and one on each Side, a vacant Space being left in the Middle; this also has a raw Appearance, and the Vacancy should be filled up with something.

A Table of five Dishes is served up in the same Manner exactly, only the fifth Dish supplies the Vacancy in the Middle. The best Shape of the Table for four Dishes, is nearly square, and for five in this Way perfectly square.

Six Dishes we rarely use, from five the Advance is to seven; and the Way of placing these is, three down the Middle, and two on each Side; the Dishes thus stand in three Rows longwise, and the best Form for the Table is square.

From seven the next Advance is to nine; we love odd Numbers: In this Case the Form of the Table is Square, and one Dish is set in the Middle and eight round it.

Our next Step is usually to thirteen Dishes; for these the Table is to be of a long square, and they are placed in three Rows; five down the Middle of the Table and four on each Side.

This is the usual Way of placing Dishes; let this be well fixed in the Memory for the present, because by complying with these Rules the Housekeeper will always avoid Blame.

MRS MARTHA BRADLEY,
The British Housewife: or the Cook, Housekeeper's, and Gardiner's Companion;
Being the Result of upwards of Thirty Years' Experience
(n.d.: probably late eighteenth century)

Manners

Loke thy naylys ben clene in blythe,
Lest thy felaghe lothe therwyth.

. . .

If thou spit over the borde or elles opone,
Thou shalle be holden an uncurtayse mon.

WYNKYN DE WORDE,
Boke of Curtasye

Dining with the Doctor

When invited to dine, even with an intimate friend, he was not pleased if something better than a plain dinner was not prepared for him. I have heard him say on such an occasion, "This was a good dinner enough, to be sure; but it was not a dinner to ask a man to." On the other hand, he was wont to express, with great glee, his satisfaction when he had been entertained quite to mind. One day when we had dined with his neighbour and landlord in Bolt Court, Mr Allen, the printer, whose old housekeeper had studied his taste in everything, he pronounced this eulogy: "Sir, we could not have had a better dinner had there been a *Synod of Cooks*."

JAMES BOSWELL,
The Life of Samuel Johnson

Autres Moeurs

After inspecting the various temples and the belfry, which contains a noble bronze bell of large dimensions, our host conducted us back to his house, where dinner was already on the table. The priests of the Buddhist religion are not allowed to eat animal food at any of their meals. Our dinner therefore consisted entirely of vegetables, served up in the usual Chinese style, in a number of small round basins, the contents of each – soups excepted – being cut up into small square bits, to be eaten with chopsticks. The Buddhist priests contrive to procure a number of vegetables of different kinds, which, by a peculiar mode of preparation, are rendered very palatable. In fact, so nearly do they resemble animal food in taste and in appearance, that at first we were deceived, imagining that the little bits we were able to get hold of with our chopsticks were really pieces of fowl or beef. Such, however, was not the case, as our good host was consistent on this day at least, and had nothing but vegetable productions at his table. Several other priests sat with us at table, and a large number of others of inferior rank with servants, crowded around the doors and windows outside. The whole assemblage must have been much surprised at the awkward way in which some of us handled our chopsticks, and, with all their politeness, I observed they could not refrain from laughing when, after repeated attempts, some little dainty morsel would still slip back again into the dish. I know few things more annoying, and yet laughable too, than attempting to eat with the Chinese chopsticks for the first time, more particularly if the operator has been wandering on the hills all the morning, and is ravenously hungry. The instruments should first of all be balanced between the thumb and fore-finger of the right hand; the points are next to be brought carefully to-gether, just leaving as much room as will allow the coveted morsel to go in between them; the little bit is then to be neatly seized; but alas! in the act of lifting the hand, one point of the chopstick too often slips past the other, and the object of all our hopes drops back again into the dish, or perhaps even into another dish on the table. Again and again the same operation is tried, until the poor novice loses all patience, throws down the chopsticks in despair, and seizes a porcelain spoon, with which he is more successful. In cases like these the Chinese themselves are very obliging, although scarcely in a way agreeable to an Englishman's taste. Your Chinese friend, out of kindness and politeness, when he sees the dilemma in which you are, reaches across the table and seizes, with his own chopsticks, which have just come out of his mouth, the wished-for morsel, and with them lays it on the plate before you. In common polite-ness you must express your gratitude and swallow the offering.

ROBERT FORTUNE,
Wanderings in China (1847)

The table is the only place where one does not suffer from *ennui* during the first hour.

BRILLAT-SAVARIN

Diversions During Dinner

'Tis common for two to breake the Merrythought of a chicken, or wood-cock, etc., the Anatomists call it Clavicula: 'tis called the merrythought because when the fowle is opened, dissected, or carv'd, it resembles the pudenda of a woman. . . .

The manner of breaking it, as I have it from the woemen, is thus: viz. One puts ye merrithought on his nose (slightly) like a paire of spectacles, and shakes his head till he shakes it off his nose, thinking all the while his Thought; then he holds one of the legs of it between his forefinger and Thumbe, and another holds the other in like manner, and breakes it; he that has the longer part, has got the Thought; then he that has got the thought putts both parts into his hand, and the other drawes (by way of Lott), and then they both Wish, and he that lost his Thought drawes; if he drawes the longest part, he has his wish, if the shorter he looses his Wish.

JOHN AUBREY,
Remaines of Gentilisme and Judaisme (1687)

Simple Manners

There is no man so feasted as the chapel pastor. His tall and yet rotund body and his broad red face might easily be mistaken for the outward man of a sturdy farmer, and he likes his pipe and glass. He dines every Sunday, and at least once a week besides, at the house of one of his stoutest upholders. It is said that at such a dinner, after a large plateful of black currant pudding, finding there was still some juice left, he lifted the plate to his mouth and carefully licked it all round; the hostess hastened to offer a spoon, but he declined, thinking that was much the best way to gather up the essence of the fruit. So simple were his manners, he needed no spoon; and, indeed, if we look back, the apostles managed without forks, and put their fingers in the dish. After dinner, the cognac bottle is produced and the pastor fills his tumbler half full of spirit, and but lightly dashes it with water. It is cognac and not brandy, for your chapel minister thinks it an affront if anything more common than the best French liquor is put before him; he likes it strong, and with it his long clay pipe. Very frequently another minister, sometimes two or three, come in at the same time, and take the same dinner, and afterwards form a genial circle with cognac and tobacco, when the room speedily becomes full of smoke and the bottle of brandy soon disappears. In these family parties there is not the least approach to over-conviviality; it is merely the custom, no one thinks anything of a glass and a pipe; it is perfectly innocent; it is not a local thing, but common and understood. The consumption of brandy and tobacco and the good things of dinner, tea, and supper (for the party generally sit out the three meals), must in a month cost the host a good deal of money, but all things are cheerfully borne for the good of the church. Never were men feasted with such honest good-will as these pastors; and if a budding Paul or Silas happens to come along who has scarce yet passed his ordination, the youthful divine may stay a week if he likes, and lick the platter clean. . . .

RICHARD JEFFRIES,
Field and Hedgerow (1889)

He who receives friends and pays no attention to the repast prepared for them is not fit to have friends.

To invite a person to your house is to take charge of his happiness as long as he is beneath your roof.

BRILLAT-SAVARIN

Hostmanship

Of doing the Honours of a Table

In the Old Times in England People thought they never entertained one another well if they did not feed them till they almost burst; as at present a Man in Germany never thinks he makes much of another if he do not make him drunk: But this is a Custom set aside for a much more reasonable Civility.

We suppose that every one who dines with us dines as well every Day at home, and therefore we make no Pother about his eating as if he were at a Feast.

It was then the Custom for the Mistress of the Table to see her Guests eat of every Dish, and eat heartily, now the true Politeness among perfectly polite People is not to regard what any one eats; but if there happen to be a Person present not so much used to Company, the Lady is to ask him without Ceremony whether she shall help him to this or that Dish. This is an Ease to the Backwardness of the Guest, and may be done in such a Manner as not to draw on the Attention of the rest of the Company.

As our Grandmothers made too much Racket with their Guests: we are in danger of making too little; so natural it is for Ladies to run from one Extreme to another: Those good old Gentlewomen were always finding Fault with their Food, and thought they shewed their own Skill in letting their Company know what was amiss, and their Civility in expressing their Concern that Things were not good enough for their Entertainment: On the other Hand, our Ladies are to apt to neglect the Thing entirely; they take no Notice of their Provision; it goes as it comes, and the Company have no Way to know they are welcome but by remembering they were asked.

A middle Practice is better: Let the truly polite Lady take some Notice of the Things, though not too much, and let her praise a Dish that is good tho' 'tis her own; 'tis civil to recommend it to her Company.

MRS MARTHA BRADLEY,
The British Housewife

The mistress of the house should always be certain that the coffee be excellent; the master that his liquors be of the first quality.

The most indispensable quality of a good cook is promptness.
It should also be that of the guests.

BRILLAT-SAVARIN

Wrongly Suspected

When I sat next the Duchess at tea,
It was just as I knew it would be,
  Her rumblings abdominal
  Were something phenomenal –
And everyone thought it was me.
                              Anon.

Oriental Hospitality

"How quick your servants are!" Miss Quested exclaimed. For a cloth had already been laid, with a vase of artificial flowers in its centre, and Mahmoud Ali's butler offered them poached eggs and tea for the second time.

"I thought we would eat this before our caves, and breakfast after."

"Isn't this breakfast?"

"This breakfast? Did you think I should treat you so strangely?" He had been warned that English people never stop eating, and that he had better nourish them every two hours until a solid meal was ready.

"How very well it is all arranged."

"That you shall tell me when I return to Chandrapore. Whatever disgraces I bring upon myself, you remain my guests." He spoke gravely now. They were dependent on him for a few hours, and he felt grateful to them for placing themselves in such a position. All was well so far; the elephant held a fresh-cut bough to her lips, the tonga shafts stuck up into the air, the kitchen-boy peeled potatoes, Hassan shouted, and Mohammed Latif stood as he ought, with a peeled switch in his hand. The expedition was a success, and it was Indian; an obscure young man had been allowed to show courtesy to visitors from another country, which is what all Indians long to do – even cynics like Mahmoud Ali – but they never have the chance. Hospitality had been achieved, they were "his" guests; his honour was involved in their happiness, and any discomfort they endured would tear his own soul.

Like most Orientals Aziz overrated hospitality, mistaking it for intimacy, and not seeing that it is tainted with the sense of possession. It was only when Mrs Moore or Fielding was near him that he saw farther, and knew that it is more blessed to receive than to give. These two had strange and beautiful effects on him – they were his friends, his for ever, and he theirs for ever; he loved them so much that giving and receiving became one. He loved them even better than the Hamidullahs, because he had surmounted obstacles to meet them, and this stimulates a generous mind. Their images remained somewhere in his soul up to his dying day, permanent additions. He looked at her now as she sat on a deck chair, sipping his tea, and had for a moment a joy that held the seeds of its own decay, for it would lead him to think: "Oh, what more can I do for her?" and so back to the dull round of hospitality.

E. M. FORSTER,
A Passage to India

Roasted Porter

Roasted porter was a fashionable fancy in Sir G. Beaumont's youth. He has now a set of silver cups made for the purpose. They were brought red hot to the table, the porter was poured into them in that state, and it was a pleasure to see with what alarm an inexperienced guest ventured to take the cup at the moment that the liquor foamed over and cooled it. The effect must have been much the same as that of putting a hot poker in, which I have often seen done at Westminster, or a piece of red hot pottery, – which we sometimes use here.

ROBERT SOUTHEY,
Common-place Book (1849-51)

Port Ritual

In the old graces and ritual of the table such as are observed in the common-rooms of Oxford and the combination-rooms of Cambridge, Port bears an important role. After dinner is concluded with a savoury, the table is cleared, the cloth is deftly removed, dishes of fruit, biscuits and nuts are laid out on the bare table where each one can help himself, and each diner is furnished with a Port glass, a Sherry glass, and a fruit plate, fork, and silver knife. A decanter of Port and one of Madeira or Sherry are placed by the Senior Fellow at the head of the table, and the servant retires, only to reappear if fresh supplies of wine are required. The Senior Fellow first fills the glass of the gentleman at his right hand, next serves himself, and then the gentleman at his left. The decanters are then slid around the polished table on padded coasters, clockwise or "with the sun", because Port will take offence at being circulated "against the sun", and go sour on you. When the head of the table judges that it is time, he starts the decanters around a second time, and sometimes there is a third round of a light sherry for "mouth-wash" after an unusually rich and fruity Vintage Port. A short glass from the bottom of the decanter is called a "buzz", and entitles the victim to another full glass, provided he has put the "buzz" away by the time the servant brings a new decanter. When everyone who wants it has had a second glass, the head of the table rings for coffee and cigarettes. Up to that point smoking is absolutely prohibited; and when I first knew Oxford, smoking was never allowed at any time in the same room where Port was drunk. One had to adjourn to another room after dinner if one wished to smoke.

In America few can afford servants with the technique of rolling up a tablecloth and whisking it over the heads of the diners, but we can see that Port is handed around "with the sun", and a little restraint in the matter of smoking will be amply repaid by full enjoyment of the delicious grapy bouquet and rich, full flavour of the Noblest of Wines.

SAMUEL E. MORISON,
Wine and Food, 19

The order of drinking is from the mildest to the most foamy and perfumed.

To wait too long for a dilatory guest shows disrespect to those who are punctual.

BRILLAT-SAVARIN

The Wedding Breakfast. Dickie Doyle, 1849.

The Wedding Feast

A wedding in Tyrol is a celebration attended by a few hundred people. They come down from the mountain and they come up from the Land. One must have endurance and good lungs just to recite the announcement of the meal:

> Twelve cooks have baked with fat and flour
> and prepared the table for this happy hour.
> They stirred and steamed and weighed things right.
> Come all of you, bring appetite;
> you have never eaten such fare –
> there's enough for a hundred pair.
> Start with the soup, eat dumplings and fish,
> calf's-head and kidneys, as much as you wish,
> roast geese and pigeons, mutton and deer,
> and wash it down with wine and beer.
> Let's make the bride's father run to the cave:
> this is no day on which to save.

And let all sorrow be forsaken –
drink when the bridal wreath is taken,
pour it down and again make room
in your cups to toast the groom.
Start the shooting and the band
for we will proclaim in all the land
that the customs of the good old days
and that our forefathers' ways
honoured are and well observed.
After that there will be served
Gugelhupf with coffee and cream.
Come on foot, come with your team;
from valleys deep, from mountains tall,
hurry and assemble all.

LUDWIG BEMELMANS,
The Snow Mountain

Drinking on the Nail

One of the great characteristics of the dinner-table in the early seventeenth century was the formality of drinking, especially that of drinking healths. . . . It was not exactly the modern practice of giving a toast, but each person in turn rose, named some one to whom he individually drank, and emptied his cup. "He that begins the health," we are told in a little book published in 1623, "first uncovered his head, he takes a full cup in his hand, and setting his countenance with grave aspect, he craves for audience; silence being once obtained he begins to breathe out the name, peradventure, of some honourable personage, whose health is drunk to, and he that pledges must likewise off with his cap, kiss his fingers, and bow himself in sign of a reverent acceptance. When the leader sees his follower thus prepared, he sups up his broth, turns the bottom of the cup upward, gives the cup a phillip to make it cry twango. And thus the first scene is acted. The cup being newly replenished to the breadth of a hair, he that is the pledger must now begin his part; and thus it goes round throughout the whole company." In order to ascertain that each person had fairly drunk off his cup, in turning it up he was to pour all that remained on his nail, and if there were too much to remain as a drop on the nail without running off, he was made to drink his cup full again. This was termed drinking on the nail, for which convivialists invented a mock Latin phrase, and called it drinking *super-nagulum* or *super-naculum*.

THOMAS WRIGHT,
Homes of Other Days (1871)

Promise of Delights

Praying you to suppe with us this night,
And ye shall have made, at your devis,
A great pudding, or a round hagis,
A French moile, a tansie, or a froise.

JOHN LYDGATE,
The Siege of Thebes (1421–2)

Grace

Before
Gloria deo, sirs, *proface*,
Attend me now whilst I say grace,
For bread and salt, for grapes and malt,
For flesh and fish, and euery dish:
Mutton and beefe, of all meates cheefe:
For Cow-heels, chitterlings, tripes and sowse
And other meate thats in the house:
For backs, for breasts, for legges, for loines,
For pies with raisons, and with proines:
For fritters, pancakes, and for frayes,
For venison pasties, and minct pies:
Sheephead and garlick, brawne and mustard,
Wafers, spiced cakes, tart and custard,
For capons, rabets, pigges and geese,
For apples, carawaies and cheese:
for all these and many moe,
Benidicamus domino

After
O Domini & Chare puter,
That giu'st vs wine in stead of water
And from the Pond and Riuer cleere
Mak'st nappie Ale and good March Beere
That send'st vs sundry sorts of meate
And euery thing we drinke or eate,
To maides, to wiues, to boyes, to men,
Laus Deo sancte Amen

JOSHUA COOKE (attrib.),
How to Chuse a Good Wife from a Bad (1602)

FOOD FOR THOUGHT

The Whale as a Dish

That mortal man should feed upon the creature that feeds his lamp, and, like Stubb, eat him by his own light, as you may say; this seems so outlandish a thing that one must needs go a little into the history and philosophy of it.

It is upon record, that three centuries ago the tongue of the Right Whale was esteemed a great delicacy in France, and commanded large prices there. Also, that in Henry VIIIth's time, a certain cook of the court obtained a handsome reward for inventing an admirable sauce to be eaten with barbacued porpoises, which, you remember, are a species of whale. Porpoises, indeed, are to this day considered fine eating. The meat is made into balls about the size of billiard balls, and being well seasoned and spiced might be taken for turtle-balls or veal balls. The old monks of Dunfermline were very fond of them. They had a great porpoise grant from the crown.

The fact is, that among his hunters at least, the whale would by all hands be considered a noble dish, were there not so much of him; but when you come to sit down before a meat-pie nearly one hundred feet long, it takes away your appetite. Only the most unprejudiced of men like Stubb, nowadays partake of cooked whales; but the Esquimaux are not so fastidious. We all know how they live upon whales, and have rare old vintages of prime old train oil. Zogranda, one of their most famous doctors, recommends strips of blubber for infants, as being exceedingly juicy and nourishing. And this reminds me that certain Englishmen, who long ago were accidentally left in Greenland by a whaling vessel – that these men actually lived for several months on the mouldy scraps of whales which had been left ashore after trying out the blubber. Among the Dutch whalemen these scraps are called "fritters"; which, indeed, they greatly resemble, being brown and crisp, and smelling something like old Amsterdam housewives' dough-nuts or oly-cooks, when fresh. They have such an eatable look that the most self-denying stranger can hardly keep his hands off.

But what further depreciates the whale as a civilized dish, is his exceeding richness. He is the great prize ox of the sea, too fat to be delicately good. Look at his hump, which would be as fine eating as a buffalo's (which is esteemed a rare dish), were it not such a solid pyramid of fat. But the spermaceti itself, how bland and creamy that is; like the transparent, half-jellied, white meat of a cocoanut in the third month of its growth, yet far too rich to supply a substitute for butter. Nevertheless, many whalemen have a method of absorbing it into some other substance, and then partaking of it. In the long try watches of the night it is a common thing for the seamen to dip their ship-biscuit into the huge oil-pots and let them fry there awhile. Many a good supper have I thus made.

In the case of a small Sperm Whale the brains are accounted a fine dish. The casket of the skull is broken into with an axe, and the two plump, whitish lobes withdrawn (precisely resembling two large puddings), they are then mixed with flour, and cooked into a most delectable mess, in flavour somewhat resembling calves' head, which is quite a dish among some epicures; and every one knows that some young bucks among the epicures, by continually dining upon calves' brains, by and by get to have a little brains of their own, so as to be able to tell a calf's head from their own heads; which, indeed, requires uncommon discrimination. And that is the reason why a young buck with an intelligent-looking calf's head before him, is somehow one of the saddest sights you can see. The head looks a sort of reproachfully at him, with an "*Et tu Brute!*" expression.

It is not, perhaps, entirely because the whale is so excessively unctuous that landsmen seem to regard the eating of him with abhorrence; that appears to result, in some way, from the consideration before mentioned: i.e. that a man should eat a newly murdered thing of the sea, and eat it too by its own light. But no doubt the first man that ever murdered an ox was regarded as a murderer; perhaps he was hung; and if he had been put on his trial by oxen, he certainly would have been; and he certainly deserved it if any murderer does. Go to the meatmarket of a Saturday night and see the crowds of live bipeds staring up at the long rows of dead quadrupeds. Does not that sight take a tooth out of the cannibal's jaw? Cannibals? Who is not a cannibal? I tell you it will be more tolerable for the Feegee that salted down a lean missionary in his cellar against a coming famine; it will be more tolerable for that provi-

dent Feegee, I say, in the day of judgment, than for thee, civilized and
enlightened gourmand, who nailest geese to the ground and feastest on
their bloated livers in thy paté-de-foie-gras.

But Stubb, he eats the whale by its own light, does he? and that is
adding insult to injury, is it? Look at your knife-handle, there, my
civilized and enlightened gourmand dining off that roast beef, what is
that handle made of? – what but the bones of the brother of the very ox
you are eating? And what do you pick your teeth with, after devouring
that fat goose? With a feather of the same fowl. And with what quill did
the Secretary of the Society for the Suppression of Cruelty to Ganders
formally indite his circulars? It is only within the last month or two that
that society passed a resolution to patronize nothing but steel pens.

HERMAN MELVILLE,
Moby Dick

Coleridge declares that a man cannot have a good conscience who
refuses apple dumplings, and I confess that I am of the same opinion.

CHARLES LAMB

The Unselfish Oyster

The grill-room clock struck eleven with the respectful unobtrusiveness
of one whose mission in life is to be ignored. When the flight of time
should really have rendered abstinence and migration imperative the
lighting apparatus would signal the fact in the usual way.

Six minutes later Clovis approached the supper-table, in the blessed
expectancy of one who has dined sketchily and long ago.

"I'm starving," he announced, making an effort to sit down gracefully
and read the menu at the same time.

"So I gathered," said his host, "from the fact that you were nearly
punctual. I ought to have told you that I'm a Food Reformer. I've ordered two bowls of bread-and-milk and some health biscuits. I hope
you don't mind."

Clovis pretended afterwards that he didn't go white above the collar-
line for the fraction of a second.

"All the same," he said, "you ought not to joke about such things.
There really are such people. I've known people who've met them. To
think of all the adorable things there are to eat in the world, and then to
go through life munching sawdust and being proud of it."

"They're like the Flagellants of the Middle Ages, who went about
mortifying themselves."

"They had some excuse," said Clovis. "They did it to save their immortal souls, didn't they? You needn't tell me that a man who doesn't love oysters and asparagus and good wines has got a soul or a stomach either. He's simply got the instinct for being unhappy highly developed."

Clovis relapsed for a few golden moments into tender intimacies with a succession of rapidly disappearing oysters.

"I think oysters are more beautiful than any religion," he resumed presently. "They not only forgive our unkindness to them; they justify it, they incite us to go on being perfectly horrid to them. Once they arrive at the supper-table they seem to enter thoroughly into the spirit of the thing. There's nothing in Christianity or Buddhism that quite matches the sympathetic unselfishness of an oyster."

SAKI,
The Chronicles of Clovis

The Oyster-Seller. Jean le Clerc, about 1600.

Meditations on Oysters

Sansom street, below Ninth, runs a modest course through the middle of the afternoon, scooped between high and rather grimy walls so that a coolness and a shadow are upon it. It is a homely little channel, frequented by laundry wagons taking away great piles of soiled linen from the rear of the Continental Hotel, and little barefoot urchins pushing carts full of kindling wood picked up from the litter of splintered packing cases. On one side of the street is a big power-house where the drone and murmur of vast dynamos croon a soft undertone to the distant clang and zooming of the trolleys. Beyond that is the stage door of a burlesque theatre, and a faint sweetness of greasepaint drifts to the nose down a dark, mysterious passageway.

We walked down this little street, noticing the For Rent sign on a saloon at the corner and the pyramided boxes of green and yellow apples on a fruit stand, and it seemed to us that there was an unmistakable breath of autumn in the air. Out beyond, where the street widens and floods itself again with sun, there were heat and shimmer and the glittering plate-glass windows of jewelry dealers, but in the narrow strip of alley we felt a premonitory tang of future frost. At the end of August the sunlight gets yellower, more oblique; it loses the pale and deadly glare of earlier days. It is shallower, more colourful, but weaker of impact. Shall we say it has lost its punch?

And then we saw a little oyster café, well known to many lovers of good cheer, that has been furbishing itself for the jolly days to come. No one knows yet whether the U-boats have frightened the oysters, whether the fat bivalves will be leaner and scarcer than in the good old days; no one knows whether there will even be enough of them to last out until next Easter; but in the meantime we all live in hope. And one thing is certain – the oyster season begins on Monday. The little café has repainted its white front so that it shines hospitably; and the sill and the cellar trapdoor where the barrels go in, and the shutters and the awning poles in front, are all a sticky glistening green. The white marble step, hollowed by thousands of eager feet in a million lunch-time forays, has been scrubbed and sandsoaped. And next Monday morning, bright and early, out goes the traditional red and green sign of the R.

The "poor patient oyster", as Keats calls him (or her, for there are ady oysters, too, did you know?), is not only a sessile bivalve mollusk, but a traditional symbol of autumn and winter cheer. Even if Mr Hoover counts out the little round crackers in twos and threes, we hope there will be enough of the thoughtful and innocent shellfish to go around.

When the cold winds begin to harp and whinny at street corners and wives go seeking among the camphor balls for our last year's overcoats, you will be glad to resume your acquaintance with a bowl of steaming bivalves, swimming in milk, with little clots of yellow butter twirling on the surface of the broth. An oyster stew, a glass of light beer and a corncob pipe will keep your blue eyes blue to any weather, as a young poet of our acquaintance puts it.

CHRISTOPHER MORLEY,
Travels in Philadelphia

How Not to Eat Oysters

In the spring of 1949 the season opened with a fair for the benefit of ex-prisoners of war, organized by the prisoners themselves. The feature of that show, for me, was the exhibition of modern tapestries from Aubusson, but there were also impressive food specialities from all regions of France. The advertisement that hit me hardest was displayed in the booth filled with delicacies from the maritime province of Finistère. The prize offering was shellfish, my favourite food, summed up so poignantly by Zola as "liquid fire".

There were two posters, a yard wide and two yards high, revealing respectively, the innards of an oyster and a mussel, each magnified about one hundred diameters. The diagrams were sketched and tinted vividly, in the minutest detail.

All my life I have been fond of oysters, and more so of mussels, which are so hard to buy in the United States because of the libelous propaganda fish dealers have spread there to discourage the consumption of any sea foods that can be sold cheaply. From earliest childhood I have been reconciled to the idea of eating bivalves alive, I am not squeamish about any good food. Rattlesnake meat à la King I have cooked, myself, and found delicious. I have consumed mountain oysters and prairie dancers that are actually poetic. I relish squid cooked in blackest ink. Eels stewed or fried, or squirrels in Brunswick pie are to my taste. Nevertheless I got a rude jolt at the Prisoners' Fair when I examined those advertising posters for oysters and mussels. Each organ and part was labelled and numbered.

The mouth of an oyster, so it seems, is near the small hinged end of the shell; just below it, if the oyster is held vertically, small end up, is the stomach. Then come the liver, the intestine, the anus and a pair of small protuberances which may, in the course of a couple of million years, develop into legs like those of a tadpole. The inner organs are enclosed in a cloak or skin. What sticks out and squirts jets through the parted shells of a clam is delicately called "the siphon".

Europeans were not deterred by those posters from sampling eagerly the oysters, clams, palourdes, cockles, mussels, snails, razor fish or sea-urchins at the booth in question, but I must confess that I, and other Americans, got out of there in a hurry and contented ourselves with hard-boiled eggs at the Alsatian bar.

ELLIOT PAUL,
Springtime in Paris

Fish for Breakfast

The divine took his seat at the breakfast-table, and began to compose his spirits by the gentle sedative of a large cup of tea, the demulcent of a well buttered muffin, and the tonic of a small lobster.

THE REV. DR FOLLIOTT. You are a man of taste, Mr Crotchet. A man of taste is seen at once in the array of his breakfast-table. . . . Chocolate, coffee, tea, cream, eggs, ham, tongue, cold fowl – all these are good, and bespeak good knowledge in him who sets them forth: but the touch-stone is fish: anchovy is the first step, prawns and shrimps the second; and I laud him who reaches even to these: potted char and lampreys are the third, and a fine stretch of progression; but lobster is, indeed, matter for a May morning, and demands a rare combination of knowledge and virtue in him who sets it forth.

MR MACQUEDY. Well, sir, and what say you to a fine fresh trout, hot and dry, in a napkin? or a herring out of the water into the frying pan, on the shore of Loch Fyne?

THE REV. DR FOLLIOTT. Sir, I say every nation has some eximious virtue; and your country is pre-eminent in the glory of fish for breakfast. We have much to learn from you in that line at any rate.

MR MACQUEDY. And in many others, sir, I believe. Morals and metaphysics, politics and political economy, the way to make the most of all the modifications of smoke; steam, gas, and paper currency; you have all these to learn from us; in short, all the arts and sciences. We are the modern Athenians.

THE REV. DR FOLLIOTT. I, for one, sir, am content to learn nothing from you but the art and science of fish for breakfast.

THOMAS LOVE PEACOCK,
Crotchet Castle

He was a bold man that first ate an oyster.

JONATHAN SWIFT

Bog Butter

Bogs hold more than turf and bogwood. It is a commonplace that bronze implements of all kinds have been found in them. Scarcely a museum that has not a specimen of one kind or another, preserved by the bacteria-free soil, of wooden bowls and platters, goblets, spades, spoons, canoes, and tunics of wool, capes of skin, or shoes of leather. One of the largest dug-out canoes ever found in western Europe, fifty-two feet in length, was taken from a bog in County Galway.

But one of the most surprising, though by no means uncommon, finds is bog butter. This is not, as one might suspect by the name, some strange fungus akin to the yellow jelly-like growth found on trees, and known as witch's butter, but the genuine churn-made products of the milk of cows, sometimes still edible. Knowing the preservative power of bogs, its owners had buried it, to await such time as they were going to market, four, five, or six months ahead. Meanwhile, death or accident intervened, and so the wooden firkin, or the skin or cloth container, with its contents, lay undisturbed, fifty, a hundred, maybe two hundred, years.

ROBERT GIBBINGS,
Lovely is the Lee

Identifying Edible Fungi

But how to tell the poisonous mushroom from the harmless variety, since both are found in the same localities, have the same habits, and the same dull look around the face? Ah – don't be surprised – the mushroom *has* a face, and if you look very closely and carefully, you will see the merest hint of an eye, two noses, and a lip. For purposes of identification, we have what we call the Alfred Zeiler test, named after Professor Schaffner of the University of Rochester. The mushrooms are boiled for twenty minutes and their jackets removed. They are then placed in a frying pan with a cubic centimetre of butter, a gramme of pepper, and a pennyweight of coarse salt, after which they are subjected to 137 degrees of heat Fahrenheit in the laboratory oven, removed, and placed on antiseptic paper plates. Fifteen minutes after they are eaten, a reaction will be noted. If the mushrooms are harmless, the subject will want to lie down, remove his or her collar, and roll over on his or her face. If poisonous, the balance of the mushrooms should be thrown out, as they are unfit to consume.

The mushroom often turns up in some really remarkable forms. Sir

Joseph Mushroom, from whom their name is derived, tells an interesting anecdote. A cask of wine had been left undisturbed in a cellar for three years, in some country other than the United States. At the end of that time, the cask was found firmly fastened to the ceiling by a large mushroom which had grown as the wine leaked out. The cask was quite empty when found and how the mushroom looked was nobody's business. Sir Joseph, by the way, no longer raises mushrooms; he has settled down quietly in Surrey, where he devotes himself to raising bees, but there is still a reminiscent gleam in his eye when Irene Adler is mentioned.

S. J. PERELMAN,
Crazy Like a Fox

No. 8

Most Westerners, except Continental people and those who have tasted Chinese delicacies in the East or in a place like China Town in New York or San Francisco, think that the best dish the Chinese cuisine can offer is what is known as "Chop Suey", which, though it can be very tasty and appetizing, is far from being a Chinese delicacy and is hardly known as such in China. It is only a made-up dish specially prepared for American customers by pioneer Chinese restaurants early set up in the United States. It consists of slices of several kinds of vegetables, such as bamboo shoot, mushroom, onion, bean sprouts, celery, cabbage, tomato, and water chestnut, cooked together with fillets of meat or chicken. . . . However, it is so popular in America and England that some Chinese restaurants in these countries sell nothing but "Chop Suey".

In connection with this dish there is a story which may now be told. The late Mr Ernest Bevin, former British Foreign Secretary, dined several times at the Chinese Embassy and, every time, was given, partly, Chinese food. One evening he was asked whether he had ever had Chinese food before, and he answered "yes", adding that he often went to Chinese restaurants before he took office. Hearing this I naturally asked him what dish he liked best and his answer was "No. 8". This sounded like a conundrum. Therefore I followed up my question with a series of queries like "Animal? Mineral? Vegetable?" In other words, I asked him whether it was meat, poultry or sea food, and his replies were a successive "No". Then I said, "I know it now!" He dined at the Embassy a few weeks later and "No. 8" prominently figured in the menu. After he had tasted it, I asked him whether it was right, and his answer was "Quite right, but you have improved it!" This was, in fact, "Chop Suey". As "No. 8" became so well known afterwards as a gastronomic choice of the Foreign Secretary, it always formed an item of the menu in subsequent "diplomatic" dinners during my term of office, even on the occasion when their Royal Highnesses, Princess Elizabeth (now Her Majesty the Queen) and the Duke of Edinburgh, honoured us with their presence at an informal dinner in April 1949.

F. T. CHENG,
Musings of a Chinese Gourmet

Good Bread

Gentle bakers, make good bread! For good bread doth comfort, confirm and doth establish a man's heart, beside the properties rehearsed. Hot bread is unwholesome for any man for it doth lay in the stomach like a sponge, causing undecoct humours; yet the smell of new bread is comfortable to the head and to the heart. Soden bread, as simnel and cracknels and bread baked upon a stone, or upon iron, and bread that saffron is in is not laudable. Burnt bread, and hard crusts and pasty crusts doth engender color, and just and melancholy humours; wherefore chip the upper crust of your bread. And who so doth use to eat the second crust after meat, it maketh a man lean.

ANDREW BOORDE,
Dyetary (1562)

There was an Old Man of Calcutta,
Who perpetually ate bread and butter;
   Till a great bit of muffin,
   On which he was stuffing,
Choked that horrid Old Man of Calcutta.

EDWARD LEAR

Food and Drink in Wales

It has been written of Iolo Morganwg, one of the lights of learning in eighteenth-century Wales, that "tea and bread and butter were his great luxuries, and of the former he would partake at all hours and in liberal quantities". He was known to drink sixteen cups of tea at one sitting. He used sugar and a copious infusion of cream, which he considered adjuncts of nutrition to the exhilarating property of the tea. Under such high auspices nothing could prevent tea from attaining its present proud position – the national beverage of Wales. Coffee has never met with much favour, its unpopularity being either a cause, or an effect, of its bad brewing. Sensible people's attitude was summed up seventy years ago by George Borrow, who, on the one occasion on which he was offered coffee in Wales, drank one cup out of courtesy, but when he was pressed to take a second, replied: "No, thank you, I have had enough." At the same time Borrow had kind words to say for Welsh food, but his appetite had been so over-sharpened by prolonged exercise in the open air that he could not be called a discriminating critic of eating. Nothing else could excuse his rhapsodies over his breakfast at Bala – "Having dressed myself I went to the coffee room and sat down to breakfast. What a breakfast! Pot of hare; ditto of trout; pot of prepared shrimps; dish of plain shrimps; tin of sardines; beautiful beefsteak; eggs, muffins, large loaf, butter, not forgetting capital tea!" Borrow was probably a better judge of beer than of food, and he spent considerable time and thought in contrasting the rival ales of Llangollen and Bala, the one so dark and rich, the other "as pale and delicate in colour as cowslip wine but of mellow flavour with scarcely any smack of the hop in it, and though so pale and delicate to the eye, nearly as strong as brandy."

IFAN KYRLE FLETCHER,
Wine and Food, 5

The pleasure of the table belongs to all ages, to all conditions, to all countries and to all eras; it mingles with all other pleasures, and remains at last to console us for their departure.

BRILLAT-SAVARIN

Cheese

Cheese, a bad supplement for a meal but a good complement.

NORMAN DOUGLAS,
An Almanac

Porridge for Breakfast

In the large kitchen, which occupied most of the middle of the house, a sullen fire burned, the smoke of which wavered up the blackened walls and over the deal table, darkened by age and dirt, which was roughly set for a meal. A snood full of coarse porridge hung over the fire, and standing with one arm resting upon the high mantel, looking moodily down into the heaving contents of the snood, was a tall young man whose riding-boots were splashed with mud to the thigh, and whose coarse linen shirt was open to his waist. The firelight lit up his diaphragm muscles as they heaved slowly in rough rhythm with the porridge.

He looked up as Judith entered, and gave a short, defiant laugh, but said nothing. Judith slowly crossed over until she stood by his side. She was as tall as he. They stood in silence, she staring at him, and he down into the secret crevasses of the porridge.

"Well, mother mine", he said at last, "here I am, you see. I said I would be in time for breakfast, and I have kept my word."

His voice had a low, throaty, animal quality, a sneering warmth that wound a velvet ribbon of sexuality over the outward coarseness of the man.

Judith's breath came in long shudders. She thrust her arms deeper into her shawl. The porridge gave an ominous, leering heave; it might almost have been endowed with life, so uncannily did its movements keep pace with the human passions that throbbed above it.

"Cur", said Judith, levelly, at last. "Coward! Liar! Libertine! Who were you with last night? Moll at the mill or Violet at the vicarage? Or, Ivy, perhaps, at the ironmongery? Seth – my son. . . ." Her deep, dry voice quivered, but she whipped it back, and her next words flew out at him like a lash.

"Do you want to break my heart?"

"Yes", said Seth, with elemental simplicity.

The porridge boiled over.

Judith knelt, and hastily and absently ladled it off the floor back into the snood, biting back her tears. While she was thus engaged, there was a confused blur of voices and boots in the yard outside. The men were coming into breakfast.

STELLA GIBBONS,
Cold Comfort Farm

Breakfast is something to which all ideas of human adjustment are inapplicable. It is like love: conversation impedes and spectators ruin it.

NICHOLAS MONSARRAT,
Corvette Command

David Copperfield and the friendly waiter: illustration by Phiz.

A Touch of the Dramatic

"You are not wounded, Holmes?" I asked, as my friend entered the room.

"Tut, it is only a scratch through my own clumsiness," he answered, nodding his good morning to us. "This case of yours, Mr Phelps, is certainly one of the darkest which I have ever investigated."

"I feared that you would find it beyond you."

"It has been a most remarkable experience."

"That bandage tells of adventures," said I. "Won't you tell us what has happened?"

"After breakfast, my dear Watson. Remember that I have breathed thirty miles of Surrey air this morning. I suppose there has been no answer to my cabman advertisement? Well, well, we cannot expect to score every time."

The table was all laid, and, just as I was about to ring, Mrs Hudson entered with the tea and coffee. A few minutes later she brought in the covers, and we all drew up to the table, Holmes ravenous, I curious, and Phelps in the gloomiest state of depression.

"Mrs Hudson has risen to the occasion," said Holmes, uncovering a dish of curried chicken. "Her cuisine is a little limited, but she has as good an idea of breakfast as a Scotswoman. What have you there, Watson?"

"Ham and eggs," I answered.

"Good! What are you going to take, Mr Phelps: curried fowl, eggs, or will you help yourself?"

"Thank you, I can eat nothing," said Phelps.

"Oh, come! Try the dish before you."

"Thank you, I would really rather not."

"Well, then," said Holmes, with a mischievous twinkle, "I suppose that you have no objection to helping me?"

Phelps raised the cover, and as he did so he uttered a scream, and sat there staring with a face as white as the plate upon which he looked. Across the centre of it was lying a little cylinder of blue-grey paper. He caught it up, devoured it with his eyes, and then danced madly about the room, pressing it to his bosom and shrieking out in his delight. Then he fell back into an arm-chair, so limp and exhausted with his own emotions that we had to pour brandy down his throat to keep him from fainting.

"There! there!" said Holmes, soothingly, patting him upon the shoulder. "It was too bad to spring it on you like this; but Watson here will tell you that I never can resist a touch of the dramatic."

Phelps seized his hand and kissed it. "God bless you!" he cried; "you have saved my honour."

"Well, my own was at stake, you know," said Holmes. "I assure you, it is just as hateful to me to fail in a case as it can be to you to blunder over a commission."

Phelps thrust away the precious document into the innermost pocket of his coat.

"I have not the heart to interrupt your breakfast any further, and yet I am dying to know how you got it and where it was."

Sherlock Holmes swallowed a cup of coffee and turned his attention to the ham and eggs. Then he rose, lit his pipe and settled himself down into his chair.

SIR ARTHUR CONAN DOYLE,
The Naval Treaty

Animals fill themselves; man eats. The man of mind alone knows how to eat.

BRILLAT-SAVARIN

I abstain from wine only on account of the expense.

RALPH WALDO EMERSON

A Melton Mowbray Pork-pie

Strange pie that is almost a passion!
  O passion immoral for pie!
Unknown are the ways that they fashion
  Unknown and unseen of the eye.
The pie that is marbled and mottled,
  The pie that digests with a sigh:
For all is not Bass that is bottled,
  And all is not pork that is pie.

RICHARD LE GALLIENNE

Salad

Oh cool in the summer is salad
  And warm in the winter is love;
And a poet shall sing you a ballad
  Delicious thereon and thereof.
A singer am I, if no sinner,
  My muse has a marvellous wing,
And I willingly worship at dinner,
      The Sirens of Spring.

Take endive – like love it is bitter,
  Take beet – for like love it is red:
Crisp leaf of the lettuce shall glitter,
  And cress from the rivulet's bed:
Anchovies, foam-born, like the lady
  Whose beauty has maddened this bard:
And olives, from groves that are shady:
      And eggs – boil 'em hard.

MORTIMER COLLINS

The Salad Bowl

Oh, green and glorious! oh, herbaceous treat!
'Twould tempt the dying anchorite to eat;
Back to the world he'd turn his fleeting soul,
And plunge his fingers in the salad bowl!

SYDNEY SMITH

110

Turtle Soup

Beautiful Soup, so rich and green
Waiting in a hot tureen!
Who for such dainties would not stoop?
Soup of the evening, beautiful Soup!
Soup of the evening, beautiful Soup!
 Beau-ootiful Soo-oop!
 Beau-ootiful Soo-oop!
Soo-oop of the e-e-evening.
 Beautiful, beautiful Soup!

Beautiful Soup! Who cares for fish,
Game, or any other dish?
Who would not give all else for twop—
 Ennyworth only of beautiful Soup?
Pennyworth only of beautiful Soup?
 Beau-ootiful Soup!
 Beau-ootiful Soup!
Soo-oop of the e-e-evening,
Beautiful, beauti-ful SOUP!

LEWIS CARROLL

Soup and fish explain half the emotions of life.
SYDNEY SMITH

Dining on Whitebait. Dickie Doyle, 1849.

I'm a Shrimp! I'm a Shrimp!

I'm a shrimp! I'm a shrimp! Of diminutive size.
Inspect my antennae, and look at my eyes;
I'm a natural syphon, when dipped in a cup
For I drain the contents to the latest drop up.
I care not for craw-fish, I heed not the prawn,
From a flavour especial my fame has been drawn;
Nor e'en to the crab or the lobster do yield,
When I'm properly cook'd and efficiently peeled.
Quick! quick! pile the coals – let your saucepan be deep,
For the weather is warm, and I'm sure not to keep;
Off, off with my head – split my shell into three –
I'm a shrimp! I'm a shrimp – to be eaten with tea.

ROBERT BROUGH

The Ballad of Bouillabaisse

A street there is in Paris famous,
    For which no rhyme our language yields,
Rue Neuve des Petits Champs its name is –
    The New Street of the Little Fields.
And here's an inn, not rich and splendid
    But still in comfortable case;
To which in youth I oft attended,
    To eat a bowl of Bouillabaisse.

This Bouillabaisse a noble dish is –
    A sort of soup, or broth, or brew,
Or hotchpotch of all sorts of fishes,
    That Greenwich never could out do:
Green herbs, red peppers, mussels, saffron
    Soles, onions, garlic, roach and dace:
All these you eat at Terré's tavern
    In that one dish of Bouillabaisse.

Indeed a rich and savoury stew 'tis;
    And true philosophers, methinks,
Who love all sorts of natural beauties,
    Should love good victuals and good drinks.
And Cordelier or Benedictine
    Might gladly, sure, his lot embrace,
Nor find a fast-day too afflicting,
    Which served him up a Bouillabaisse.

I wonder if the house still there is?
    Yes, here the lamp is, as before;
The smiling red-cheeked *écaillère* is
    Still opening oysters at the door.
Is Terré still alive and able?
    I recollect his droll grimace:
He'd come and smile before your table
    And hope you liked your Bouillabaisse.

We enter – nothing's changed or older.
   "How's Monsieur Terré, waiter pray?"
The waiter stares, and shrugs his shoulder –
   "Monsieur is dead this many a day."
"It is the lot of saint and sinner,
   So honest Terré's run his race."
"What will Monsieur require for dinner?"
   "Say, do you still cook Bouillabaisse?"

"Oh, oui, Monsieur", 's the waiter's answer;
   "Quel vin Monsieur désire-t-il?"
"Tell me a good one." – "That I can, Sir:
   The Chambertin with yellow seal."
"So Terré's gone," I say and sink in
   My old accustom'd corner-place;
"He's done with feasting and with drinking,
   With Burgundy and with Bouillabaisse."

My old accustom'd corner here is,
   The table still is in the nook;
Ah! vanished many a busy year is
   This well-known chair since last I took.
When first I saw ye, *cari luoghi*,
   I'd scarce a beard upon my face,
And now a grizzled, grim old fogy,
   I sit and wait for Bouillabaisse.

Where are you, old companions trusty
   Of early days here met to dine?
Come, waiter! quick, a flagon crusty –
   I'll pledge them in the good old wine.
The kind old voices and old faces
   My memory can quick retrace;
Around the board they take their places,
   And share the wine and Bouillabaisse.

There's Jack has made a wondrous marriage;
   There's laughing Tom is laughing yet;
There's brave Augustus drives his carriage;
   There's poor old Fred in the *Gazette*;

On James's head the grass is growing:
　Good Lord! the world has wagged apace
Since here we set the claret flowing,
　And drank, and ate the Bouillabaisse.

Ah me! how quick the days are flitting!
　I mind me of a time that's gone,
When here I'd sit, as now I'm sitting,
　In this same place – but not alone.
A fair young form was nestled near me,
　A dear dear face looked fondly up,
And sweetly spoke and smiled to cheer me
　– There's no one now to share my cup.

　　　. . . . .

I drink it as the Fates ordain it.
　Come, fill it, and have done with rhymes:
Fill up the lonely glass, and drain it
　In memory of dear old times.
Welcome the wine, whate'er the seal is;
　And sit you down and say your grace
With thankful heart, whate'er the meal is.
　– Here comes the smoking Bouillabaisse!

　　　　　　W. M. THACKERAY

To the Immortal Memory of the Halibut

On which I dined this day, Monday, April 26, 1784

Where hast thou floated, in what seas pursued
Thy pastime? when wast thou an egg new spawn'd
Lost in th' immensity of ocean's waste?
Roar as they might, the overbearing winds
That rock'd the deep, thy cradle, thou wast safe –
And in thy minnikin and embryo state,
Attach'd to the firm leaf of some salt weed.
Didst thou outlive tempests, such as wrung and rack'd
The joints of many a stout and gallant bark,
And whelm'd them in the unexplored abyss.

Indebted to no magnet and no chart,
Nor under guidance of the polar fire,
Thou wast a voyager on many coasts,
Grazing at large in meadows submarine,
Where flat Batavia, just emerging, peeps
Above the brine – where Caledonia's rocks
Bear back the surge – and where Hibernia shoots
Her wondrous causeway far into the main.
  – Wherever thou hast fed, thou little thought'st,
And I not more, that I should feed on thee.
Peace, therefore, and good health, and much good fish
To him who sent thee! and success, as oft.
As it descends into the billowing gulf,
To the same drag that caught thee! – Fare thee well!
Thy lot thy brethren of the slimy fin
Would envy, could they know that thou wast doom'd
To feed a bard, and to be praised in verse.

WILLIAM COWPER

In Praise of Turtle

Of all the things I ever swallow
Good, well dressed turtle beats them hollow
It almost makes me wish, I vow,
To have two stomachs, like a cow.

THOMAS HOOD

DINNER IS SERVED

Three Unforgettable Dinners

In 1884, when in Shanghai, I became friendly with the brother of the Chinese Interpreter at the British Legation in Peking and himself no mean student of the language.

Finding life monotonous that summer when most of the residents had gone to Chefoo to enjoy the sea bathing, we decided to charter a houseboat and go up country for a few days' shooting.

There are hardly any roads in that part of China and one travelled by water in comfortable boats, at least for Europeans. You took your boy and your cook with you, and a lowdah or head boatman helped by two coolies worked in the stern an enormous scull which propelled the boat at the rate of five or six miles an hour. This was slow going, but neither my friend nor myself were in a hurry and we had made up our mind to enjoy every minute of our trip, which we did, except one evening when we accepted an invitation to a native dinner with disastrous result as we shall see presently.

We passed by Woosee and its ruined pagoda on the top of a hill, we went across Lake Chao, we entered through a water-gate the fascinating abandoned town of Kahding; where we found plenty of game among its ruins and pools: pheasants, teal and three civet cats, yah mows in Chinese. We passed through another water-gate into the walled town of Soochow, renowned for the fairness of its women, and so on. At night we made fast to the bank of the canal wherever we were, we had our dinner and went to bed early.

One morning at the crack o' dawn we had the surprise of our lives. Somewhere, not far off, a bugler was sounding the reveille. It was so extraordinary, so unexpected, that my friend and I jumped out of our bunk and climbed the bank to find out where that call came from, and there, in front of us, was a camp of Chinese soldiers, in the centre of which stood the fine tent of their commander. Curious to know something about the then Chinese Army we decided to pay him a visit. So after breakfast we walked across to the parade ground and watched some comic drilling with antiquated guns of varied patterns for which, by the way, there was no ammunition. The commander, dressed in Mandarin robes and wearing a hat with peacock feathers and cloth top boots with thick white soles, greeted us with profound bows, his arms crossed and his hands hidden in his spacious sleeves.

He and my friend started jabbering and got on well together. After we had had a good look round we asked him whether he would like to see the houseboat. He assured us that nothing would give him more pleasure. So it was arranged that he should come that afternoon. After more bowing and scraping we parted.

He arrived about tea-time accompanied by a couple of nondescript officers and two or three privates. He left his retinue on the bank and came aboard alone. We did not know what to offer him, but my friend produced a bottle of Chartreuse, several sherry glasses of which he drank without turning a hair. He soon after this became friendly and lively and, among other things we talked about, he gave us the explanation of the reveille. Some years back, he told us, to quash the revolt of the Taipings, the Chinese Government asked the help of Britain, and Gordon and a few officers and men were sent to reorganize the Chinese Army. Among the men were buglers who brought with them the British regimental calls, and these remained. All the same, it was weird to hear that reveille in a strange land thousands of miles from where it originated.

When we said good-bye to the Mandarin soldier, to whom we presented the rest of the Chartreuse, there was more bowing and scraping, and he made us promise to come and have a meal with him that night. We accepted with misgivings, knowing what strange things the Chinese eat. However, we turned up at the hour appointed and after the usual salaams we sat down on uncomfortable stools in the beautifully decorated tent.

There were two other guests besides ourselves, one of whom was the Taotai or Magistrate of a nearby village. We were first served in exquisite celadon bowls, a kind of white broth in which floated strips of brown somethings about the thickness of a pencil, which we did not ancy much. The orthodox roast duck followed; a dish I am not partial to in native China because the bird is torn to pieces by the cook and served by him or boys with dirty fingers. This was accompanied by bamboo shoots and kromakis. Two dishes came next, but I cannot recollect what they consisted of. For a wonder we had no birds' nests nor sharks' fins – we were too far from the shops. Of course, sticky rice, so different from the steamed India preparation, were by us all the time in place of bread. One sweet I remember specially – big cabbage rosebuds preserved in thick syrup. For drinks we had bowls of hot samshoo constantly replenished.

Something unusual took my fancy at that meal. Small thick linen or cotton squares, piled on a plate and steaming hot, were passed round between the courses. You took one, buried your face in it for a moment and dropped it on a plate held by a second boy. It gave you a most pleasant and refreshing sensation. I heartily recommend this practice to Corporations for their heavy banquets.

We ended the meal with tea without milk and sugar, of course, and made individually in each cup. The saucer, placed upside down on the top and held with two fingers while you sipped the brew, prevented the leaves getting in your mouth. This was accompanied by the gurgling of the quaint bubble-bubble Chinese pipes and the native guests' eructations in appreciation of a good feed.

It was than that I most unfortunately asked my friend to find out the ingredients of that white broth and specially what the brown things were.

"A great delicacy", said the Mandarin, "I am glad you liked them. They are a kind of fat palm caterpillar."

My friend looked at me, I looked at him! With one accord we rose, mumbling some kind of excuse; we rushed out of the tent just in time to bring up a dinner we had, after all, enjoyed. Such is the power of imagination.

Another dinner which I shall never forget was given somewhere in Turkey in Asia by a high official of one of the vilayets. That was many years ago. The guests were four officers, one of whom a fat major, and myself.

Before we sat down to the meal, a great quantity of raki, a very potent spirit akin to the Spanish aguardiente, was consumed and the poor major, who had already celebrated some birthday or something somewhere else, got decidedly fuddled, so much so, in fact, that when dinner was announced by a smart Kavass, his brother officers had to hoist him up from his chair and half carry him to his seat at the table, to the accompaniment of much laughter and encouragement. When we were settled, a plate of thick soup made of bamians and decorated with pimientos, was placed in front of each of us. At that moment the major, unable to keep his balance any longer, fell forward, his face right in it. His comrades thought this extremely funny and screamed with merriment at the blowing and spluttering of the poor major, who was, without a doubt, drowning in his soup. His face, usually very red, was getting purple and big veins stuck out on his temples. I could stand it no longer. I got up and, going round the table, I caught him by the hair and lifted his face from the plate. The others realized at last, that the joke had gone too far.

We carried him to a sofa and, unbuttoning his uniform, we tried to revive him by throwing several glasses of water in his face. This had no effect and we all got scared. In the end a doctor had to be called.

As to we four remaining guests, being unable to give any more help, we decided to leave the patient with his host and the doctor, and we went home on an empty stomach and in sober mood, notwithstanding the amount of raki consumed.

For myself, although very sorry for the major, I regretted the big lump of halva and the baklavas, my favourite Turkish sweets, which I had spotted on a side table when we entered the dining room.

I am glad to add that the major recovered and felt no ill-effect from his "drowning".

It was in Las Palmas, Grand Canary, in the 'nineties that I sat down, with my wife this time, to my third unforgettable dinner.

We were the only guests that night of Mr and Mrs Swanston, a most popular couple. Mr Swanston was then, if I remember rightly, in charge of the British Consulate. Cocktails were unknown in those days, but we were offered some of the famous old Blandy Brothers' Madeira. One or two members of the Blandy family actually resided in Grand Canary.

Then we sat down to what I expected to be a recherché little dinner as the Swanstons kept an excellent cook. The soup, quite a surprise, was a delicious cream of fresh ground nut, always in great demand on the West Coast, not far off. And, *apropos* of ground nut, it reminds me that the first time I dined at Government House, Sierra Leone, Colonel Cardew's A.D.C., no doubt in honour of a French guest, wrote the menu cards in French, and I was much puzzled by the first item, which read: *Potage de noix terrestres*!

To return to our unfortunate dinner, we had hardly finished our soup and the Canarian servant, after removing our plates, was passing round a succulent dish, judging by its *fumet*, when suddenly our hostess sprang up and, pointing to the ceiling, drew our attention to a curious cracking or tearing sound. "Quick, let's all clear out" she screamed like one demented.

I thought the poor lady had really gone crazy, yet there was something so compelling in her anxiety to see us out of the room that we all followed her, wondering what was going to happen next.

Well, we had hardly passed out when the whole ceiling came down with an appalling crash and everything in the room was absolutely flattened out. Moreover, a tremendous whirlwind of thick white dust blew us along the passage outside, where, covered with plaster from head to foot, we thanked Mrs Swanston for saving our lives. We had had, indeed, a narrow escape.

But what about our poor dinner! What about that lovely dish which, coming after that rare potage, promised to be something equally special! (By the way, I never knew what it was) and what about the rest of that precious Madeira and also the bottle of Hiedsieck Monopole I had seen on the table near our host. What a tragedy, without counting the crockery, the glass, the furniture reduced to pulp!

However, we soon got over our shock and sat down in another room to an impromptu meal of tinned stuff.

But how did Mrs Swanston know about the ceiling, I hear you say. This is the explanation. She was in Nice in the earthquake of 1886, I think, when many were killed. She had never forgotten the ominous crackings in a house where she herself just escaped death, and when she heard something similar in her Canarian dining room, she immediately thought that an earthquake was coming.

And now about the ceiling itself. The houses in the Canaries have no real roofs. They are built on the Eastern model with terraces instead. These are coated with a kind of clay which is beaten and rolled till it becomes waterproof. But the strong summer sun cracks it. So a new coat has to be laid on the old before the rainy season. When this has been going on for years the terrace becomes too heavy for its rafters. It collapses and now and again one heard of people being crushed to death. I daresay the modern houses in the Fortunate Isles are safer now.

BARON DE BELABRE,
Wine and Food, 34

No mean woman can cook well. It calls for a generous spirit, a light hand and a large heart.

EDEN PHILLPOTTS

A Consular Menu

May 1676

9. We had a breakfast, but no sett dinner; but all the nation was invited at Assera to a treat of our Consull's providinge; but such a on as I never saw before. The particulars whereof you may see below as they stood on the table.

A Dish of Turkeys		A Dish of Tarts
	A Plate of Sauceages	
A Dish of Gellys		A Dish of Gammons and Tongs
	A Bisqué of Eggs	
A Dish of Geese		A Dish of Biscotts
	A Plate of Anchovies	
A Dish of Hens		A Venison Pasty
	A Plate of Anchovies	
A Dish of Biscotts		A Dish of Green Geese
	A Great Dish with a Pyramid of Marchpane	
A Dish of Tarts		A Dish of Hens
	A Dish of Hartichocks	
A Pasty		A Dish of Marchpane in Cakes
	A Dish of Sauceages	
A Dish of Gammons		A Dish of Biscott
	A Plate of Herrings	
A Dish of Geese		A Dish of Turkeys
	A Plate of Anchovies	
A Dish of Marchpane		A Pasty
	Hartichocks	
A Dish of Hens		A Dish of Gellys
	A Pyramid of Marchpane	
A Dish of Biscott		A Dish of Gammons
	Anchovies	

THE REVEREND HENRY TEONGE,
Chaplain on board His Majesty's Ships *Assistance, Bristol* and *Royal Oak*, 1675–9,
Adventures of a Naval Chaplain

Dining Under Difficulties

September 1675

30. A brave gale all night, which brought us this morning nearer Candia, to a small iland called Goza, and another a little more eastward, called Anti-Goza. More myrth at dinner this day then ever since wee cam on board. The wind blew very hard, and wee had to dinner a rump

of Zante beife, a little salted and well rosted. When it was brought in to
the cabin and set on the table (that is, on the floore, for it could not
stand on the table for the ship's tossing), our Captaine sent for the
Master, Mr Fogg, and Mr Davis, to dine with him selfe and my selfe,
and the Leiuetenant and the Pursor. And wee all sat closse round about
the beife, som securing themselves from slurring by setting their feete
against the table, which was fast tyd downe. The Leiuetenant set his
feets against the bedd, and the Captaine set his back against a chayre
which stood by the syd of the ship. Severall tumbles wee had, wee and
our plates, and our knives slurrd oft together. Our liquor was white
rubola, admirable good. Wee had also a couple of fatt pullets; and whilst
wee were eating of them, a sea cam, and forced into the cabin through
the chinks of a port hole, which by lookeing behind me I just discovered
when the water was coming under mee. I soone got up, and no whitt
wett; but all the rest were well washed, and got up as fast as the could,
and laughed on at the other. Wee dranke the King's and Duke's healths,
and all our wives particularly; and cam out at 2 a clock, and were com
as far as Sugar-lofe hill in Candia. Severall seas com over our ship, and
cause much myrth to see the water flee as high as the mainmast, and to
wash as many as was under it.

Ibid.

Show me another pleasure like dinner which comes every day and
lasts an hour.

TALLEYRAND

A Roman Meal

. . . the hour being arrived, he conducted them to the hotel where the physician lodged, after having regaled their expectations with an elegant meal in the genuine old Roman taste; and they were received by Mr Pallet, who did the honours of the house, while his friend superintended the cook below. By this communicative painter, the guests understood that the doctor had met with numerous difficulties in the execution of his design; that no fewer than five cooks had been dismissed, because they could not prevail upon their own consciences to obey his directions in things that were contrary to the present practice of their art; and that although he had at last engaged a person, by an extraordinary premium, to comply with his orders, the fellow was so astonished, mortified and incensed at the commands he had received that his hair stood on end, and he begged, on his knees, to be released from the agreement he had made; but finding that his employer insisted upon the performance of his contract, and threatened to introduce him to the commissaire, if he should flinch from the bargain, he had, in the discharge of his office, wept, sung, cursed, and capered, for two whole hours without inter-mission.

While the company listened to this odd information, by which they were prepossessed with strange notions of the dinner, their ears were invaded by a piteous voice, that exclaimed in French, "For the love of God! dear sir! for the passion of Jesus Christ! spare me the mortifica-tion of the honey and oil!" Their ears still vibrated with the sound, when the doctor entering, was by Peregrine made acquainted with the strangers, to whom he, in the transports of his wrath, could not help complaining of the want of complaisance he had found in the Parisian vulgar, by which his plan had been almost entirely ruined and set aside. The French marquis, who thought the honour of his nation was con-cerned at this declaration, professed his sorrow for what had happened, so contrary to the established character of the people, and undertook to see the delinquents severely punished, provided he could be informed of their names and places of abode.

The mutual compliments that passed on this occasion were scarce finished, when a servant, coming into the room, announced dinner; and the entertainer led the way into another apartment, where they found a long table, or rather two boards joined together, and furnished with a variety of dishes, the steams of which had such evident effect upon the nerves of the company, that the marquis made frightful grimaces, under pretence of taking snuff; the Italian's eyes watered; the German's visage underwent several distortions of feature; our hero found means to exclude the odour from his sense of smelling, by breathing only through his mouth; and the poor painter, running into another room, plugged his nostrils with tobacco. The doctor himself, who was the only person then present whose organs were not discomposed, pointing to a couple of couches placed on each side of the table, told his guests that he was sorry he could not procure the exact triclinia of the ancients, which were somewhat different from these conveniences, and desired they would have the goodness to repose themselves without ceremony, each in his respective couchette, while he and his friend Mr Pallet would place themselves upright at the ends, that they might have the pleasure of serving those that lay along. This disposition, of which the strangers had no previous idea, disconcerted and perplexed them in a most ridiculous manner; the marquis and baron stood bowing to each other, on pretence of disputing the lower seat, but in reality with a view of profiting by the example of each other, for neither of them understood the manner in which they were to loll; and Peregrine, who enjoyed their confusion, handed the count to the other side, where, with the most mischievous politeness, he insisted upon his taking possession of the upper place.

In this disagreeable and ludicrous suspense, they continued acting a pantomime of gesticulations, until the doctor earnestly entreated them to waive all compliment and form, lest the dinner should be spoiled before the ceremonial could be adjusted. Thus conjured, Peregrine took the lower couch on the left-hand side, laying himself gently down, with his face towards the table. The marquis, in imitation of this pattern, though he would have much rather fasted three days than run the risk of discomposing his dress by such an attitude, stretched himself upon the opposite place, reclining upon his elbow in a most painful and awkward situation, with his head raised above the end of the couch, that the economy of his hair might not suffer by the projection of his body. The Italian, being a thin limber creature, planted him-self next to Pickle, without sustaining any misfortune, but that of his stocking being torn by a ragged nail of the seat, as he raised his legs on a level with the rest of his limbs. But the baron, who was neither so wieldy nor supple in his joints as his companions, flounced himself down with such precipitation, that his feet, suddenly tilting up, came in furious contact with the head of the marquis, and demolished every curl in a twinkling, while his own skull, at the same instant, descended upon the side of his couch with such violence, that his periwig was struck off, and the whole room filled with pulvilio.

The drollery of distress that attended this disaster entirely vanquished the affected gravity of our young gentleman, who was obliged to suppress his laughter by cramming his handkerchief in his mouth; for the bareheaded German asked pardon with such ridiculous confusion, and the marquis admitted his apology with such rueful complaisance, as were sufficient to awake the mirth of a Quietist.

This misfortune being repaired as well as the circumstances of the occasion would permit, and every one settled according to the arrangement already described, the doctor graciously undertook to give some account of the dishes as they occurred, that the company might be directed in their choice; and with an air of infinite satisfaction, thus began, "This here, gentlemen, is a boiled goose, served up in a sauce composed of pepper, lovage, coriander, mint, rue, anchovies and oil! I wish, for your sakes, gentlemen, it was one of the geese of Ferrara, so much celebrated among the ancients for the magnitude of their livers, one of which is said to have weighed upwards of two pounds; with this food, exquisite as it was, did the tyrant Heliogabalus regale his hounds. But I beg pardon, I had almost forgot the soup, which I hear is so necessary an article at all the tables in France. At each end there are dishes of the salacacabia of the Romans; one is made of parsley, pennyroyal, cheese, pinetops, honey, vinegar, brine, eggs, cucumbers, onions and hen livers; the other is much the same as the soup-maigre of this country. Then there is a loin of boiled veal with fennel and carraway seed, on a pottage composed of pickle, oil, honey and flour, and a curious hashish of the lights, liver, and blood of a hare, together with a dish of roasted pigeons. Monsieur le baron, shall I help you to a plate of this soup?" The German, who did not at all disapprove of the ingredients, assented to the proposal, and seemed to relish the composition; while the marquis being asked by the painter which of the silly-kickabys he chose, was, in consequence of his desire, accommodated with a portion of the soup-maigre; and the count, in lieu of spoon meat, of which he said he was no great admirer, supplied himself with a pigeon, therein conforming to the choice of our young gentleman, whose example he determined to follow through the whole course of the entertainment.

The Frenchman having swallowed the first spoonful, made a full pause, his throat swelled as if an egg had stuck in his gullet, his eyes rolled, and his mouth underwent a series of involuntary contractions and dilations. Pallet, who looked steadfastly at this connoisseur, with a view of consulting his taste, before he himself would venture upon the soup, began to be disturbed at these emotions, and observed with some concern, that the poor gentleman seemed to be going into a fit; when Peregrine assured him, that these were symptoms of ecstasy, and for further confirmation asked the marquis how he found the soup. It was with infinite difficulty that his complaisance could so far master his disgust, as to enable him to answer, "Altogether excellent, upon my honour!" And the painter being certified of his approbation, lifted the spoon to his mouth without scruple; but far from justifying the eulogium of his taster, when this precious composition diffused itself upon his palate, he seemed to be deprived of all sense and motion, and sat like the leaden statue of some river god, with the liquor flowing out at both sides of his mouth.

The doctor, alarmed at this indecent phenomenon, earnestly inquired into the cause of it; and when Pallet recovered his recollection and swore that he would rather swallow porridge made of burning brimstone, than such an infernal mess as that which he had tasted, the physician, in his own vindication, assured the company that, except the usual ingredients, he had mixed nothing in the soup but some sal-ammoniac, instead of the ancient nitrum, which could not now be procured; and appealed to the marquis, whether such a *succedaneum* was not an improvement on the whole. The unfortunate *petit-maître*, driven to the extremity of his condescension, acknowledged it to be a masterly refinement; and deeming himself obliged, in point of honour, to evince his sentiments by his practice, forced a few more mouthfuls of this disagreeable potion down his throat, till his stomach was so much offended, that he was compelled to start up of a sudden, and, in the hurry of his elevation, overturned his plate into the bosom of the baron. The emergency of his occasions would not permit him to stay and make apologies for this abrupt behaviour; so that he flew into another apartment, where Pickle found him puking, and crossing himself with great devotion; and a chair, at his desire, being brought to the door, he slipped into it more dead than alive, conjuring his friend Pickle to make his peace with the company, and, in particular, excuse him to the baron, on account of the violent fit of illness with which he had been seized. It was not without reason that he employed a mediator; for when our hero returned to the dining-room, the German got up, and was under the hands of his own lacquey, who wiped the grease from a rich embroidered waistcoat, while he, almost frantic with his misfortune, stamped upon the ground, and, in High Dutch, cursed the unlucky banquet, and the impertinent entertainer, who all this time, with great deliberation, consoled him for the disaster, by assuring him that the damage might be repaired with some oil of turpentine and a hot iron. Peregrine, who could scarce refrain from laughing in his face, appeased his indignation by telling him how much the whole company, and especially the marquis, was mortified at the accident; and the unhappy *salacacabia* being removed, the places were filled with two pies – one of dormice, liquored with syrup of white poppies, which the doctor had substituted in the room of toasted poppy-seed, formerly eaten with honey, as a dessert; and the other composed of an hock of pork baked in honey.

Pallet hearing the first of these dishes described, lifted up his hands and eyes, and, with signs of loathing and amazement, pronounced, "A pie made of dormice and syrup of poppies! – Lord in heaven! what beastly fellows those Romans were!" His friend checked him for his irreverent exclamation with a severe look, and recommended the veal of which he himself cheerfully ate, with such encomiums to the company, that the baron resolved to imitate his example, after having called for a bumper of burgundy, which the physician, for his sake, wished to have been the true wine of Falernum. The painter, seeing nothing else upon the table which he would venture to touch, made a merit of necessity, and had recourse to the veal also; although he could not help saying that he would not give one slice of the roast beef of Old England for all the dainties of a Roman emperor's table. But all the doctor's invitations and assurances could not prevail upon his guests to honour the hashis and the goose; and that course was succeeded by another, in which he told them were divers of those dishes, which, among the ancients, had obtained the appellation of *politeles*, or magnificent. "That which smokes in the middle", said he, "is a sow's stomach filled with a composition of minced pork, hog's brains, eggs, pepper, cloves, garlic, aniseed, rue, ginger, oil, wine and pickle. On the right-hand side are the teats and belly of a sow, just farrowed, fried with sweet wine, oil, flour, lovage, and pepper. On the left is a *fricasee* of snails, fed, or rather purged, with milk. At that end, next Mr Pallet, are fritters of pompions, lovage, origanum, and oil; and here are a couple of pullets, roasted and stuffed in the manner of Apicius."

The painter, who had, by wry faces, testified his abhorrence of the sow's stomach, which he compared to a bagpipe, and the snails which had undergone purgation, no sooner heard him mention the roasted pullets, than he eagerly solicited a wing of the fowl; upon which the doctor desired he would take the trouble of cutting them up, and accordingly sent them round, while Mr Pallet tucked the tablecloth under his chin, and brandished his knife and fork with singular address; but scarce were they set down before him, when the tears ran down his cheeks, and he called aloud in a manifest disorder, "Zounds! this is the essence of a whole bed of garlic!" That he might not, however, disappoint or disgrace the entertainer, he applied his instruments to one of the birds; and, when he opened up the cavity, was assaulted by such an irruption of intolerable smells, that, without staying to disengage himself from the cloth, he sprung away, with an exclamation of

"Lord Jesus!" and involved the whole table in havoc and confusion.

Before Pickle could accomplish his escape, he was sauced with a syrup of the dormice pie, which went to pieces in the general wreck. And as for the Italian count, he was overwhelmed by the sow's stomach, which bursting in the fall discharged its contents upon his leg and thigh, and scalded him so miserably, that he shrieked with anguish, and grinned with a most ghastly and horrible aspect.

TOBIAS SMOLLETT,
The Adventures of Peregrine Pickle

"On second thoughts, Norris, we'll just have a chop."

A Soupçon of Kerosene

Dinner had to be cooked – and what a dinner too! Our Chief had most kindly brought with him from Ocean Island an exquisite little shoulder of frozen lamb, *and* some onions, *and* potatoes, AND a tin of real French *petits pois*. We ourselves could put up such things as mint sauce or red-currant jelly, as well as olives, salted almonds and the rest; beyond which, to crown perfection with beauty's ultimate grace, there was our plum pudding, tinned, but delicious. It was so delicious, in fact, that we had decided to hoard this last of six trial tins for Christmas. I grudged the premature sacrifice of it at first, but Olivia was more generous. The Old Man liked a good sweet, she said: and anyhow, her argument ran on, what sort of a main course were we going to get at Christmas comparable to roast lamb. Why not decide to look on this night's feast as our Christ-mas dinner in advance and make an artist's job of it, soup, joint and pudding in one sweet symphony. I thought of the *allegretto* of the soup, the pastoral *andante* of the lamb and little peas, the *scherzo* of almonds and wittily stuffed olives running into the rollicking *rondo* of the pud-ding. My mouth watered. I withdrew my niggardly objections.

The joint was popped into the oven about an hour and a half before dinner, with Sila on guard. Faasolo was quiet now, he said. Last in-structions were given. We bathed, changed, had a final look at the dinner-table, saw that it looked nice with our best glass and rose candle-shades, felt young and adult and proud, passed out to the cool down-staris loggia, were presently joined there by our Chief, and relaxed a while with pleasant drinks beside us.

. . . As we took our seats at the rose-lit dining-table, I felt that we were all one together for always in this land that was no strange land now for any of us. And the soup, when it appeared, looked a creamy dream to me. Olivia always could do heavenly things with chicken stock, asparagus and tinned milk. Sila, too, had become an adept at it.

But Sila's unhappy Faasolo had crept into the kitchen while we were at drinks and asked him to refill her hurricane lamp. I, for my part, never did much mind a *soupçon* of kerosene in any food except fish, so I went on with my helping. Olivia and the Old Man chose to abandon theirs in favour of sherry, toast and *jeux d'esprit*. That seemed rather a pity, but neither said a word about the soup. What was there to worry about, anyhow, with lamb and plum pudding still in prospect?

I was lapping up the last spoonsful when Sila appeared at the door naked to the waist in a not very clean state. He made no apology for intruding like that, but spoke in English, presumably in honour of our guest: "Missus, come quick!" he cried urgently. "Gravy, no bloody good!" and bolted back to the kitchen.

Olivia rushed wildly after him. The Old Man lit a cigarette and sat mum. I became aware of tension in his silence. I was tense myself. Gravy is important.

Looking back from now to then, I realize that Sila's report did little justice to himself. For gravy to be good or bad there must *be* some of it, and in this case there was none at all. That was his real problem, and it was one that no cook on earth could have solved in the circumstances. As for blaming anyone else, I can see that if he was innocent so also was poor Faasolo. She, like him was, in the last analysis, but the driven puppet of calamity. She had come to the kitchen at seven o'clock intending to leave as soon as he filled her lamp. But she was a woman, and what woman in her place could have resisted the temptation that assailed her then? Her heart was bursting with heavy new thoughts about his lady visitor. She stayed to confide them to him. He paused in his work to reply. One thing led to the next; she went on, he went on. They lost themselves in each other, oblivious to all else until disaster fell upon them. It was the ooze of greasy fumes from the oven that told them what had happened. The shoulder of our little lamb was burned to a cinder. One cannot make gravy with ashes.

If this had been fiction, my story would have ended with the walk-out of our furious Chief when cold bullimacow and beetroot were laid before him. But real list has small regard for climax and anti-climax; it just goes on, as the meal went on. We finished our gross substitutes for lamb and *petits pois* with little gaiety. He did, indeed, rise at the end and say he thought that would be about enough for that evening. Olivia, I could see, was keen to let him go, and be damned to the plum pudding. But something in me rebelled at the total waste of that one remaining treasure. So I told him the history of it, despite her reproachful glances. In the end, I was glad I had done so, because he consented with visible softening of temper to stay on. We all sat down again.

There was a longish wait before the pudding arrived. Sila came along at last himself to explain the delay. His first attempt at sauce had gone wrong, so he had made another just as good.

"Well, well, better late than never!" observed the Old Man brightly when it was uncovered. "And, my word! what have we here? The sauce looks very handsome, I must say." And so it did, swimming crimson-red around the pudding's foot.

"Yes, he good Sah," volunteered Sila, "I makem myself. I boilem with plenty sugar."

"Some kind of wine sauce eh?" The Old Man had recaptured his benevolence with extraordinary decency. I could see Olivia was glad now that I had got him to stay.

"No Sah," replied Sila, "he not wine – he juice. He beetroot juice outem tin."

It was then that the Old Man walked out, and Olivia wept.

SIR ARTHUR GRIMBLE,
A Pattern of Islands

Vegetable Luxury

One of the greatest luxuries in dining is to be able to command plenty of good vegetables well served up. But this is a luxury vainly hoped for at set parties. The vegetables are made to figure in a very secondary way, except, indeed, whilst they are considered as great delicacies, which is generally before they are at their best – excellent potatoes, smoking hot and accompanied by melted butter of the first quality would alone stamp merit on any dinner.

THOMAS WALKER,
The Art of Dining (1835)

A City Feast

The napkins were folded on every plate
Into castles and boats, and the devil knows what –

Then each tuck'd his napkin under his chin,
That his holyday band might be kept very clean;
And pinn'd up his sleeves to his elbows, because
They should not hang down, and be greased in the sauce.

When done with the flesh, then they clawed off the fish,
With one hand at mouth, and the other in dish.
When their stomachs were closed, what their bellies denied,
Each clapt in his pocket to give to his bride,
With a cheesecake and custard for my little Johnny,
And a handful of sweetmeats for poor daughter Nanny.

ROBERT SOUTHEY
Common-place Book (1849–51)

Watching a Dinner

Oh! Johnnie! 'ere's a dinner party – Look at all them things!
Oh! look at all them dishes – Wot that powdered footman brings!
Well, if they eat all that there food – 'Ow poorly they will be
'Ere, jump upon my back, Johnnie! – Now, then, you can see!
Oh! Johnnie! look at that ole gent, – They've took 'is plate away!
Afore 'e's finished 'arf 'is food, – That is a game to play!
No! that ain't beer they're drinkin' of – Not likely, why, that's fizz!
Oh! look at that great pink thing there, – That's salmon fish, that is!
I think there's some mistake 'ere, Johnnie! – We ain't arst to-night!
We could a-pick'd a bit, eh! Johnnie? – We've got the appetite!
Seein' all that food there makes yer 'ungry, that it do!
We ain't had no dinner-parties lately! Johnnie! me and you!
Oh! Johnnie! look at that ole gal, – With only 'arf a gown,
The hice she's swaller'd must 'ave cost, ah! well nigh 'arf-a-crown.
She's 'avin' 'arf a quartern now, and wants it, that she do,
When I've eat too much hice myself, – I've 'ad that feelin' too!
Oh! Johnnie! they've pulled down the blind, – I call it nasty mean.
They're all ashamed, that's wot they is, – Ashamed o' bein' seen.
A-eatin' all that food like that, – 'Tain't decent, that it ain't!
We wouldn't pull no blinds down – If we'd 'arf o' their complaint!
So come along, let's 'oof it, Johnnie, – 'Oof it to the Strand,
Now don't yer go a-cryin', Johnnie, – 'Ere, give me your 'and.
'Ungry, Johnnie? So am I, – We'll get a brown or two,
A-callin' "Keb or Kerridge, Captain!" Johnnie! me and you!

Anon.

Eating on Stage

Other great actors, again, aid themselves in the matter of eating by
thinking out devices beforehand. Thus in *Gringoire*, the late Sir Herbert
Tree, playing one of his most famous character studies – that of a penni-
less poet at the court of Louis XI – found himself faced with the problem of being a starving man on whom a meal is suddenly bestowed. He
had to eat, for he believed in realism; he *had* to tackle a whole chicken,
with his hands. He solved the difficulty by causing to be constructed for
himself a fine, plump, hollow pullet of *papier maché*, the breast being
composed of two lids. He then filled it every night with real slices of
excellent cold chicken and was thus able, when the moment came, to
fling himself on the bird, tackle it with his fingers, and eat it with a
proper relish and abandon in front of an enthusiastic audience. In addition, he concluded this banquet with a whole bunch of genuine grapes.
The wine, however, which accompanied all this food, consisted of
coloured water – except when one evening, by mistake, turpentine was
substituted for it. Unfortunately Sir Herbert swallowed a great gulp from
his glass before he discovered the nature of its contents. With remarkable
fortitude, however, he continued to act, although he was all the time
suffering the greatest agony, until the end of the play.

This meal was a feat, but how much endurance, coupled with an equal
art – and more appetite – it must take to have an entire dinner served to
you upon the stage, and to consume it. Yet, in spite of the difficulties,
in spite of superstitions, and stage managers, it has several times been
successfully accomplished. Thus, in that popular play *The Man from
Blankley's*, the late Sir Charles Hawtrey devoured his way right through
the menu of a normal burgess dinner of pre-war days, with the custom-
ary number of courses – soup, fish, chicken, sweet, savoury – served in
the traditional manner. Notwithstanding the apparent ease and enjoyment with which he ate, and for all the smoothness with which the scene
was presented, this was a triumphant achievement – but then Hawtrey
and his stage manager were both accomplished technicians.

Such repasts, such single dishes, that are what they pretend to be,
constitute, nevertheless, a rarity in stage history. Though we may have
listened with sympathy at the beginning of this essay to the complaint
of Monsieur Clary, it was never, in fact, justified, and we come back to
the two great categories already mentioned, into which the generality
of theatrical food is still divided; pasteboard and one edible material
masquerading as another. When we see actors or actresses eating, undoubtedly eating, we can, if we hold the cypher, translate the outward

semblance of the food on their side of the mirror into its reality on ours; just as, to take another sense, that of sound, instead of taste, if we see a stage crowd in riot or panic, the faces contorted, the air full of shouts, we wonder what the words are that they utter, and then recall that the answer is "Rhubarb!", "Rhubarb!", or "Rhabarbet", as some say; for that, I know not why, is the convention. Similarly caviare on the boards turns into black-currant jam off them, and meat – a particularly difficult substance to swallow while talking – is always represented by a kind of pink mousse or jelly. The part of wine is nearly always taken by coloured water, though ginger-ale, as a rule, passes for champagne. (Admirers of Miss Tallulah Bankhead will, on the other hand, remember with pleasure how often they have seen her drink *real* champagne in one of the plays in which she appeared in London.) There are, however, common exceptions; tea is always tea, frequent, hot and plentiful, but weak; and chocolates are chocolates all the stage over – the contents, it can be confidently stated of no box, however vast in size, ever seeing the light of the following day.

SIR OSBERT SITWELL,
Sing High! Sing Low!

Ancient Customs

The table was covered with wreaths, greens, cups and ewers. Slaves brought woven baskets filled with bread light as snow. Fat eels sprinkled with seasonings, wax-colored alphests and sacred callichthys were brought in upon platters of painted earthenware.

Thus too were served a pompilos, a purple fish believed to be born of the same foam as Aphrodite, boops and bedradones, a gray mullet flanked with cuttle-fish, and multicolored scorpoeni. In order that they might be eaten burning hot, slices of fat tunnyfish, and soft warm pulps with tender arms were presented in little casseroles. And, at the last, the belly of a white torpedo, round as that of a beautiful woman.

Such was the first course, from which the guests selected the good morsels in little fragments and left the rest for the slaves . . .

The second course was coming to an end. Pheasants had been served, sand-grouse, a magnificent red and blue porphura and a swan with all its feathers which had been cooked for forty-eight hours in order not to scorch its wings. Upon upcurved platters lay waterplants, pelicans and a white peacock which seemed to brood eighteen roasted and larded balls of sperm – in short, food enough to nourish an hundred persons with the fragments which were left, when the choice morsels had been set aside. But all this was nothing beside the last dish.

This masterpiece (for nothing such had been seen at Alexandria for a long time) was a young pig, half of which had been roasted and the other half stewed in bouillon. It was impossible to distinguish where it had been killed or how they had filled its belly with all it contained. It was stuffed with round quails, the breasts of fowls, larks, succulent sauces, slices of vulva and minced meat, the presence of which, in the intact animal, seemed inexplicable.

There was a general cry of admiration and Faustina resolved to ask for the recipe. Phrasilas smilingly uttered metaphorical sentences: Philodemos improved a distich where the word *"choiros"* was taken in turn by its two meanings, which made the already drunken Seso laugh until she cried; but as Bacchis had given the order to pour out seven rare wines in seven cups for each banqueter, the conversation degenerated.

PIERRE LOUYS,
Aphrodite

"Of course we really only bother with Christmas for the child's sake."

The Prince of Wales' Irish Friend

O'Byrne, a native of Ireland . . . without talents, morals, connections, rank or education, he contrived to attain a certain degree of celebrity, acquired a very considerable fortune, entertained with splendid profusion and was received among persons of the highest rank, who even courted his society. He was accustomed to tell the Prince of Wales many bold as well as unpalatable truths . . . I have already mentioned O'Byrne's skill in the science of cookery or gastronomy; he lived in very familiar habits with the late Duke of Orleans, too well known by the part which he took in the French Revolution. As O'Byrne passed much of his time in the capital of France between 1782 and 1788, he frequently dined with the Duke either at the Palais Royal or at the voluptuous retreat at Monceaux, without the barrier of Paris. O'Byrne told me that dining at the latter place in a select company where a superb repast was served, all the guests vied in their enconiums on the delicacy with which the dishes were prepared. "*Monseigneur, vous êtes bien servi*", said they; "*on ne peut rien goûter de mieux apprêté.*" The Marquis de Sillery, one of them, and he only, dissented from the general opinion. "*Non, monseigneur*", said he, "*vous êtes mal servi; vous ne savez pas vivre; je vous donnerai à manger, et à toute cette compagnie; alors, vous verrez, messieurs, ce que c'est que d'être servi comme il faut.*" "We all stared at each other," added O'Byrne, "but a day was named and the company met. Never did I taste such cookery. Only two dishes were ever placed on the table at the same time; they were, however, exquisite. We sat down at three o'clock and continued eating till nine. Every individual present admitted that Sillery had made good his promise and outdone the Duke of Orleans."

Memoirs of Sir Nathaniel William Wraxall (1815)

Christmas Dinner in the Arctic Seas

Dec. 25 (1829). It was Christmas day. There are few places on the civilized earth in which that day is not, perhaps, the most noted of the year; to all, it is at least a holiday; and there are many to whom it is somewhat more. The elements themselves seemed to have determined that it should be a noted day to us, for it commenced with a most beautiful and splendid aurora, occupying the whole vault above. At first, and for many hours, it displayed a succession of arches, gradually increasing in altitude as they advanced from the east and proceeded towards the western side of the horizon; while the succession of changes were not less brilliant than any that we had formerly witnessed. The church service allotted for this peculiar day was adopted; but, as is the etiquette of the naval service, the holiday was also kept by an unusually liberal dinner, of which, roast beef from our Galloway ox, not yet expended, formed the essential and orthodox portion. I need not say that the rule against grog was rescinded for this day, since, without that, it would not have been the holiday expected by a seaman. The stores of the *Fury* rendered us, here, even more than the reasonable service we might have claimed; since they included mince pies, and, what would have been more appropriate elsewhere, though abundantly natural here, iced cherry brandy with its fruit; matters, however, of amusement, when we recollected that we were rioting in the luxuries of a hot London June, without the heat of a ball in Grosvenor Square to give them value, and really without any especial desire for sweetmeats of so cooling a nature. I believe that it was a happy day for all the crew: and happy days had a moral value with us, little suspected by those whose lives, of uniformity, and of uniform ease, peace, and luxury, one or all, render them as insensible to those hard-won enjoyments, as unobservant of their effects on the minds of men. To display all our flags was a matter of course; and the brilliancy of Venus was a spectacle which was naturally contemplated as in harmony with the rest of the day.

SIR JOHN ROSS,
Narrative of a Second Voyage in Search of a North-west Passage and of a Residence in the Arctic Regions During the Years 1829, 1830, 1831, 1832, 1833 (1835)

A Night of Destruction

November 1675

9. I was invited to dinnar with our Captaine, and our Doctor, our Pursor, Capt. Mauris, and Capt. North, to our Consulls on shoare; where wee had a princelike dinnar: and every health that wee dranke, every man broake the glasse he drank in; so that before night wee had destroyed a whole chest of pure Venice glasses; and when dinnar was ended, the Consull presented every one of us with a bunch of beads, and a handfull of crosse, for which he sent to Jherusalem on purpose, as he tolde us afterwards.

THE REVEREND HENRY TEONGE,
Chaplain on board His Majesty's Ships *Assistance*, *Bristol* and *Royal Oak*, 1675-9,
Adventures of a Naval Chaplain

EATING OUT

Lunch with Ronald Firbank

Some months later he appealed – yes, that is the word – to me to lunch
with him again. But would I mind the Café Royal. He liked the Café
Royal. Was I sure I wouldn't mind? At that time the Café Royal had a
very mixed clientele. Firbank evidently had a vogue of his own in that
gilded saloon, the domino room or café itself. Our entry was much observed. We found a table. Cocktails, of course. No, the ordinary lunch
wasn't good enough for us. While our special food was being cooked
we sat and looked on at the curious medley of painters, young officers,
models and daughters of joy. C. R. W. Nevinson drifted by, nodding to
me as he passed. He returned: "You haven't seen John, have you –
Augustus John? I'm lunching with him here."

I had not. He stood for a minute and I introduced him to Firbank.
"I don't like that fellow," my host said, as Nevinson left us; "I think
he's sinister."

In a few minutes Nevinson, who had been roaming about like a lost
spirit, returned: "I don't think John's coming. Can I lunch at your
table, Grant?"

I assented with rather a poor grace, indicating that Firbank, as my
host, was really the man to ask. After all, I was in a difficulty, since my
host had said he didn't like Nevinson. Nor did Firbank help. He glared.
I said something that implied that Nevinson had been a soldier, that he
had been invalided out and that he was not anxious to return to any kind
of battlefield now or at any time. Firbanks face brightened. Evidently
the painter was a fellow sufferer fearing the same enemy. Nevinson must
have a cocktail. The waiter must bring double martinis for all three of
us. Nevinson must be his guest . . . Painter and writer became as thick

as thieves, bosom friends in the twinkling of an eye. Left alone with Nevinson for a minute, I told him who Firbank was, indicating that he was a possible patron as he was interested in the arts. Later, Firbank insisted on knowing where his guest was going. To the New English Art Club show. Could he come too? "Yes, do go," I broke in, "and buy one of Nevinson's paintings." Firbank looked, unsteadily, at his watch. Good God! Was it really half-past three? He must get to Coutts' to cash a cheque. He'd break the door down with a hatchet rather than be balked. I had time to tell Nevinson to look after him a bit. "He's got to get back to Oxford", I added, for Firbank was then living in Oxford, occupying, I believe, a whole large house at the bottom of the High, where he hoped that the military authorities had lost sight of him.

GRANT RICHARDS,
Author Hunting

Lunch with a Great Dane

It was when Xavier, the dog, showed signs of being famished, that Christophe was driven to action. He could starve himself, out of pique, but not a noble animal. Dark thoughts began to churn in Christophe's mind and all of them centred around Busse. Busse wanted to destroy him, and had taken steps to do so. What were the facts? Christophe was not insolvent. A week's wages were due to him, fifteen hundred francs. If Madame Berthelot owed him that sum, and Busse owed her much more than that, Christophe was justified, he thought, in collecting from Busse by any means at all. Busse was manager of the hotel and restaurant, the Mont Souris. For 1,500 francs a sound meal could be had. Christophe rose, and the dog whined approvingly.

Leading the Great Dane to the Hôtel de Mont Souris, Christophe passed through the lobby, head held higher than a Prime Minister's. The huge padded feet of the Dane skidded on the polished parquet. The clerk, Ribou, was absent from his desk. No guests were seated among the palms and rubber plants. Busse was nowhere to be seen.

Christophe went on into the dining-room, which was deserted at that hour. The Great Dane, smelling food from the kitchen, let out one deep resonant bark that echoed through the building.

Busse, two flights upstairs, still staring at the painting "La Chasse Spirituelle", which was propped on his camouflaged *bidet*, turned pale and trembled. He knew he should investigate and assert himself, and had to admit that he lacked the courage. He wished, as he did so many times each day, that he had been born brave.

The regular waiters in the dining-room of the Mont Souris had been excused for a couple of hours and an extra colleague sent by the union was left on guard. When the strange waiter saw a tall man, well dressed and correct, entering with a prize dog on a leash he bowed and advanced. The dining-room was fragrant. All the tables were carefully set. The linen was white, the silver caught glints in the dimness. The curtains of the courtyard windows were slightly parted. There were bouquets of spring flowers at regular intervals, in ranks and files. As their hues and their fragrance assailed Christophe, he straightened and ground his teeth.

"An admirable dog, monsieur," the extra waiter said.

"He's hungry," Christophe said nonchalantly. "A couple of pounds of raw meat and a bone or two if you please."

"By all means," said the waiter, "I'll fetch them from the kitchen . . . And for Monsieur?"

"Come to think of it, I haven't lunched today," Christophe said.

The waiter gestured toward the expanse of unoccupied tables. "Would monsieur prefer to sit by a window?" he asked.

Somehow Christophe preferred not to go too far into the room. He indicated a table near the door which led to the bar, and the waiter installed him there. Xavier, convinced that all was well, stretched out at full length, his huge head on his front paws.

"This will do," said Christophe.

"And what will you have?" the waiter asked.

From somewhere far back in Christophe's memory came recollections of food and wine.

"Have you a plump young guinea hen which could be halved and grilled rather lightly?" Christophe asked.

"We have a chicken of Bresse now being roasted," the waiter said.

"Precisely. A chicken of Bresse. And while I am waiting for the chicken, a rabbit pâté and bread with a bottle of Pouilly."

"The pâté is excellent. I've tried it myself," the waiter said. He hurried away to the kitchen, returned with the bread and pâté, excused himself, came back once more with the wine and a platter on which were raw meat scraps for Xavier.

Christophe was turning the wine bottle in its bucket of ice; "This is cool enough," he said. The waiter started to pull the cork and showed no astonishment when Christophe forgot himself, grabbed a piece of bread and tore off a huge mouthful which he chewed ravenously.

"It's not often one sees a healthy appetite these days," said the waiter. The old man had tucked his napkin into his collar, and had eaten half the bread and most of the pâté. When the waiter started pouring the white wine into a wine glass, Christophe substituted the water tumbler, and when it was filled, tossed it off.

"Is it to your taste, Monsieur?" the waiter asked.

Christophe was on his second tumbler. He swallowed it and nodded.

The waiter glanced down at the dog, who had cleaned the platter in three gulps. "You're feeding your dog rather early, if you wish a tranquil night."

"I do not want a tranquil night," Christophe said. He had eaten the pâté, the bread, the fine aspic jelly, and the lettuce. "More wine if you please."

"With the fowl you'll want a red," the waiter suggested.

"Bordeaux," said Christophe.

"Lafitte, monsieur?"

Christophe shrugged assent. "What time is best for feeding dogs, and how much should one like this be fed?" he asked.

"About seven in the evening. Raw meat is best. Five hundred grams for each fifty kilos the animal weighs," the waiter replied.

That caused Christophe to bristle. "With beef at 450 francs the kilo? How much will this dog weigh?"

"About eighty kilos, I should judge," said the waiter.

"In other words, 350 francs for each meal. I shall present him to the Fourth Republic," Christophe said.

"The Government accepts no dogs at the Jardin des Plantes or the Jardin d'Acclimatation," the waiter said.

"One must resort to bribery, I suppose," Christophe said. There was a signal from the kitchen and the waiter went back to get the chicken. Christophe picked up the menu and read the figures. With the wine he had ordered, and the brandy he was going to order, the check would come to well over 1,500 francs. Why not?

ELLIOT PAUL

Springtime in Paris

The Turn of the Tide

The news from Toulon had not yet come in, on the night of November 27, 1942; that amazing November when the tide of war began to turn. Four of us were dining at Boulestin's; the basis of excuse for the small party was because our host wanted to open a magnum of very special Bordeaux, a 1911 Château Chevalier, to find out if it were still holding up; as we began the meal with oysters, we drank a white Burgundy before the claret; a 1929 Chablis le Pinet Blanc, which for some unknown reason captured my palate and my imagination more than the Château Chevalier. About that Chablis was a haunting far-away loveliness . . . Trying to be matter-of-fact and not mix it up with the old days and forlorn causes, I asked my host: "I hope they've still got plenty more in the cellar?" He replied gravely: "This is the last bottle." I said nothing, but picked up the cork and put it in my handbag. "As a souvenir?" asked Kate Mary Bruce, who with her husband made up the quartette. "No", I replied, lying glibly, "to stick between my teeth and bite hard in case of an air-raid. They say you should and I've lost the one I had". Allied to the Château Chevalier, we had roast pheasant, *choux de Bruxelles en purée* and an excellent *mousse au chocolat*, creamy with a crisp surface. Naturally we paused over drinking the claret while we ate the sweet, but afterwards I produced a glass jar of medlars, which I had brought along remembering that nowadays after a sweet we could not order cheese. Our host, a sophisticated connoisseur of wine and food, had apparently never yet eaten a medlar. Surprised I waited for his verdict. He thought nothing or less than nothing of their mysterious attraction.

"And I usually like fruit", he complained; "raspberries, gooseberries, nectarines – "

"But, my good man" – (or I may have said "My good fellow") – "you must not think of medlars as *fruit*."

"They're not vegetable; they're not nuts; what are they, then?"

I made an effort: "They mean the same as olives, only at the end of a meal."

Definition is the very devil, and how hard to explain the glamour of a medlar if you yourself have grown up with it. Medlars, mulberries, quinces, they should all three grow in the perfect garden which one has never had. Medlars, walnuts and the bouquet of wine; evening-clothes, damask and Royal Worcester and cut-glass and crystal chandeliers . . . Never medlars alone, but in complement to the bouquet of wine; their rough, husky flavour serves to bring it out like a charm. But I was alone in my championship; the others still went on saying: "But *what* is it about them?" So I quoted Rosalind and hoped for the best: "I'll graff it with you, and then I shall graff it with a medlar; then it will be the earliest fruit i' the country: for you'll be rotten e'er you be half ripe, and that's the right virtue of the medlar."

When I came home after that dinner, I heard the news of the French battleships at Toulon. Had we only known a couple of hours sooner, there would have been no irony in toasting that valiant hopeless gesture in the last bottle of Chablis le Pinet Blanc, 1929. It was a curious little counter-comment, that a bottle of Châteauneuf du Pape, 1933, which had been given to me on my fiftieth birthday, had perished when I came to open it. Nor was it corked; no reason why it should not have held up as well or better than the Chablis le Pinet Blanc, except the unreasonable, superstitious fancy that 1940 had been a bad year for France and June 17th a bad date for a gift from France.

G. B. STERN,
Trumpet Voluntary

Al Fresco

Nevertheless, for happiness give me (when again you can) a summer among many summers in the South of France. Towards evening we would drive inland up into the hills to one of those little walled Provençal villages and have supper: omelette, and fresh sardines fried, and *fromage du pays* and *vin rosé du pays*, and fruit in abundance; sitting out of doors under a pergola by the low wall of the friendly little restaurant; a yoke of white oxen or a shepherd and his flock plodding patiently up from the valley along the winding mountain road just below; a lemon-coloured moon floating as though in mid-air, shedding its pale pure light on the islands of St Honoré and St Marguerite that were lightly sketched between sea and sky.

Ibid.

Gourmandise is an act of our judgment, in obedience to which we grant a preference to things which are agreeable over those which have not that quality.

BRILLAT-SAVARIN

Poor Man's Puggatory

"London is a grand place to be sure; but oh, my beloved 'earers, there is no misery like that of solitude in a crowd, or inconwenience like that of livin' with men without being able to afford to partake of their pleasures. London is the rich man's paradise, the poor man's puggatory! yet how many fools, who can ill afford it, think it necessary to make a hannual pilgrimage once a year to the shrine of her monstrosity. Hup they come, leavin' their quiet country 'omes just as their sparrowgrass is ready for eatin' and their roses begin to blow, – neglectin' their farms – maybe their families – leavin' bulls to bail themselves, cattle to get out of the pound and wagrants into the stocks, as they can; hup, I say, they come to town, to get stuck in garrets at inns with the use of filthy, cigar-smokin', spitty, sandy-floored, sawdusty coffee-rooms, a hundred and seventy-five steps below, and never a soul to speak to. Vot misery is theirs! Down they come of a mornin' after a restless, tumblin', heated, noisy night, to the day den of the establishment, with little appetite for breakfast, but feelin' the necessity of havin' some in order to kill time. A greasy-collared, jerkin', lank-'aired waiter, coasts a second-'and, badly-washed web over a slip of a table, in a stewy, red-curtained box, into which the sun beats with unmitigated wengeance. A Britannia-metal tea-pot, a cup, a plate, a knife, and a japanned tea-caddie, make their appearance. Then comes a sugar-basin, followed by a swarm of flies, that 'unt it as the 'ounds would a fox, and a small jug of 'sky-blue', which the flies use as a bath after their repast. A half-buttered muffin mounts a waterless slopbasin; a dirty egg accompanies some toasted wedges of bread; the waiter points to a lump of carrion wot he calls beef, on a dusty sideboard, and promises to bring the 'Post' as soon as it is out of 'and.

". . . Now for a chop house or coffee-room dinner! Oh, the 'orrible smell that greets you at the door! Compound of cabbage, pickled salmon, boiled beef, saw-dust, and anchovy sarce. 'Wot will you take, sir?' inquires the frowsy waiter, smoothin' the filthy cloth, 'soles, macrel, vitin's – werry good, boiled beef – nice cut, cabbage, weal and 'am, cold lamb and sallard.' – *Bah* the den's 'ot to suffocation – the kitchen's below – a trap door vomits up dinners in return for bellows down the pipe to the cook. Flies settle on your face – swarm on your head; a wasp travels round; everything tastes flat, stale, and unprofitable. As a climax he gets the third of a bottle of warm port as a pint, and to prevent jealousy between body and mind, gives the latter a repast on second-hand news, by goin' through the columns of an evenin' paper. This, too, from a man wot can hardly manage a three-days-a-week one in the country."

ROBERT SMITH SURTEES,
Handley Cross

The Salmi of Life

(What the Soul of the Young Man Said to the Waiter)

Tell me not in figures wavy
    That my bill is twelve-and-nine,
When I had but soup of gravy,
    Steak, potatoes, cheese, and wine.

I'm a poet, I'm a rhymer,
    Hardly versed in traders' tricks,
But a pint of *Laubenheimer*
    Ought not to be four-and-six.

Though I'm not at all unwilling
    To assist you to success,
I must say I think a shilling
    Far too much for watercress.

Bills are long, and cash is fleeting,
    And I wish to make it clear
That the bill you are receipting
    Is the last I settle here.

When you've fleeced your guests and fined them,
   I may venture to explain,
They will shake the dust behind them,
   And they won't come back again.

So I leave you, poorer, sadder,
   Lest you make me poorer still;
Sharper than the biting adder
   Is the adder of the bill.

ADRIAN ROSS

Les Garçons. Drawing by Aubrey Beardsley.

Experiences of Doubtful Worth
in New York

In foreign parts the wise course is to forget one's native customs and eat and drink according to local usage. I'm doing pretty well out of it.

In The Four Seasons on Park-avenue I had some very passable clams and oysters, followed by breast of chicken stuffed with harvest vegetables.

In Luchow's on 14th Street, the pork tenderloin on wild rice with raisins and sour cream sauce was by no means uneatable.

The deep-fried scallops and eggs Benedict at Sardi's did not at all disgrace the establishment.

At the Warwick I ate slices of delicious ham cut so thinly that you could have made a lampshade out of them.

The food is, of course, titanic. My companion at dinner last night was given a steak the size and roughly the shape of his foot. If the rest of the chicken I ate was in proportion to its heart the man who killed it must have had quite a fight.

At first the size is a bother, you wish you could wrap up the half you don't eat and post it to Sicily.

I record without comment that my stomach adjusted to the problem after a day or two. Whether it will stay adjusted or react is a stage of my trip yet to be reached.

The meals from which I have just quoted were taken in restaurants of considerable splendour and expense (at The Four Seasons they change the entire decor four times a year to match the seasonal hues).

I should be deceiving you if I pretended that they represented typical American food. For this you go to the automats, the coffee houses, the chain restaurants such as Rikers and the Chock Full o' Nuts, and the food bars such as those on Grand Central Station.

In one of these I ate, just to say I had, a cheeseburger, an experience of doubtful worth. Knowing that a hamburger is filled with meat, you would deduce that a cheeseburger would be based on cheese. Not so.

It is made from meat and toasted cheese, set between two halves of a soft bun.

It seemed to need a good deal of room to eat, and extensive mopping-up afterwards. It was tacky too—every time I closed my jaws on a piece I had to force them apart again with a knife-handle.

Another disappointment was the famed pumpkin pie with whipped cream, ingested in a restaurant just off Times-square.

It tasted of nothing much flavoured with cinnamon, and repeated on me rather noticeably during the evening.

My contacts say I was unlucky and should try again, but I don't know. The great triumph of American food is its salads.

Something in the air of New York – probably the humidity – keeps lettuces crisply succulent. The dressing is made usually with lemon juice instead of vinegar, and everywhere is consistently good.

Even in the grade one restaurants few people drink wine. The American attitude to this amenity is one of wilful ignorance. They don't want to know, and restaurants abet them by absurd over-charging.

This is despite the good range of American wines – the naïve, domestic Burgundies of Thurber's cartoon.

In the liquor stores you can buy a half-gallon bottle – a very handy size I'd say – of Californian Chianti for a dollar and a half.

Restaurants sell it only by the glass at 50 cents. So I do as everybody else does, and drink iced water.

PETER BLACK,
Article in the Daily Mail, 8th October, 1960

Vins du Pays

I am not prone to recommend restaurants, or to discommend them, for the simple reason that, if they have proved bad, I smile to think of other men being poisoned and robbed as well as myself; as to the good ones – why, only a fool would reveal their whereabouts. Since, however, I hope so to order my remaining days of life as never to be obliged to return to these gimcrack regions, there is no inducement for withholding the name of the Merle Blanc at Monte Carlo, a quite unpretentious place of entertainment that well deserves its name – white blackbirds being rather scarcer here than elsewhere. The food is excellent – it has a cachet of its own; the wine more than merely good. And this is surprising, for the local mixtures (either Italian stuff which is dumped down in shiploads at Nice, Marseille, Cette, etc., or else the poor though sometimes aromatic product of the Var) are not gratifying to the palate. One imbibes them, none the less, in preference to anything else, as it is a peculiarity of what goes under the name of wine hereabouts that the more you pay for it the worse it tastes. If you adventure into the Olympic spheres of Château Lafite and so forth, you may put your trust in God or in a blue pill. Château Cassis would be a good name for these finer vintages, seeing that the harmless black currant enters largely into their composition, though not in sufficient quantity to render them wholly innocuous. Which suggests a little problem for the oenophilist. What difference of soil or exposure or climate or treatment can explain the fact that Mentone is utterly deficient in anything drinkable of native origin, whereas Ventimiglia, a stone's throw eastwards, can boast of its San Biagio, Rossese, Latte, Dolceacqua and other noble growths, the like of which are not to be found along the whole length of the French Riviera?

NORMAN DOUGLAS,
Alone

FOOD FIT FOR KINGS

A Palatial Meal

Footmen were rolling in long buffet tables, glittering with gold and silver; Hornblower forced himself to watch keenly, so as to commit no breach of etiquette. To one side the royal party had taken their seats, Empresses and Czar in armchairs and the princes and princesses in upright chairs, and everyone had to be careful always to face in that direction so as not to commit the heinous crime of letting royalty see a human back. People were beginning to take food from the buffets, and, try as he would, Hornblower could see no sign at all of any attention to precedence. But there was the Persian Ambassador munching something from a gold plate, so that he was justified in making a move in the same direction. Yet all the same this was the most curious dinner he had ever attended, with everyone standing up except royalty; and royalty, he could see, were eating nothing at all.

"May I offer you my arm, Countess?" he said as the group began to drift towards a buffet.

The courtiers by dint of long practice had seemingly mastered the art of eating while standing up and while holding their hats under their arms, but it was not easy. His dangling sword was liable to trip him, too, and that infernal pistol in his waistband was digging uncomfortably into his side. The footmen serving at the buffets understood no French, and the Countess came to Hornblower's rescue with an order.

"That is caviare," she explained to him, "and this is vodka, the drink of the people, but I think you will find that the two are admirably suited to each other."

The Countess was right. The grey, unappetizing-looking stuff was perfectly delicious. Hornblower sipped cautiously at the vodka and in his present high strung condition hardly noticed the fierce bite of the liquor; but there was no doubt that vodka and caviare blended together exquisitely. He felt the warm glow of the alcohol inside him, and realized that he was desperately hungry. The buffet was covered with foods of all kinds, some being warm in chafing dishes, some cold; under the tutelage of the Countess, Hornblower went a fair way towards tackling them all. There was a dish apparently of stewed mushrooms that was excellent, slices of smoked fish, and unidentifiable salad, some varieties of cheese, eggs both hot and cold, a sort of ragout of pork. There were other liquors as well, and Hornblower ate and drank with his spirits rising momentarily, playing his part in the conversation and feeling more and more warmly grateful to the Countess. It might be a queer way to have dinner, but Hornblower thought he had never tasted such delicious food. His head began to whirl with the liquor; he knew that danger signal of old, although this time he did not resent it quite so bitterly as usual, and he checked himself in the midst of a laugh in time not to be too unrestrained. Laughter, chatter, and bright lights; this was one of the jolliest parties he had ever attended. . . . Hornblower replaced his lovely porcelain plate on the buffet, among the gold dishes, and wiped his mouth with one of the silken napkins that lay there. He was comfortably replete, with the gratifying sensation of having eaten just too much and having drank just enough; he supposed coffee would be served soon, and a cup of coffee was all he needed to complete his internal gratification.

"I have dined extremely well", he said to the Countess.

The most remarkable expression passed over the Countess's face. Her eyebrows rose, and she opened her mouth to say something and then shut it again. She was smiling and puzzled and distressed all at the same time. She again started to speak, but her words were cut short by the ceremonial opening of yet another pair of doors from which twenty or thirty footmen emerged to form an avenue leading into the next room. Hornblower became conscious that the royal party had risen from their chairs and were falling into formation, and the complete cessation of conversation told Hornblower that some specially solemn moment had arrived. Couples were moving about the room like ships jockeying for position. The Countess laid her hand on his arm with a gentle pressure as if to lead him. By George, a procession was forming behind the royal party! There went the Persian Ambassador, a smiling girl on his arm. Hornblower just had time to lead his own partner forward to join the procession next, and after two or three more couples had joined behind him the procession began to move forward, its tail being steadily lengthened as it went. Hornblower kept his eyes on the

Persian Ambassador before him; they passed down the avenue of foot-men, and entered the next room.

The procession was breaking off to left and to right in alternate couples as though in a country dance; the Persian Ambassador went to the left, and Hornblower was ready to go to the right without the prompt-ing of the gesture of the Grand Marshal, who was standing there ready to direct anyone in doubt. It was another enormous room, lit by what seemed to be hundreds of cut-glass chandeliers dangling from the roof, and all down the length of it ran a vast table – miles long, it seemed, to Hornblower's disordered imagination – covered with gold plate and crystal and embanked with flowers. The table was shaped like a T with a very small crosspiece, and the royal party had already taken their seats at the head; behind every chair all the way down stood a white-wigged footman. It dawned upon Hornblower that dinner was about to begin; the food and drink which had been served in the domed hall had been something extra and introductory. Hornblower was ready to laugh at himself for his idiotic lack of comprehension at the same time as he was ready to groan with despair at the thought of having to eat his way through an Imperial dinner in his present distended condition.

Save for royalty, the men were standing at their chairs while the ladies sat; across the table the Persian Ambassador was bending affably over the young woman he had brought in, and the aigrette in his turban nodded and his diamonds flashed. The last woman took her seat, and then the men sat down together – not quite so simultaneously as marines presenting arms, but almost so. A babble of conversation began im-mediately, and almost immediately a golden soup plate was put under Hornblower's nose and a golden soup tureen full of pink soup was offered to him for him to help himself from. He could not help glancing down the table; everyone had been given soup at the same moment – there must be two hundred footmen at least waiting at table. . . .

There was a cool, pleasant yellow wine in a tall glass before Horn-blower, and he sipped it.

"My experience today", he said, "is that Russians are the most de-lightful people in the world, and Russian women the most charming and most beautiful."

The Countess flashed a glance at him from her sultry eyes, and, it seemed to Hornblower, set his brains creeping about inside his skull. The golden soup plate was whisked away and replaced by a golden dinner plate. Another wine was poured into another glass before him – cham-pagne. It effervesced just as his thoughts appeared to him to be doing. His footman spoke to him in Russian apparently offering him a choice, and the Countess settled the problem without referring to him.

Wild Boar à la Troyenne; a Roman extravaganza.

"As this is your first visit to Russia," she explained, "I could be sure that you have not yet tasted our Volga River trout."

She was helping herself to one as she spoke, from a golden dish. Hornblower's footman was presenting another golden dish.

"A gold service looks very well," said the Countess sadly, "but it allows the food to grow unfortunately cold. I never use mine in my house save when I entertain His Imperial Majesty. As that is the case in most houses I doubt if His Imperial Majesty ever has a hot meal."

The gold knife and fork with which Hornblower dissected his fish were heavy in his hands, and scraped oddly against the gold plate.

"You have a kind heart, madame," he said.

"Yes," said the Countess, with deep significance.

Hornblower's head whirled again; the champagne, so cold, so delicate, seemed perfectly adapted to put this right, and he drank of it thirstily.

A couple of fat little birds on toast followed the trout; they melted delicately in the mouth; some other wine followed the champagne. And there was a venison stew, and a cut of some roast which might be mutton but which was borne on Pegasus-wings of garlic beyond mundane speculation. Somewhere in the procession of food appeared a pink water ice, only the third or fourth which Hornblower had ever tasted ...

The Countess beside him was pressing his foot under the table; and a little electric thrill ran through him and his steadiness vanished once more. He smiled at her beatifically. She gave him a long look with lowered lids and then turned away to address a remark to her neighbour on her other side, a tactful hint for Hornblower to pay a little attention to the Baroness to whom he had hardly spoken a word. Hornblower plunged feverishly into conversation, and the general in the outlandish dragoon uniform on the far side of the Baroness joined in with a question about Admiral Keats, whose acquaintance he had made in 1807. The footman was offering a new dish; his hairy wrist was exposed between his cuff and his white glove, and that wrist was spotted with flea bites. Hornblower remembered having read in one of the books he had been studying about the northern powers that the farther east one travelled the worse the vermin became – the Polish flea was bad, but the Russian flea was unbearable. If it was any worse than the Spanish flea, with which Hornblower had an intimate acquaintance, it must be a remarkably well developed flea.

C. S. FORESTER,
The Commodore

A Dinner at Karnak

No one who was present will forget the occasion. Only those who had not been invited thought it a "desecration". It was full moon. The guests had all been called for by carriages. We all arrived together at about seven o'clock and were received by the Carnarvons in the Temple of Ramesses, to the right of the large entrance gate to Karnak.

Most of the staff of the Winter Palace were there, costumed as for a performance of *Aïda*. It was as unreal as a scene from the *Arabian Nights* to look from the double line of standing figures of Ramesses to the very long table, perfectly appointed with glass, cutlery, china, and linen, as imposing as though it had been laid in a great banquet hall in England.

The food was hot and unbelievably good, and the service noiseless, as delicacies and choice wines appeared and disappeared. Maspero, the guest of honor, was in fine form as he led the conversation, which was mostly about Karnak. Many of the Egyptologists present had had some connection with Karnak during long careers in Egypt, and interesting and amusing anecdotes about excavations, conducted at various periods, flew back and forth among the guests. Maspero's comments were brilliant and to the point.

By a little after nine the guests were in the great Hypostyle Hall, which was illuminated by artificial light in addition to the moon. No one before had attempted such a combination, which was extraordinarily successful in bringing out details on the tall columns.

The beauty of the night and the light of the full moon tempted us all to wander far afield, over the vast confines of the temple enclosure. Past the pylons and obelisks to the distant Bubastis Gate, then back to the entrance to Karnak, to climb to the top of the pylon and look across the Nile to the high gebel above the Theban Plain, with the dim outlines of temples visible, or on the Luxor side of the river, to see the bold peaks beyond the town. By mutual accord the party got to the Sacred Lake and there stayed on in silent enjoyment until our host tactfully indicated it was time to go home.

Outside the Temple of Ramesses a servant handed me my hat and Corinna's wrap. Maspero happened to be at my side. We both looked at the great court and the standing figure of Ramesses where we had recently feasted. The table had vanished, so had the chairs. There was no sign of anyone's having been there.

Maspero rubbed his eyes: "An unexpected and a perfect climax!" he said.

JOSEPH LINDON SMITH,
Tombs, Temples and Ancient Art

A Carthaginian Feast

There were men of all nations there, Ligurians, Lusitanians, Balearians, Negroes, and fugitives from Rome. Beside the heavy Dorian dialect were audible the resonant Celtic syllables rattling like chariots of war, while Ionian terminations conflicted with consonants of the desert as harsh as the jackal's cry. The Greek might be recognized by his slender figure, the Egyptian by his elevated shoulders, the Cantabrian by his broad calves. There were Carians proudly nodding their helmet plumes, Cappadocian archers displaying large flowers painted on their bodies with the juice of herbs, and a few Lydians in women's robes, dining in slippers and earrings. Others were ostentatiously daubed with vermilion, and resembled coral statues.

They stretched themselves on the cushions, they ate squatting round large trays, or lying face downwards they drew out the pieces of meat, and sated themselves, leaning on their elbows in the peaceful posture of lions tearing their prey. The last-comers stood leaning against the trees, watching the low tables half hidden beneath the scarlet coverings, and awaiting their turn.

Hamilcar's kitchens being insufficient, the Council had sent them slaves, ware, and beds, and in the middle of the garden, as on a battle-field when they burn the dead, large bright fires might be seen at which oxen were roasting. Anise-sprinkled loaves alternated with great cheeses heavier than discuses, crateras filled with wine, and cantharuses filled with water, together with baskets of gold filigree-work containing flowers. Every eye was dilated with the joy of being able at last to gorge at pleasure, and songs were beginning here and there.

First they were served with birds and green sauce in plates of red clay relieved by drawings in black, then with every kind of shell-fish that is gathered on the Punic coasts, wheaten porridge, beans and barley, and snails dressed with cumin on dishes of yellow amber.

Afterwards the tables were covered with meats: antelopes with their horns, peacocks with their feathers, whole sheep cooked in sweet wine, haunches of she-camels and buffaloes, hedgehogs with garum, fried grasshoppers, and preserved dormice. Large pieces of fat floated in the midst of saffron in bowls of Tamrapanni wood. Everything was running over with wine, truffles, and asafoetida. Pyramids of fruit were crumbling upon honeycombs, and they had not forgotten a few of those plump little dogs with pink silky hair and fattened on olive lees – a Cartha-ginian dish held in abhorrence among other nations. Surprise at the novel fare excited the greed of the stomach. The Gauls with their long hair drawn up on the crown of the head, snatched at the water-melons and lemons and crunched them up with the rind. The Negroes, who had never seen a lobster, tore their faces with its red prickles. But the shaven Greeks, whiter than marble, threw the leavings of their plates behind them, while the herdsmen from Brutium, in their wolf-skin garments, devoured in silence with their faces in their portions.

Night fell. The velarium, spread over the cypress avenue, was drawn back, and torches were brought.

The apes, sacred to the moon, were terrified on the cedar-tops by the wavering lights of the petroleum as it burned in the porphyry vase. They uttered screams which afforded mirth to the soldiers.

Oblong flames trembled in cuirasses of brass. Every kind of scintilla-tion flashed from the gem-encrusted dishes. The crateras with their borders of convex mirrors multiplied and enlarged the images of things;

the soldiers thronged around, looking at their reflections with amazement, and grimacing to make themselves laugh. They tossed the ivory stools and golden spatulas to one another across the tables. They gulped down all the Greek wines in their leathern bottles, the Campanian wines enclosed in amphoras, the Cantabrian wines brought in casks, with the wines of the jujube, cinnamomum and lotus. There were pools of these on the ground that made the foot slip. The smoke of the meats ascended into the foliage with the vapour of the breath. Simultaneously were heard the snapping of jaws, the noise of speech, songs, and cups, the crash of Campanian vases shivering into a thousand pieces, or the limpid sound of a large silver dish.

In proportion as their intoxication increased they more and more recalled the injustice of Carthage.

GUSTAVE FLAUBERT,
Salammbô

The guests are met, the feast is set.

S. T. COLERIDGE,
The Ancient Mariner

A masquerade at a feast; a drawing by Hans Burghmair,
German, 16th century.

Before the Deluge

On the third day this fierce round of festivities was wound up with an immense dinner given by the Haritonenkos, the sugar kings of Moscow, I describe it in some detail because it gives an amazing picture of the Moscow which existed before the war and which will never come again.

The Haritonenkos' house was an immense palace on the far side of the river just opposite the Kremlin.

To meet the British delegates every official, every notable, every millionaire, in Moscow, had been invited, and when I arrived I found a throng like a theatre queue struggling on the staircases. The whole house was a fairyland of flowers brought all the way from Nice. Orchestras seemed to be playing in every ante-chamber.

When finally I made my way upstairs, I was lost in a crowd in which I knew no one. I doubt even if I shook hands with my host and hostess. But at long narrow tables vodka and the most delicious "zakuski", both hot and cold, were being served by scores of waiters to the standing guests. I took a glass of vodka and tried several of the unknown dishes. They were excellent. Then an English-speaking Russian took pity on my loneliness, and I had more vodka and more "zakuski". It was long past the appointed hour for dinner, but no one seemed to be moving, and presently it struck me that perhaps in this strange country the people dined standing up. I had another vodka and a second portion of reindeer tongue. Then, when my appetite was sated, a footman came along and handed me a card with a plan of the table and my own particular place, and a few minutes later a huge procession made its way to the dining-room. I do not wish to exaggerate. I say truthfully that I cannot remember the number of courses or the different varieties of wine which accompanied them. But the meal lasted till eleven o'clock and would have taxed the intestines of a giant. My immediate neighbours were a Miss von Meck, the daughter of a railway magnate, and Commander Kahovsky, the Russian flag-lieutenant, who had been attached to Lord Charles Beresford.

Miss von Meck spoke excellent English, and under the warm glow of her unaffected volubility my shyness soon melted. Before the meal was half-way through she had given me a lightning survey of Anglo-Russian relations, a summary of the English and Russian characters, a thumbnail sketch of everyone in the room, and a detailed account of all her own realized and unrealized desires and ambitions.

Kahovsky, however, seemed nervous and ill-at-ease. I was soon to discover why. During dinner he was called away from the room and never returned. The next day I learnt that he had gone to the telephone to speak to his mistress, the wife of a Russian Governor, who lived in St Petersburg. They had been on bad terms for some time, and with dramatic instinct she had chosen this moment to tell him that all was over. Kahovsky had then pulled out his revolver and, still holding the receiver, had put a bullet through his brain. It was very sad, very Russian, very hard on Lord Charles Beresford, and by way of example a little dangerous for a young and highly impressionable Vice-Consul.

R. H. BRUCE LOCKHART,
Memoirs of a British Agent

Two Hundred Pound Suppers

Humour. I'll bring thee
Into the court of Winter; there thy food
Shall not be sickly fruits, but healthful broths,
Strong meat and dainty.
Folly. Pork, beef, mutton, very sweet mutton, veal, venison,
capon, fine fat capon, partridge, snipe, plover, larks, teal,
admirable teal, my lord.
Humour. Mystery there, like to another nature,
Confects the substance of the choicest fruits
In a rich candy, with such imitation
Of form and colour, 'twill deceive the eye,
Until the taste be ravish'd.
Folly. Comfits and caraways, marchpanes and marmalades, sugar-plums
and pippin-pies, ginger-bread and walnuts.
Humour. Nor is his bounty limited; he'll not spare
To exhaust the treasure of a thousand Indies.
Folly. Two hundred pound suppers, and neither fiddlers nor broken
glasses reckoned; besides, a hundred pound a throw, ten times together,
if you can hold out so long.

JOHN FORD and THOMAS DEKKER,
The Sun's Darling—A Moral Masque (1617)

COOKS AND COOKERY

Advice to Cooks

Most knowing Sir! the greatest part of Cooks
Searching for truth, and couzan'd by its Looks,
One wou'd have all things little, hence has try'd
Turkey Poults fresh from th' Egg in Batter fry'd
Others, to shew the largeness of their Soul,
Prepare you Muttons swol'd and Oxen whole.
To vary the same things some think is Art.
By larding of Hogs-feet and Bacon Tart.
The Tast is now to that Perfection brought
That care, when wanting Skill, creates the Fault.

Be cautious how you change old Bills of Fare,
Such alterations shou'd at least be rare;
Yet credit to the Artist will acrue,
Who in known things still makes th' appearance new,
Fresh Dainties are by Britain's Traffik known,
And now by constant Use familiar grown;
What Lord of old wou'd bid his Cook prepare
Mangoes, Botargo, Champignons, Caviare?
Or wou'd our thrum-cap'd Ancestors find fault
For want of Sugar-Tongs or Spoons for Salt.

DR WILLIAM KING,
The Art of Cookery (1709)

As Cooks Go

That Philomène was a manic-depressive in the downhill phase was, of course, instantly apparent to a boy of five. Several boys of five who happened to be standing around and were by way of being students of psycho-pathology, stated their belief to me in just those words: "Manic depressive, downhill phase". At the close of business every evening, Philomène retired to her room armed with a sixteen-inch steak knife, doubtless to ward off an attack by her Poltergeist. She then spent the best part of an hour barricading her door with dressers, armoires, and other heavy furniture, preparatory to sleeping with the lights on. I say "sleeping" utterly without conviction, she undoubtedly moulded lead statues of her employer and crooned to them over a slow fire.

But if her behaviour was erratic, there was no lack of consistency in Philomène's cuisine. Meat loaf and cold fried chicken succeeded each other with the deadly precision of tracer bullets. At last, when blood and sinew could stand no more and I was about to dissolve the union, I suddenly discovered that this female Paul Bunyan had grown to womanhood under the bright skies of Martinique, and I knew a moment of elation. I let it be bruited through the servant's hall that I would look tolerantly on fried plantain, yams, and succulent rice dishes. That afternoon the kitchen was a hive of activity. The air was heavy with saffron, pimento, and allspice. I heard snatches of West Indian Calypsos, caught a glimpse of Philomène's head swathed in a gay bandanna. With the care befitting a special occasion, I dressed negligently but with unimpeachable taste in whites and cummerbund, mixed myself several excellent stengahs, and sauntered in to dinner for all the world like an up-country tea-planter. A few moments later Philomène entered with what might be called a smoking salver except for the circumstance that it was stone cold. On it lay the wing and undercarriage of an even colder chicken, flanked by two segments of meat loaf.

After five minutes of reflection, during which, I am told, my features closely resembled a Japanese print, I arose, and, throwing out my tiny chest, marched into the kitchen. The maledictions withered on my lips. Seated at the table, my black hibiscus blossom was tucking in a meal consisting of *potage Parmentier avec croûtons*, a crisp *gigot*, *salade fatiguée*, and *pot de crème au chocolat*.

"You – thing", I said at length, and five minutes later Philomène was on her way back to St Pierre.

S. J. PERELMAN,
Crazy Like a Fox

A cook thei hadde with them for the nonce,
To boyle chikens and the marrow bones,
And to make powders swete and tasten wel.
Wel coude he knowe a draught of London ale.
He coude roste, sethe, broille, and frie,
Make soupe and brawn and bake wel a pye.
But gret harm was it, as it semed me,
That on his shin a sore wound had he;
For blankemange he made with the beste.

GEOFFREY CHAUCER,
The Canterbury Tales

A Short-tempered Chef

Ude was quick to resent any real or imagined slight on his handiwork. One day at Crockford's a member ordered a red mullet, and Ude himself dressed it with a delicious sauce. The price on the *carte* for mullet was two shillings, and when an extra sixpence was demanded for the sauce the diner refused to pay it. Ude was furious. "The *imbécile*", he cried, "the *imbécile* apparently believes that the red mullets come out of the sea with my sauce in their pockets!"

Ude was always greedy about money – almost miserly – but once every year economy was forgotten, and some twenty of his disciples and their wives were invited to his birthday dinner. Each was expected to send a gift in advance, and it was whispered that in this way Ude's expenses were repaid with interest. No trouble, however, was spared in the preparations, and every dish was the best of its kind, exquisitely chosen and impeccably served. But "better is a dinner of herbs where love is than a stalled ox and hatred therewith"; rarely did the occasion pass off without a family quarrel.

One year an unfortunate young man trod on the paw of Madame's favourite dog, Vermilion. The dog bit him – he pushed his chair back and kicked out – several other dogs joined in – Madame shouted at her husband through the din:

"Oh, you stupid old man! Why did you not lock the dogs upstairs as I told you to?"

"Be quiet madame. This is my birthday, and I won't have any quarrelling."

"No more will I; but why did you not lock up your dogs?"

"Well, madame, they were quiet enough till that stupid young man trod on Vermilion's paw!"

"Stupid young man, did you say? M. Ude, pray, how dare you insult my relations! If anyone is stupid here it is you M. Ude!"

"Will you be quiet, madame?"

"No, I will not."

"Not on my birthday? There, take that!", and he flung some almonds at her. His wife replied with a roll snatched up at random, the dogs leapt about barking, the whole party was thrown into confusion. Despite the profuse apologies of the wretched young man who had been bitten, order was not restored for an hour. The dinner, which had been perfection, was delayed, was served up cold, and was entirely spoiled.

Another year a guest who had been asked to carve a haunch of venison cracked several plates over the plate-warmer before realizing that they were cold. Ude leapt up in a passion. "What do I hear M. M — ? *Il faut que vous soyez bien maladroit* to break seven plates before you found out that they were cold! Do you know, sir, that each of them cost me two guineas at the late Duke of York's sale? You are – you are – you are a donkey, sir!" The whole party spent some time soothing and flattering their host, finally drinking his health – "and may he never break peace with China more!"

Hardly had they begun again when a guest, not liking the venison, attempted to dispose of it quietly by giving a piece to one of the dogs. The poor beast choked, Madame Ude ran to it in despair, remedies were applied, but before long it was dead, and she retired weeping, followed by most of the ladies, and another feast was ruined.

HELEN MORRIS,
Wine and Food, 18

There was an Old Man of Peru,
Who watched his wife making a stew,
But once by mistake,
In a stove she did bake
That unfortunate Man of Peru.

EDWARD LEAR

Old Williamsburg Cookery

Virginia hospitality is as old as Virginia itself. It is one of the first characteristics which the Virginians developed and one of the first things that
the visitor to Virginia notices. Since people from Williamsburg approach
their problems from the past, it is impossible to discuss the operations
of taverns and ordinaries in Williamsburg without getting entangled
with a history of Virginia hospitality and with the Williamsburg Art of
Cookery.

One of the first laws passed by the General Assembly of Virginia
which convened at Jamestown was one intended to protect strangers
from avaricious persons. It was called "An Act concerning Entertainment of Strangers". It provided that "every one shall be reputed to
entertayne those of Curtesie with whome they make not a certaine
Agreement".

There were very few of the avaricious persons who had to be put
down by law, if we can believe the letters, diaries and journals of that day.
In 1705, in a *History of Virginia*, Robert Beverley said of the Virginians:

"The Inhabitants are very courteous to Travellers, who need no other
Recommendation but the being human Creatures. A Stranger has no
more to do, but to inquire upon the Road, where any Gentleman, or
good Housekeeper lives, and there he may depend upon being received
with hospitality."

A journal of a British traveller, who had enjoyed the famed Virginia
hospitality, printed in the *London Magazine* in 1746 gives a vivid picture
of the nature of this entertainment:

"All over the Colony, an universal Hospitality reigns; full Tables and
open Doors, the kind Salute, the generous Detention, speak somewhat
like the old Roast-beef Ages of our Forefathers, and would almost persuade one to think their Shades were wasted into these Regions to enjoy
with greater Extent, the Reward of their Virtues. (What is said here is
most strictly true, for their Manner of living is quite generous and open:
Strangers are sought after with Greediness, as they pass the Country,
to be invited. Their Breakfast Tables had generally the cold Remains of
the former Day, hash'd or fricasseed; Coffee, Tea, Chocolate, Venison-
pasty, Punch, and Beer, or Cyder, upon one Board: their Dinner, good
Beef, Veal, Mutton, Venison, Turkies and Geese, wild and tame, Fowls
boil'd and roasted; and perhaps somewhat more, as Pies, Puddings, etc.,
for Dessert; Suppers the same, with some small Addition, and a good
hearty Cup to precede a Bed of Down; And this is the constant Life they
lead, and to this Fare every Comer is welcome."

When the capital of Virginia was removed from Jamestown in 1699, a new city was created and named Williamsburg to serve as a capital. The new city of Williamsburg became by law the centre, not only of the colony's political life, but its economic and social centre as well. It was actually planned to accommodate the thousands who poured into it in "Publick Times", and in a few years a magnificent palace was erected for the royal governors who there entertained the ladies and gentlemen of the colony.

Williamsburg was a city where public houses and taverns flourished. In restoring the city of Williamsburg to its appearance during the years when it served as a capital of the Virginia colony, many beautiful and historic old taverns and public houses have been restored.

There is first of all the Raleigh, which was the most noted and well-accustomed tavern in the town. It was first built before 1742 and one of its early keepers was Henry Wetherburn, who started to build a tradition for hospitality that has always clung to the place. He made an arrack punch so good that two hundred acres of Goochland County land were sold in 1738 by William Randolph of Tucahoe, to Peter Jefferson, father of Thomas Jefferson, in exchange for "Henry Wetherburn's biggest bowl of arrack punch". Other travellers spoke of the comforts and luxuries of the old Raleigh and still others praised its "exceeding good Madeira". Above the mantel in the Raleigh's famous Apollo Room was carved and gilded a Latin motto, which translated means "Jollity is the offspring of wisdom and good living". The Raleigh is now one of the exhibition buildings on the Williamsburg Restoration, and is furnished with handsome antique furniture in accordance with the inventories of Henry Wetherburn and other early keepers.

Another famous tavern which has been restored is the Market Square Tavern which has operated almost continuously since 1749 as a public house. Visitors to present-day Williamsburg may sleep there in modern comfort in tester beds, in what keeper Gabriel Maupin advertised in 1771 as "the best accommodations". Modern accommodations are provided in a large, new air-conditioned Williamsburg Inn – just at the edge of the Restoration area.

The Travis House, which was erected in 1765, has been restored as a public eating place. After its architectural restoration was completed, after it had been suitably and handsomely furnished and a garden of holly hedges, lawn and box surrounded it – it was decided to restore the old cookery there. That is not so easy as it sounds, because to do so successfully one would have to restore the eighteenth-century way of life and the eighteenth-century appetite. But in any case it was assumed that in the colonial period Virginia could not have been so famous for

hospitality and good food without some real substantial reason
for it.

The Research Department of the Williamsburg Restoration had been
engaged for some time in studying the manners and customs of the Virginians. They knew the foodstuffs available, the method of cookery, and
even the favourite cook books of the period. In fact, the distinction of
publishing the first cook book in America belongs to Williamsburg,
where William Parks in 1742 printed *The Compleat Housewife, or Accomplished Gentlewoman's Companion.*

So experimental work was begun. Inexperienced cooks using the old
cook books are often baffled by the two dozen eggs and pound of
butter for a simple cake; the variety of culinary herbs and seeds needed;
or the overwhelming bulk of a single dish which results from following
given quantities. An experienced and well-trained experimental cook,
however, was available, and a well-equipped modern kitchen was established in the old restored outside kitchen of the Market Square Tavern.

The object of the experimental cookery was to obtain a wide selection
of tasty, appetizing dishes suitable for serving in the Travis House. It
was to be a serious effort to restore old cookery to a restored city in
order to enable visitors to Williamsburg to partake of authentic Virginia hospitality.

The experimental cook had to make some allowance for the decadence
of the present generation – the degeneration of fine living into a matter
of budgets and calories-counting. Allowance also had to be made for a
change in taste – the average person would not relish "humble-pie" and
other similar delicacies which the old-fashioned cook contrived from
the portions the modern butcher now discards.

The twentieth century has a few advantages from the cook's stand-
point – yeast in a little package instead of a smelly frothy mass in a
bucket from the brewer's; sugar finely granulated instead of being in
hard loaves needing interminable pounding; electric stoves instead of
open fires; to name several.

Some of the old recipes indeed called for "much Nicety of Hand",
and the ultimate result was often intended to please the eye more than
the palate. If the pudding smacked strongly of the "Spinage" that had
been used to make it a "lively green", or if the flavour of the beets was
as predominant as the colour, it was politely overlooked by the pleased
guest, who saw such architectural marvels as *Solomon's Temple in Flummery* rise from the centre of the table.

There were nourishing medicinal broths which the old authors com-
mend as having recovered many from the beginnings of severe con-
sumptions. The directions begin with instructions for pounding thirty

garden snails in a marble mortar with the hinder legs of thirty frogs, and add embellishments of turnips, leeks, pearl barley and saffron.

There are calf's head "soops" with careful directions to the cook not to break the eyes, which are "esteemed a great delicacy" and which, no doubt, looked out reproachfully from a tureen of what otherwise might have been a tempting savoury soup.

The next step was to develop menus based upon these adapted recipes, and then to try them at the Travis House. Eighteenth-century menus were out of the question. Here, for example, is a sample menu, taken from the first cook book in America. It is a menu for January:

First Course

Collar of Brawn
Bisque of Fish
Soup with Vermicelly
Orange-pudding with Patties
Chine and Turkey
Lamb Pasty
Roasted Pullets with Eggs
Oyster-Pie
Roasted Lamb in Joints
Grand Sallad, with Pickles

Second Course

Wild Fowl of all Sorts
Chine of Salmon broil'd with Smelts
Fruit of all Sorts
Jole of Sturgeon
Collar'd Pig
Dried Tongues, with salt Sallads
Marinated Fish

These menus seemed beyond the scope of a modern tea room, but here is a typical Travis House dinner menu. When it is presented to the guests it is handwritten in old script; and even the paper on which it is written is a reproduction of old paper. The paper has old chain and laid marks, a watermark of the arms of Virginia and a crown and cypher – W.P. – the initials of the printer, William Parks, who, in addition to publishing America's first cook book, made paper in 1744 in a Williamsburg Paper Mill.

The Travis House menu reads:

*Pocket Soup
*Savoury Tomato Soup
*Frosted Mint Shrub
*Filet of Trout
*Southern Fried Chicken
*Old Virginia Ham
*Southern Fried Chicken with Virginia Ham
*Glazed Sweet Potatoes
Creamed Celery with Almonds   *Spiced Beets
*Sally Lunn   *Corn Sticks
*Corner Dishes
*Deep Dish Apple Pie
*Green Gage Plum or Mocha Ice Cream
with
*Travis House Pecan Cookies
*Orange Sherbert
Tea   Coffee   Milk

*Derived or adapted from early Virginian Recipes taken from a Restoration Research Collection.

The pocket soup has an interesting history and is the ideal soup for travellers. In the eighteenth century, forehanded travellers carried little concentrated patties of veal glue in their pockets and dissolved them in a bowl of boiling water in order to produce a flavourful soup – thus anticipating the modern *bouillon* cube by some centuries. Foresters and others who chewed up the cakes of pocket soup might be said to have anticipated jellied *consommé*. In either case, served hot or cold, the old recipes for pocket soups have proven both unusual and popular.

Ham and chicken – separate or in combination – are an inevitable choice on any menu which pretends to observe tradition. The famous Virginia ham, made from a peanut-fed, razor-backed hog, and smoked and cured for at least two years, is a delicacy with a deserved reputation. The Virginia way of frying chicken justifies its popularity throughout Virginia.

And what could any meal be without hot bread? Certainly generations of Virginians have made hot bread an indispensable part of every meal. As early as the year 1724, the Reverend Hugh Jones noticed this Virginia food habit: "And as they brew, so do they bake daily, Bread or

Cakes, eating too much hot and new Bread, which cannot be wholesome, tho' it be pleasanter than what has been baked a Day or two". The Virginians, who were viewed with alarm in 1724 for eating hot bread, have been munching on it contentedly ever since, And, it might be added, with much better digestion than those addicted to worrying about this particular food. Any good Virginian can tell you that any indigestion caused by eating hot bread is probably owing to the Yankee cook's lack of skill and practice. The Virginia phrase, which is always passed with the hot biscuits, corn bread, muffins, etc., is still "Take two and butter 'em while they're hot".

The Sally Lunn has become a prime favourite at the Travis House – and well it might. When Miss Emma Lou's mother was a girl it was an old favourite family recipe to serve for Sunday morning "company" breakfast, or when the minister came to tea. Miss Emma Lou's mother had an enviable reputation for her skill in baking this delicious light bread and her time-tried special recipe has been used with great success. Small Sally Lunn moulds are used, and the hot, fresh cake is passed on a board on which it has been cut. They say that left-over Sally Lunn is a real delicacy toasted for tea, but we are still waiting for the day when there will be enough left over to try.

Garden-stuff, as the vegetables were called, offer a handsome variety to be tastily prepared by cooking, or to be served raw in delicious salads. Asparagus, string beans, broccoli, celery, beets, tomatoes, Lima beans, corn, radishes, spinach, endive, cress, cabbages, Irish and sweet potatoes, and practically any choice one could make to-day were available to the "compleat housewife" of long ago. No greasy, heavy mayonnaise drenched her crisp well-selected greens; there were delicious French dressings, boiled dressings, and salad dressings made of eggs and sour cream.

In the good old days a dessert had to be rich, sweet and satisfying (particularly as part of one of the old menus) or it had to have some pretensions to beauty. For example, there was *Solomon's Temple in Flummery* a magnificent architectural monument in brightly coloured stiff jellies. Or such a fancy dish as one young Williamsburg bride wrote in her cook book in 1801 – *A Hen's Nest*. To make this, first a blancmange was prepared laboriously, with isinglass to congeal it; then several dozen eggs were blown and filled with it. A nest was made by partly filling a bowl with jelly, on the top of which a straw made of shredded orange and lemon peel was placed – then the eggs were laid in the straw and jelly was poured over it to hold them in place. The realistic sculpture in jelly was then turned out in a china dish and garnished with green sweetmeats.

We have been lucky in Virginia in that heaven has supplied us with good cooks as well as good meat. Those of you who may visit Williamsburg should test the truth of this statement in person and should dine on fried chicken, ham, Sally Lunn and other good foods of the past.

JOHN DISMUKES GREEN,
Wine and Food, 25

tailleuét
Grant cuifinyer ou
Royde France.

An illustration from Taillevant Grant's cookery book,
Paris, between 1511 and 1521.

A Royal Dish

Take hens and pork, and boil them together. Take the flesh and hew it small, and grind it all to dust. Take grated bread, and mix it with the broth, and add to it yolks of eggs. Boil it, and put therein powder of ginger, sugar, saffron and salt – and look that it be stiff.

Cookery Book of King Richard II

What to Get for the Cook to Read on Sunday?

The trouble is she doesn't care for fiction. She evidently is a woman of literary culture, somehow, because she said one day that she had read the whole of Shakespeare and thought it very good. In the library of Dogblastit itself, which is a really beautiful room done in Japanese oak with leaded windows to represent the reading room of a settler's cabin, there are practically no books that suit the cook. In fact, there are nothing but the Blue Book (one needs that to look up people in) and the Pink Book and the Red Book, and, of course, the Automobile Rude Book and then some Guide Books such as *The Perfect Bartender*, and the *Gentleman's Cellar* and *Cocktails for All Occasions*. Beyond that there are, of course, all the new books – the new fiction – because there is a standing order with Spentano to send up fifty pounds of new fiction by express once a week. None of the guests of the house ever care to read any book more than three weeks old, as they are quite worthless for conversation.

An order was sent to Boston for the Harvard Classics, but the cook says she doesn't care for the way they are selected. The only compromise so far is to get her books about the South Seas. She says she is just crazy over the South Sea literature. So we have given her *Six Weeks in the Marquesas Islands* and *Four Days in Fiji, Half Hours in Hoo-Poo*. But all that will only last her less than seven weeks, and after that we don't know what to do . . . .

My visits to my fashionable friends have been so much disturbed by perpetual conversation on these problems that I have decided to give them up altogether and to get back into my own class of society. I have some friends, real ones, who have a wooden house on an island where there is no electric light within twenty miles and where they use rain water out of a barrel.

They have coal-oil lanterns to see by; they wear flannel collars and they pass the soap from one room to another as it is needed. The men cut the firewood, as required, and never keep more than half an hour's supply on hand, and the girls do all the work because help can't be got and they know ten different ways of cooking canned salmon.

I am going back there.

STEPHEN LEACOCK,
Winnowed Wisdom

Escape Route

I have never been able to find in writing the escape from external things that I find in cooking. Cooking takes my mind off everything but itself, for the reason that I am not a seasoned cook and therefore have to think and concentrate. At the same time this concentration is effortless – unlike the concentration involved in literary work, which is so very effortful that if there be any real opposition from outside I can make no headway against it. There is, too, in writing an emotional drain which can eventually bring about complete exhaustion; but in cooking, fatigue is bodily and passes away with rest.

SHEILA KAYE-SMITH,
Kitchen Fugue

Philosophical Principles

The subject of cookery having been very naturally introduced at a table where Johnson, who boasted of the niceness of his palate, avowed that "he always found a good dinner," he said, "I could write a better book about cookery than has ever yet been written; it should be a book upon philosophical principles. Pharmacy is now made much more simple. Cookery may be so too. A prescription, which is now compounded of five ingredients, had formerly fifty in it. So in Cookery. If the nature of the ingredients is well known, much fewer will do. Then, as you cannot make bad meat good, I would tell what is the best butcher's meat, the best beef, the best pieces; how to choose young fowls; the proper seasons of different vegetables; and how to roast, and boil, and compound."

JAMES BOSWELL,
The Life of Samuel Johnson

Luncheon Chez Swann

But – and this more than ever from the day on which fine weather definitely set in at Combray – the proud hour of noon, descending from the steeple of Saint-Hilaire which it blazoned for a moment with the twelve points of its sonorous crown, would long have echoed about our table, beside the "holy bread", which too had come in, after church, in its familiar way; and we would still be found seated in front of our Arabian Night plates, weighed down by the heat of the day, and even more by

A cartoon by Henri Toulouse-Lautrec, artist and gourmet.

our heavy meal. For upon the permanent foundation of eggs, cutlets, potatoes, preserves, and biscuits, whose appearance on the table she no longer announced to us, Françoise would add – as the labour of fields and orchards, the harvest of the tides, the luck of the markets, the kindness of neighbours, and her own genius might provide; and so effectively that our bill of fare, like the quatrefoils that were carved on the porches of cathedrals in the thirteenth century, reflected to some extent the march of the seasons and the incidents of human life – a brill, because the fish-woman had guaranteed its freshness; a turkey, because she had seen a beauty in the market at Roussainville-le-Pin; cardoons with marrow, because she had never done them for us in that way before; a roast leg of mutton, because the fresh air made one hungry and there would be plenty of time for it to "settle down" in the seven hours before dinner; spinach, by way of a change; apricots, because they were still hard to get; gooseberries, because in another fortnight there would be none left; raspberries, which Mr Swann had brought specially, cherries, the first to come from the cherry-tree, which had yielded none for the last two years; a cream cheese of which in those days I was extremely fond; an almond cake, because she had ordered one the evening before; a fancy loaf, because it was our turn to "offer" the holy bread. And when all these had been eaten, a work composed expressly for ourselves, but dedicated more particularly to my father, who had a fondness for such things, a cream of chocolate, inspired in the mind, created by the hand of Françoise would be laid before us, light and fleeting as an "occasional piece" of music, into which she had poured the whole of her talent. Anyone who refused to partake of it, saying: "No, thank you, I have finished; I am not hungry," would at once have been lowered to the level of the Philistines who, when an artist makes them a present of one of his works, examine its weight and material, whereas what is of value is the creator's intention and his signature. To have left even the tiniest morsel in the dish would have shown as much discourtesy as to rise and leave a concert hall while the "piece" was still being played, and under the composer's very eyes.

MARCEL PROUST,
Swann's Way

God sends meat, and the devil sends cooks.
Old Adage

A cook may be taught, but a man who can roast is born with the faculty.
BRILLAT-SAVARIN

The Meaning of Cookery

What does cookery mean? It means the knowledge of Medea and of Circe, and of Calypso, and Sheba.

It means knowledge of all herbs, and fruits, and balms and spices, and of all that is healing and sweet in grapes and savoury in meat.

It means carefulness, and inventiveness, watchfulness, willingness, and readiness of appliances.

It means the economy of your great-grandmother and the science of modern chemistry, and French art, and Arabian hospitality.

It means, in fine, that you are to see imperatively that everyone has something nice to eat.

JOHN RUSKIN

On Cooking

"All culinary tasks should be performed with reverential love, don't you think so? To say that a cook must possess the requisite outfit of culinary skill and temperament – that is hardly more than saying that a soldier must appear in uniform. You can have a bad soldier in uniform. The true cook must have not only those externals, but a large dose of general worldly experience. He is the perfect blend, the only perfect blend, of artist and philosopher. He knows his worth; he holds in his palm the happiness of mankind, the welfare of generations yet unborn. That is why you will never obtain adequate human nourishment from a young girl or boy. Such persons may do for housework, but not in the kitchen. Never in the kitchen! No one can aspire to be a philosopher who is in an incomplete state of physical development. The true cook must be mature; she must know the world from her social point of view; however humble it may be; she must have pondered concerning good and evil, in however lowly and incongruous a fashion; she must have passed through the crucible of sin and suffering or, at the very least – it is often the same thing – of married life. Best of all, she should have a lover, a fierce and brutal lover who beats and caresses her in turns; for every woman worthy of the name is subject and entitled to fluctuating psychic needs – needs which must be satisfied to very core, if the master is to enjoy sound, healthy fare."

"We don't always allow them to fulfil that last condition", observed Mr Heard.

"I know we don't. That is precisely why we are so often poisoned or starved, instead of being cheered with wholesome food."

"You were speaking of woman-cooks?" asked van Koppen.

"I was. But it stands to reason that no woman can be trusted with so responsible a task – so sacred a mission I ought to call it – in regions south of Bordeaux or east of Vienna. Among many other reasons the whole sex is too drowsy, outside that radius. And if she drinks a little – "

"Drinks a little?"

"If she drinks a little, why, it is all to the good. It shows that she is fully equipped on the other side of her dual nature. It proves that she possesses the prime requisite of the artist; sensitiveness and a capacity for enthusiasm. Indeed, I often doubt whether you will ever derive well-flavoured victuals from the atelier of an individual who honestly despises or fears – it is the same thing – the choicest gift of God. Andrea, my man here, is abstemious to the last degree; not, I am glad to say, from conviction or ill-health – it is the same thing – but because he is incurably desirous of saving my money. What is the consequence? You can taste his self-imposed asceticism in the very *zabbaglione*, for which I must really apologize! It speaks to the eye, but not to the heart. Let us hope the coffee will be more harmonious."

"Would you not include some of our American dishes in your bill of fare?"

"To be sure I would; a fine selection. I have most pleasant recollections of the cuisine of Baltimore."

"You can get all those things in New York."

"No doubt, no doubt. But one thing invariably distresses me in trans-atlantic dinners; the unseemly haste in rising. One might really think the company were ashamed of so natural and jovial a function as that to which a dining-room is consecrated. And then, have you not noticed that sitting at table, a certain intellectual tone, an atmosphere of a definite kind, is insensibly generated among the guests, whatever the subject of conversation may be: They are often quite unaware of its existence, but it hangs, none the less, about the room and binds the inmates together for the time being. Suddenly we are bidden to rise and betake ourselves elsewhere; to sit on other chairs in a different temperature among different surroundings. It is a wrench. That peculiar atmosphere is dissipated; the genius of the earlier moment driven out beyond recapture; we must adapt ourselves to other conditions and begin anew, often with a good deal of trouble – often, how often, against our inclination! I call that a perverse custom. Every state of the mind, whether we are in society or alone, should be pressed to the last drop, irrespective of whether we happen to have swallowed a final mouthful of food or not.

When the conversation has died, as everything must die, from sheer inability to draw further breaths of life, then is the time to break up that old encircling dome of thought; to construct a fresh one, if need be, in a fresh environment."

"I confess," said the American, "it has always struck me as rather barbarous – this running away. I like to linger. But the ladies don't. They know that their dresses show off better in a parlour than under the boards of a mahogany table; perhaps their conversation, too, sounds better among arm-chairs and rugs. So we run after them, as we generally do; instead of making them run after us" ("as I do," he added to himself).

"But Count! If you like our American dishes, why not get this man of yours to learn a few from the Duchess? I know she would gladly teach him; she is not jealous of her knowledge like a professional chef."

"I would have asked her that favour long ago, if Andrea had been a born cook, like Keith's man. Unfortunately he is quite different. The philosopher is represented in his nature, but not the artist. He is only a devoted Arcadian, overflowing with good intentions."

"And are they of no avail?" queried the bishop.

"I have been told that, in art and literature, they will atone for deficiency of natural talent. It may be so; some persons, at least, have been able to cajole their brain into believing this. However that may be, I do not think the rule can be extended into the domain of cookery. Good intentions – no. Nobody need attempt such an imposture on his stomach, an upright and uncompromising organ, which refuses to listen to nonsense. Or let them try the experiment. Gastritis will be the result of good intentions. . . ."

NORMAN DOUGLAS,
South Wind

New England Dishes

Upon making known our desires for a supper and a bed, Mrs Hussey, postponing further scolding for the present, ushered us into a little room, and seating us at a table spread with the relics of a recently concluded repast, turned round to us and said – "Clam or cod?"

"What's that about Cods, ma'am?" said I, with much politeness.

"Clam or Cod?" she repeated.

"A clam for supper? a cold clam; is *that* what you mean, Mrs Hussey?" says I; "but that's a rather cold and clammy reception in the winter time ain't it, Mrs Hussey?"

But being in a great hurry to resume scolding the man in the purple shirt, who was waiting for it in the entry, and seeming to hear nothing but the word "clam", Mrs Hussey hurried towards an open door leading to the kitchen and, bawling out "clam for two", disappeared.

"Queequeg," said I, "do you think that we can make out a supper for us both on one clam?"

However, a warm savoury steam from the kitchen served to belie the apparently cheerless prospect before us. But when that smoking chowder came in, the mystery was delightfully explained. Oh, sweet friends! hearken to me. It was made of small juicy clams, scarcely bigger than hazel nuts, mixed with pounded ship biscuit, and salted pork cut up into little flakes; the whole enriched with butter, and plentifully seasoned with pepper and salt. Our appetites being sharpened by the frosty voyage, and in particular, Queequeg seeing his favourite fishing food before him, and the chowder being surpassingly excellent, we despatched it with great expedition: when leaning back a moment and bethinking me of Mrs Hussey's clam and cod announcement, I thought I would try a little experiment. Stepping to the kitchen door, I uttered the word "cod" with great emphasis, and resumed my seat. In a few moments a savoury steam came forth again, but with a different flavour, and in good time a fine cod-chowder was placed before us.

We resumed business; and while plying our spoons in the bowl, thinks I to myself, I wonder now if this here has any effect on the head? What's that stultifying saying about chowder-headed people? "But look, Queequeg, ain't that a live eel in your bowl? Where's your harpoon?"

Fishiest of all fishy places was the Try Pots, which well deserved its name; for the pots there were always boiling chowders. Chowder for breakfast, and chowder for dinner, and chowder for supper, till you began to look for fish-bones coming through your clothes. The area before the house was paved with clam-shells. Mrs Hussey wore a polished necklace of codfish vertebra; and Hosea Hussey had his account books bound in superior old shark-skin. There was a fishy flavour to the milk, too, which I could not at all account for, till one morning happening to take a stroll along the beach among some fishermen's boats, I saw Hosea's brindled cow feeding on fish remnants, and marching along the sand with each foot in a cod's decapitated head, looking very slip-shod, I assure ye.

HERMAN MELVILLE,
Moby Dick

My Chinee Cook

They who say the bush is dull are not so very far astray,
For this Eucalyptic cloisterdom is anything but gay;
But its uneventful dulness, I contentedly could brook,
If I could only get back my lost, lamented Chinee cook.

We had tried them without number, – cooks to wit – my wife and I
One a week, then three a fortnight, as my wife can testify;
But at last we got the right one; I may say 'twas by a fluke,
For he dropped in miscellaneous-like, that handy Chinee cook.

He found the kitchen empty, laid his swag down and commenced;
My wife, surprised, found nothing to say anything against;
But she asked him for how much a year the work he undertook, –
"Me workee for me ration," said that noble Chinee cook.

Then right off, from next to nothing, such a dinner he prepared,
That the Governor, I'm certain, less luxuriously fared;
And he waited, too, in spotless white, with such respectful look,
And bowed his head when grace was said, that pious Chinee cook.

He did the work of man and maid, – made beds and swept out rooms;
Nor cooled he in his zeal as is the manner of new brooms;
Oh, he shed celestial brightness on the most sequestered nook,
For his mop and pail were everywhere, my cleanly Chinee cook.

We got fat upon his cooking, we were happy in those days,
For he tickled up our palates in a thousand pleasant ways.
Oh, his dinners! Oh, his dinners! They were fit for any duke!
Oh, delectable Mongolian! Oh, celestial Chinee cook!

There was nothing in creation that he did not put to use,
And the less he got to cook with, all the more he could produce.
All nature was his kitchen range, likewise his cookery book.
Neither Sozer nor Meg Dod could teach that knowing Chinee cook.

And day by day upon my wife and me the mystery grew,
How his virtues were so many and his earnings were so few;
And we laid our heads together to find by hook or crook,
The secret of the cheapness of that priceless Chinee cook.

And still the sense of mystery grew on us day by day,
Till it came to be a trouble and we wished him well away;
But we could not find a fault in one so far above rebuke –
Ah, we did not know the value of that valuable cook.

But one day when I was out he brought my wife a lot of things,
Turquoise earrings, opal bracelets, ruby brooches, diamond rings,
And he ran their various prices o'er as glibly as a book,
And dirt cheap were the jewels of that jewel of a cook.

I returned, and just in time to stop the purchase of the lot.
And to ask him where on earth these costly jewels he had got.
And when I looked him in the face, good gracious, how he shook!
And he says, says he "Me bought him," did that trembling Chinee cook.

And I a justice of the peace! Oh, fortune, how unkind!
For a certain Sidney robbery came rushing to my mind.
"You bought them! Ah, I fear me, John, you paid them with a hook;
I am bound to apprehend you, oh, unhappy Chinee cook!"

So the mystery was solved at length, the secret now we saw:
John used us as a refuge from the clutches of the law;
And now, alas, too late, would I his frailty overlook,
He's gone and I am left without my skilful Chinee cook.

Oh, could I taste again of those delicious luscious things,
I could pardon him the robbery of other people's rings;
I exaggerated principle, my duty I mistook,
When I handed over to the law my peerless Chinee cook.

What would I not give now for one of his superb ragouts,
His *entremets*, his *entrées*, his incomparable stews!
Oh, art and taste and piquancy my happy board forsook,
When I came the J.P. over my lamented Chinee cook.

Take away the hateful letters. 'Twas my justice robbed my peace.
Take my name from the commission, and my matchless cook release.
But I fear my Johnnie's dead, for I am haunted by a spook,
With oblique eyes and a pig-tail, like my lost, my Chinee cook.

J. B. STEPHENS

Dashing in
and
Dishing up

*A guide
to the culinary art
by Ronald Searle*

LITERARY:
Food is just fuel after all

IMPROVISATION:
Cuppa soup'll settle me

INITIATION:
It never did that to mother

EXPERIMENTAL:
Fudge – oh boy !

UTILITARIAN:
'Ow many 'ands d'yer think I got ?

INSUFFICIENCY:
Hello, Rosemary! Surprise – surprise!

IDEAL:
An amusing little sauce !

Barometer Soup

I hunted up another barometer; it was new and perfect. I boiled it half
an hour in a pot of bean soup which the cooks were making. The result
was unexpected: the instrument was not affected at all but there was such
a strong barometer taste to the soup that the head cook, who was a most
conscientious person, changed its name in the bill of fare. The dish was
so liked by all that I ordered the cook to have barometer soup every day.

MARK TWAIN,
A Tramp Abroad

Chinese Cooking

In cookery the Chinese hold a middle position, below the French and
above the English. There is a certain degree of philosophy in a Chinaman's smallest act – he never does anything for which he cannot give a
reason. He sees an especial connection between cookery and civilization
– wherein he agrees with some great names among ourselves – and he
conceives that the English must be very low in the intellectual scale, and
must hold their high rank only by brute force. An Englishman's mode
of feeding is, says John Chinaman, the nearest approach to that of the
savages of Formosa. He does the chief work of the slaughter-house upon
his dinner-table, and he remits the principal work of the kitchen to his
stomach. "In remote ages, before we became civilized", a polite Chinaman once informed me, "we used knives and forks, as you do, and had
no chopsticks. We still carry a knife in our chopstick case; but it is a
remnant of barbarism, – we never use it. We sit down to table to eat,
not to cut up carcases."

Sedentary and dyspeptic men of every race will think with the
Chinese, that legs, shoulders, loins, heads, limbs, directly suggestive of
the living animal are common only to the banquet of an Englishman
and a beast of prey. "Plain wholesome food" means a slice of red flesh
and a crudely-prepared vegetable, and requires animal heat, intensified
by labour or exercise, to digest and assimilate it. It is the food of man in
a state of nature. This "plain food" is only wholesome in comparison
with those poisonous compounds of grease and carbonised or saturated
meat which in our inferior households are so fitly designated "made
dishes".

In London, where people's occupations do not prepare them to "eat
like a hunter," civilization is invading the kitchen. Bad housewives say

that "travel and the clubs have spoiled the men," they will no longer contentedly feed like dogs or tigers. Young men, who in the aggregate rule society, vote a household careless of the *cuisine*, to be *mauvais genre*; and old men, each potent in his particular circle, have learned from those great practical chymists, Ure, and Soyer, and Francatelli, that it is possible to enjoy the pleasures of the table without the penalty of an after-sensation of looming apoplexy.

In China, however, the natives see and are taught English cookery in its worst possible form. In Hongkong and Shanghai a dinner-table at the summer season is a melancholy spectacle of spoiled food. The creatures to be eaten were necessarily killed the same day, and the tough tissues are as hard as death stiffened them. This is not the fault of the Chinese cooks. Every Chinaman has a natural aptitude for cookery. I know one little, lean thread-paper anatomy at Hongkong, whose only teaching has been half a dozen lessons administered to him from the pages of a French cookery-book, and who will send you up a *consommé aux œufs pochés*, a fillet of beef *aux champignons*, a salmi of teal, a salad, waferlike fried potatoes, and a sweet omelette in a style certainly not inferior to Vefour; for the salmi I'd back him against the world, and for the salad against any Englishman who ever inverted that best of Italian proverbs, "*Molto d'olio, poco d'aceto*".

I dare say my hint that English cookery is not quite a perfect art will be considered very impertinent; but it has been so much the habit to ridicule the Chinese as filthy feeders, that if we are about seriously to consider their methods of preparing their food as one of the articles of their civilization, we must cast a glance homeward, lest we try them by a wrong standard. GEORGE WINGROVE COOKE,
China: The Times *Special Correspondence from China in the Years 1857–58* (1858)

Hare and Pudding

"Now there's fifteen eggs I want beaten for thirty-five minutes. Get the cream pot and whisk and break the eggs one a time into the basin, so that there isn't a bad one amongst them, or it will spoil them all, and if any little bits of shell get in, take them out with this spoon."

Nessel did so with very aching arms, but she carefully broke the eggs into the basin and then slid them into the cream pot. When all fifteen were in the pot she took the whisk and began to beat them round and round, round and round, till the pot became nearly full of golden froth.

Facing: Back from the Market by Chardin (1699-1779). *Louvre.*

The child stopped. "Is it thirty-five minutes, Rachel?" she asked. "My arms are fit to drop out."

"There's another ten minutes," answered Rachel. "I'll tell you when it's time to leave off." And so she did and Nessel was very glad of a nice hot cup of coffee and a raspberry tart or two, for she was nearly exhausted, beating eggs and chopping meat – they are two hard tasks. She went and stood by the cooking board; on the flour bin on a large dish lay a curious-looking object. It was dark red, quite flat, except for its head, which was either a rabbit's or hare's, and it had its ears on. Nessel inspected it and then said to Rachel, "Is it a hare? Why is it so flat? Did it get run over or crushed under the roll?"

"None of those silly things," said Rachel. "I've just had Charles take all the bones out of the biggest hare Spider ever caught. It was a beauty, and I'm making it into a Florentine hare. You can stand and see me do it, only put out all those cats – they'll craze me, for they love hare." So Nessel picked up Skirrywinks, Muskrat, Chinnie, and Bud, and Bee, one at a time, and put them out into the pump-yard, then came back to Rachel and the old hare.

"I am now going to make the forcemeat stuffing. Half a pound of chopped veal, half a pound of chopped suet, pepper and salt; chop four small shallots, a small bunch of parsley, thyme and half a dozen nice-sized mushrooms, two large breakfast cups of finely rubbed breadcrumbs, soak them in hot milk, press out the milk, and add to it a quarter of a pound of butter and a spoonful of the liquor the hare's bones have been stewed in; put all into a saucepan and stir it over the stove until it dries; take it out and pound it well in a mortar with the hare's liver, some finely chopped ham and powdered spice made of cloves, mace and nutmeg; mix all together with a glass of good port wine. Mix all these ingredients together, then having wiped your boned hare dry, take a wooden spoon and thickly spread the forcemeat on the hare; roll up the hare close to the head and fasten with skewers and tie round with broad tape; wrap it in a clean cloth and cover with two quarts of boiling water. As soon as the liquor is reduced to a quart by gentle stewing, put in a pint of red wine, a large spoonful of lemon pickle, one of mushroom ketchup, and the same of browning, then stew it till the liquor be reduced to a pint and thicken it with butter rolled in flour. Dish it up and lay round it four slices of the forcemeat, which has been cooked in a caul of veal. When you dish it up draw the jawbones and stick them in the sockets for eyes, and let the ears lie back on the roll; stick a sprig of myrtle in its mouth. Strain your sauce in which it was stewed and pour over it and garnish with cranberries and parsley. Send to table very hot; lay round the dish about six or eight morels and serve with redcurrant jelly. This is a very good dish accompanied with mashed and roast potatoes, cauliflowers, parsnips, or artichokes.

"There," said Rachel, "the hare is ready to be cooked. I do hope it will turn out well. Now for the pudding. It's to be a Fine Amber Pudding. Put a pound of butter into a saucepan with three-quarters of a pound of loaf sugar, finely powdered; mix well together, as they melt; add fifteen eggs well beaten and as much fresh candied orange as will add colour and flavour to it. Beat the orange candy to a fine paste, line the dish with the paste and fill with the egg, butter, and sugar mixture; make a very rich, short crust and lay over as if for a pie and bake in a slow oven. This is delicious hot or cold. There," said Rachel, "Aunt Fanny will be pleased with this, and we will have a cranberry pie and custard and bullace tart and cream."

"That will make a lovely dinner," said the child, "I feel quite hungry."

"Well," said her sister, "it's no use being hungry. You must go up on the horse pasture and get your flail basket full of morels. Ride up on old Jenny, for it's nearly our dinner-time, and it's hot roast stuffed leg of pork to-day and apple sauce and hot stewed pears and cream."

MATHENA BLOMFIELD,
Nuts in the Rookery

Christmas Fare

At Christmas time be careful of your fame;
See the old tenant's table be the same.
Then if you would send up the brawner's head,
Sweet rosemary and bays around it spread;
His foaming tusks let some large pippin grace,
Or mid'st those thund'ring spears an orange place,
Sauce like himself, offensive to its foes,
The roguish mustard, dang'rous to the nose,
Sack and the well spiced Hippocras the wine.
Wassail the bowl with ancient ribbands fine,
Porridge with plumbs, and turkeys with the chine.

DR WILLIAM KING,
The Art of Cookery (1709)

The discovery of a new dish confers more happiness on humanity than the discovery of a new star.

BRILLAT-SAVARIN

Frogs' Legs

Put three dozen frogs' legs in a saucepan with a dozen chopped mushrooms, four shallots also chopped, and two ounces of butter. Toss them on a fire for five minutes; then add a tablespoon of flour, a little salt and pepper, grated nutmeg; and moisten with a glass of white wine and a teacupful of consommé.

Boil for ten minutes, meanwhile mix the yolks of four eggs with two tablespoonfuls of cream. Now remove the frogs' legs and the other ingredients from the fire, then add the eggs and cream, stirring continually until thoroughly mixed, and serve.

A noble aphrodisiac.

Venus in the Kitchen or Love's Cookery Book
Edited by NORMAN DOUGLAS

Oven Cooking Abhorred

The old idea of cooking meat was to employ a naked flame. Ovens of any kind were at first resented, and one must admit that a joint, so long as it is sufficiently large, is undoubtedly far superior when roasted in front of a fire on a jack. Anyone who really appreciates cooked meat must surely prefer a steak or chop grilled, to anything cooked in an oven or fried.

My grandfather would not tolerate oven-cooking, but naturally women preferred it because it meant less dirt and bother. One day a roast leg of lamb was placed before him, which he commenced to carve as usual, but when he had eaten some he could tell at once it was oven-cooked, so in a rage he told my aunt, who kept house for him, to send for the cook. When she came into the room he seized the leg of lamb and hurled it through the window. I am not able to record his exact words, but they must have been fairly strong and much to the point, because the cook gave in her notice there and then, and my aunt burst into tears. So, to pacify the cook, he gave her a guinea, and the price of my aunt overlooking the incident was a new silk dress. And, of course, the window had to be repaired. But man's ideas of cooking cannot stay the hand of so-called progress for long and where is the man, if he be a man, who can remain unmoved by the sight of a woman's tears! It does not matter if a new method of cooking is inferior to the old method or not; if it saves work and worry, that new idea will come into general favour in spite of men's disapproval. Gradually, indeed, the taste becomes confused, and people come to prefer the new flavour to the old. Large numbers of people today prefer the flavour of canned vegetables and fruit to the fresh article! Many even prefer the flavour of tinned salmon to the freshly cooked fish. During the Second World War many London evacuee children would not eat fresh vegetables, because they had never been taught to enjoy them, and they actually refused roast chicken, and other foods which were regarded as luxuries. They preferred tinned meats, fish and chips, and manufactured biscuits. These were their delicacies.

MONTAGU C. ALLWOOD,
English Countryside and Gardens

Rôti sans Pareil

Take a large olive, stone it and stuff it with a paste made of anchovy, capers and oil.
Put the olive inside a trussed and boned bec-figue (garden warbler).
Put the bec-figue inside a fat ortolan.
Put the ortolan inside a boned lark.
Put the stuffed lark inside a boned thrush.
Put the thrush inside a fat quail.
Put the quail, wrapped in vine-leaves, inside a boned lapwing.
Put the lapwing inside a boned golden plover.
Put the plover inside a fat, boned, red-legged partridge.

Put the partridge inside a young, boned, and well-hung woodcock.

Put the woodcock, rolled in bread-crumbs, inside a boned teal.

Put the teal inside a boned guinea-fowl.

Put the guinea-fowl, well larded, inside a young and boned tame duck.

Put the duck inside a boned and fat fowl.

Put the fowl inside a well-hung pheasant.

Put the pheasant inside a boned and fat wild goose.

Put the goose inside a fine turkey.

Put the turkey inside a boned bustard.

Having arranged your roast after this fashion, place it in a saucepan of proper size with onions stuffed with cloves, carrots, small squares of ham, celery, mignonette, several strips of bacon well seasoned, pepper, salt, spice, coriander seeds, and two cloves of garlic.

Seal the saucepan hermetically by closing it with pastry. Then put it for ten hours over a gentle fire and arrange it so that the heat penetrates evenly. An oven moderately heated would suit better than the hearth.

Before serving, remove the pastry, put your roast on a hot dish after removing the grease, if there is any, and serve.

Venus in the Kitchen or Love's Cookery Book
Edited by NORMAN DOUGLAS

Scripture Cake

1. 4½ cups of Kings iv. 22 v.
2. 1½ cups of Judges v. 25 v.
3. 2 cups of Jeremiah vi. 20 v.
4. 2 cups of I Samuel xxv. 18 v.
5. 2 cups of Nahum iii. 12 v.
6. 1 cup of Numbers xvii. 8 v.
7. 2 tablespoonsful I Sam. xiv. 25 v.
8. Season to taste II Chron. ix. 9 v.
9. 6 cups Jeremiah xvii. 11 v.
10. 1 pinch Leviticus ii. 13 v.
11. 1 cup of Judges iv. 19 last clause.
12. 3 teaspoonsful Amos iv. 5 v.
13. Follow Solomon's prescription for the making of a good boy and you will have a good cake, see Proverbs xxiii. 14 v.

AMY ATKINSON and GRACE HOLROYD,
Practical Cookery

MERRY ENGLAND

The Hunt-dinner

Meanwhile the savoury smell of dinner fighting its way up the crowded staircase, in the custody of divers very long-coated post-boys turned waiters, and a most heterogeneous lot of private servants, some in top-boots, some in gaiters, some few in white cotton stockings, and the most out-of-the-way fitting liveries, entered the waiting-room, and the company began to prepare for the rush. All things – soup, fish, joints, vegetables, poultry, pastry and game – being at length adjusted, and the covers taken off to allow them to cool, Mr Snubbins borrowed a candle from the low end of the table, and forthwith proceeded to inform Mr Jorrocks that dinner was served.

Great was the rush! The worthy citizen was carried out of the waiting-room, across the landing, and half-way up to the dining-room, before he could recover his legs, and he scrambled to his seat at the head of the table, amidst loud cries of "Sir, this is my seat! Waiter, take this person out."—"Who are you?" – "You're another!" – "Mind your eye!" – "I *will* be here!" – "I say you won't though!" – "That's my bread!" Parties at length got wedged in. The clamour gradually subsides into a universal clatter of plates, knives and forks, occasionally diversified by the exclamation of *"Waiter!"* or, "Sir, I'll be happy to take wine with you." Harmony gradually returns, as the dinner progresses, and ere the chopped cheese makes its appearance, the whole party is in excellent humour. Grace follows cheese and the "feast of reason" being over, the table is cleared for the "flow of soul."

ROBERT SMITH SURTEES,
Handley Cross

Wanity Warm

"Wot's your usual tap, sir?" replied Sam.

"Oh, my dear young friend," replied Mr Stiggins, "all taps is vanities!"

"Too true, too true, indeed," said Mrs Weller, murmuring a groan, and shaking her head assentingly.

"Well," said Sam, "I des-say they may be, sir; but which is your partickler wanity? Vich wanity do you like the flavour on best, sir?"

"Oh, my dear young friend," replied Mr Stiggins, "I despise them all. If," said Mr Stiggins – "if there is any one of them less odious than another, it is the liquor called rum – warm, my dear young friend, with three lumps of sugar to the tumbler."

"Wery sorry to say, sir," said Sam, "that they don't allow that particular wanity to be sold in this here establishment."

"Oh, the hardness of heart of these inveterate men!" ejaculated Mr Stiggins; "oh, the accursed cruelty of these inhuman persecutors!"

With these words, Mr Stiggins again cast up his eyes, and rapped his breast with his umbrella; and it is but justice to the reverend gentleman to say that his indignation appeared very real and unfeigned indeed.

After Mrs Weller and the red-nosed gentleman had commented on this inhuman usage in a very forcible manner, and had vented a variety of pious and holy execrations against its authors, the latter recommended a bottle of port wine, warmed with a little water, spice, and sugar, as being grateful to the stomach and savouring less of vanity than many other compounds. It was accordingly ordered to be prepared. Pending its preparation the red-nosed man and Mrs Weller looked at the elder W. and groaned.

"Well Sammy," said that gentleman, "I hope you'll find your spirits rose by this here lively wisit. Wery cheerful and improvin' conwersation, ain't it, Sammy?"

"You're a reprobate," replied Sam; "and I desire you won't address no more o' them ungraceful remarks to me."

So far from being edified by this very proper reply, the elder Mr Weller at once relapsed into a broad grin; and this inexorable conduct causing the lady and Mr Stiggins to close their eyes, and rock themselves to and fro on their chairs in a troubled manner, he furthermore indulged in several acts of pantomime, indicative of a desire to pommel and wring the nose of the aforesaid Stiggins, the performance of which appeared to afford him great mental relief. The old gentleman very narrowly escaped detection in one instance; for Mr Stiggins happening to give a start on the arrival of the negus, brought his head in smart contact with the clenched fist with which Mr Weller had been describing imaginary fireworks in the air, within two inches of his ear, for some minutes previous.

"Wot are you a-reachin' out your hand for the tumbler in that 'ere sawage way for?" said Sam with great promptitude. "Don't you see you've hit the gen'l'm'n?"

"I didn't go to do it, Sammy," said Mr Weller, in some degree abashed by the very unexpected occurrence of the accident.

"Try an in'ard application, sir," said Sam, as the red-nosed gentleman rubbed his head with a rueful visage. "Wot do you think o' that, for a go o' wanity warm, sir."

Mr Stiggins made no verbal answer, but his manner was expressive. He tasted the contents of the glass which Sam had placed in his hand; put his umbrella on the floor, and tasted it again, passing his hand placidly across his stomach twice or thrice; he then drank the whole at a breath, and smacking his lips, held out the tumbler for more.

Nor was Mrs Weller behindhand in doing justice to the composition. The good lady began by protesting that she couldn't touch a drop – then took a small drop – then a large drop – and then a great many drops; and her feelings being of the nature of those substances which are powerfully affected by the application of strong waters, she dropped a tear with every drop of negus, and so got on, melting the feelings down, until at length she had arrived at a very pathetic and decent pitch of misery.

The elder Mr Weller observed these signs and tokens with many manifestations of disgust, and when, after a second jug of the same, Mr Stiggins began to sigh in a dismal manner, he plainly evinced his disapprobation of the whole proceedings by sundry incoherent ramblings of speech, among which frequent angry repetitions of the word "gammon" were alone distinguishable to the ear.

"I'll tell you wot it is, Samivel, my boy," whispered the old gentleman into his son's ear, after a long and steadfast contemplation of his lady and Mr Stiggins: "I think there must be somethin' wrong with your mother-in-law's inside, as vell as in that o' the red-nosed man."

"Wot do you mean?" said Sam.

"I mean this here, Sammy," replied the old gentleman, "that wot they drink don't seem no nourishment to 'em; it all turns to warm water, and comes a-pourin' out o' their eyes. 'Pend upon it, Sammy, it's a constitootional infirmity. "

Mr Weller delivered this scientific opinion with many confirmatory frowns and nods, which Mrs Weller remarking, and concluding that they bore some disparaging reference either to herself or to Mr Stiggins, or to both, was on the point of becoming infinitely worse when Mr Stiggins, getting on his legs as well as he could, proceeded to deliver an edifying discourse for the benefit of the company, but more especially of Mr Samuel, whom he adjured in moving terms to be upon his guard in that sink of iniquity into which he was cast; to abstain from all hypocrisy and pride of heart; and to take in all things exact pattern and copy by him (Stiggins), in which case he might calculate on arriving, sooner or later, at the comfortable conclusion that, like him, he was a most estimable and blameless character, and that all his acquaintance and friends were hopelessly abandoned and profligate wretches; which consideration, he said, could not but afford him the liveliest satisfaction.

He furthermore conjured him to avoid, above all things, the vice of intoxication, which he likened unto the filthy habits of swine, and to those poisonous and baleful drugs which, being chewed in the mouth, are said to filch away the memory. At this point of his discourse the reverend and red-nosed gentleman became singularly incoherent, and staggering to and fro in the excitement of his eloquence, was fain to catch at the back of a chair to preserve his perpendicular.

CHARLES DICKENS,
Pickwick Papers

Old English Style

We had an excellent repast, in the old English style, of abundant profusion, which I so greatly admire – pig at the top, pig at the bottom, and myself on one side – turkey to remove one, and a couple of hares to supplant the other. For side dishes, there were what I never saw before in any country – a round of beef, cut in two, one half placed on each side of the table; on inquiry, I found it was to get the real juicy part of the beef, without the salt. In addition to these there were two pork-pies.

But my readers will naturally inquire, "Had you, Ego, with all this eating, anything like drinking in proportion?" Oh, indeed, I answer yes – *Oceans of Port*! We drank "Fox-hunting" again, and again, and again. In short, whenever my inestimable host found himself at a loss for a joke, a toast, or a sentiment, he invariably exclaimed, "Come Mr Ego, let's drink Fox-'untin' again!" Particulars I will not enter into, but I may be allowed to speak of myself! Ego's forehead fancied the vine-crown around it! But he trusts he never in his moments of deepest hilarity, forgot what was due to beauty and moral worth!

ROBERT SMITH SURTEES,
Handley Cross

My-dearer and Sober-water

There were two soups – at least two plated tureens, one containing pea-soup, the other mutton-broth. Mr Jorrocks said he didn't like the latter, it always reminded him of "a cold in the 'ead". The pea-soup he thought werry like 'oss-gruel: – that he kept to himself.

"Sherry or *My*-dearer?" inquired the stiff-necked boy, going round with a decanter in each hand, upsetting the soup-spoons and dribbling the wine over people's hands.

Mr Jorrocks gets My-dearer down his sleeve.

While these were going round, the coachman and Mr De Green's boy entered with two dishes of fish. On removing the large plated covers, six pieces of skate and a large haddock made their appearance. Mr Jorrock's countenance fell five-and-twenty per cent, as he would say. He very soon dispatched one of the six pieces of skate, and was just done in time to come in for the tail of the haddock. . .

"The Duke'll come on badly for fish, I'm thinkin'," said Mr Jorrocks, eyeing the empty dishes as they were taken off.

"Oh, Marmaduke don't eat fish," replied Mrs M.

"Oh, I doesn't mean your Duke, but the Duke o' Rutland," rejoined Mr Jorrocks.

Mrs Muleygrubs didn't take.

"Nothin' left for *manners*, I mean," said Mr Jorrocks, pointing to the empty dish.

Mrs Muleygrubs smiled, because she thought she ought, though she didn't know why.

"Sherry or My-dearer, sir?" inquired the stiff-necked boy, going his round as before.

Mr Jorrocks asked Mrs Muleygrubs to take wine, and having satisfied himself that the sherry was bad, he took My-dearer, which was worse.

"Bad ticket, I fear," observed Mr Jorrocks aloud to himself, smacking his lips. "Have ye any swipes?"

"Sober-water and Seltzer-water," replied the boy.

"'Ang your sober-water!" growled Mr Jorrocks.

After a long pause, during which the conversation gradually died out, a kick was heard at the door, which the stiff-necked foot-boy having replied to by opening, the other boy appeared, bearing a tray, followed by all the other flunkies, each carrying a silver-covered dish.

"Come, *that's* more like the thing," said Mr Jorrocks aloud to himself, eyeing the procession.

A large dish was placed under the host's nose, another under that of Mrs Muleygrubs.

"Roast beef and boiled turkey?" said Mr Jorrocks to himself, half inclined to have a mental bet on the subject. "May be saddle o' mutton and chickens," continued he, pursuing the speculation.

Four T. Cox Savory side-dishes, with silver rims and handles, next took places, and two silver-covered china centre dishes completed the arrangement.

"You've lots o' plate," observed Mr Jorrocks to Mrs Muleygrubs, glancing down the table.

"Can't do with less," replied the lady.

Stiff-neck now proceeded to uncover, followed by his comrade. He began at his master, and, giving the steam-begrimed cover a flourish in the air, favoured his master's bald head with a hot shower-bath. Under pretence of admiring the pattern, Mr Jorrocks had taken a peep under the side-dish before him, and seeing boiled turnips, had settled that there was a round of beef at the bottom of the table. Spare ribs presented themselves to view. Mrs Muleygrub's dish held a degenerate turkey, so lean and so lank that it looked as if it had been starved instead of fed. There was a rein-deer tongue under one centre dish, and sausages under the other. Potatoes and turnips, stewed celery and pig's feet and ears occupied the corner dishes.

"God bless us! what a dinner!" ejaculated Mr Jorrocks, involuntarily.

"Game and black-puddings coming isn't there, my dear?" inquired Mr. Muleygrubs of his wife.

"Yes, my dear," responded his obedient half.

"'Murder most foul, as in the best it is;
But this most foul, base, and unnatural.'"
muttered Mr Jorrocks, running his fork through the breast of the unhappy turkey. "Shall I give you a little *ding dong*?"

"It's turkey," observed the lady.

"True!" replied Mr Jorrocks; "*ding dong's* French."

Conversation was very dull, and the pop and foam of a solitary bottle of champagne, handed round much after the manner of liqueur, did little towards promoting it. Mr Jorrocks was not the only person that wondered "what had set him there."

"The few remnants of that course being removed, a large, richly ornamented cold game-pie made its appearance, and was placed before Mr Muleygrubs.

"Large tart!" observed Mr Jorrocks, thinking if he could help himself he might manage to make up his lee-way: "Thought there was dark puddin's comin'," observed he to his hostess.

"*Game* and *black* puddings," replied Mrs Muleygrubs. "This comes between courses always."

"Never saw it afore," observed Mr Jorrocks.

Mr Marmaduke helped the pie very sparingly, just as he had seen the butler at Ongar Castle helping a *pâté de fois gras*; and putting as much onto a plate as would make about a mouthful and a half to each person, he sent Stiff-neck round with a fork to let people help themselves. Fortunately for Mr Jorrocks, neither Mr nor Miss De Green, nor Miss Slowman nor Mr Muleygrubs, took any, and the untouched plate coming to him, he very coolly seized the whole, while the foot-boy returned to the dismayed Mr Muleygrubs for more. Putting a few more scraps on a plate, Mr Muleygrubs sent off the pie, lest any one should make a second attack.

The second course consisted of a brace of partridges and a snipe, and three links of black-pudding, which were removed by a cold omelette and fondieu. Stewed celery, fried potatoes, puffs, and tartlets, formed the side dishes.

"Vot, have you nothin' but puffs?" exclaimed Mr Jorrocks, as the stiff-necked boy brought him the two last in succession.

Chopped-cheese, celery, and sour beer, closed the repast. The cloth was left on, and Mr Jones delivered a long, energetic grace. Four little Muleygrubs being delivered at the door, went the round of the room, as the apples and oranges, figs and raisins, and a large sponge-cake, were set on the table.

ROBERT SMITH SURTEES,
Handley Cross

Meals En Route

"The coach stops here half an hour, gentlemen; dinner quite ready."
'Tis a delightful sound. And what a dinner! What a profusion of substantial delicacies. What mighty and iris-tinted rounds of beef! What vast
and marble-veined ribs! What gelatinous veal-pies! What colossal hams!
Those are evidently prize cheese! And how invigorating is the perfume
of those various and variegated pickles! Then the bustle emulating the
plenty; the ringing of bells, the clash of thoroughfare, the summoning of
ubiquitous waiters, and the all-pervading feeling of omnipotence from
the guests, who order what they please to the landlord, who can produce
and execute everything they can desire. 'Tis a wondrous sight!

BENJAMIN DISRAELI

. . . .

The place: a restaurant car in the 5.20 p.m. from Euston.
The date: 6 November 1936.
The guests: a middle-aged business man; a young Mayfair man;
   the Mayfair man's mother; myself.
The fare: Consommé Julienne.
       Petite Sole Colbert.
       Braised Ox-tongue Florentine.
       Roast Pheasant; Parmentier Potatoes; Fresh Beans.
       Bananas Glacé Chantilly; Vanilla Wafers.
       Cheese, Biscuits, Salad.
       Dessert.
       Coffee.

Of my company, it is sufficient to say that we were all strangers to each
other, except, of course, the young man and his mother, who appeared
to know each other quite well; conversation was largely monopolized
by the young man, in spite of a sore throat, and we were all glad to listen,
except the business man, who ignored all points of contact. It soon
transpired that he had already dined at a previous service and was
presumably digesting.

Before dinner, Sherry was offered, a graceful privilege of the first
class, which was much appreciated and refused by all.

No grace was said, and we proceeded at once to the Julienne, an
English and ladylike soup, full of goodness, unctuous, tasty. Common or
garden vegetables were recognized by all, swimming in slices amid the
brown liquid. Whisked, a few bubbles appeared, showing that the

209

proper use of soap had been made in washing the plates. If any criticism was offered, it was of the smallness of the portion – a rare discourtesy, possibly attributable to the fact that the Company were not paying a dividend on their Ordinary Stock.

If the soup was an English lady, the sole was a true Englishman, fat and tough withal, and browned to a manly tan; in the melted butter swam a few specks of parsley, adding that aphrodisiac quality required to relieve the heavier substance of the fish. With this course my Guinness was served – statesman among drinks, that can keep his head and has none of that tiredness which may overcome a milk stout in the course of a long railway journey. The Mayfair man chose gin, that poor relation among spirits, yet with many good qualities that are admirably set off by a splash of tonic, most amorous of *apéritifs*. The lady, with a figure to preserve, did not drink, and the business man was now smoking a cigar, in contravention of the notice on the menu that lay before him: "In the general interest passengers are requested to refrain from smoking immediately prior to and during the service of meals."

The ox-tongue was then served, of familiar Kiwi red; florentine, of course, means an accompaniment of spinach. The medicinal qualities of spinach are well known, and it is for this reason that the description referred to the greatest of Florentine families. It was felt, too, that spinach, with its large iron content, was the most appropriate of vegetables to serve on a railway whose origin and development are due to that metal.

Finally came the pheasant, and, as we saw the dissected corpse, the Mayfair man was moved to speak of his life and habits; even yesterday, it may be, the young bird was dozing in some dry shrubbery or quietly eating raisins in a Hampshire field, when suddenly came the loud explosion, the hail of pellets, the agonized run, the line of blazing sportsmen, perhaps, and the final death from the teeth of a gamekeeper's dog. Nevertheless, while my neighbour was speaking of the bird's life, I was more preoccupied with her usefulness after death. She was a fat bird and rightly served nude. Her body showed no crease or sign of wear; just hemmed by time with autumn leaves' tints, it retained both the fresh firmness of youth with the fuller ripeness of age; a sweet and gracious lady, whose flesh we rightly proceeded to consume in silence. Close examination showed that she had never been a mother. The accompanying condiments were excellent; the beans were runners – fleeter of foot than the fleet-foot kid, as the poet says.

At this point the train reached Crewe; the young man and his mother left, and I moved my seat to avoid the business man and his cigar. The sweet, however, was rather an anti-climax, and the array of cheese, from which sanctions has banished Gorgonzola, served only to fill up chinks. Interest revived with the fruit, the three musketeers of English winter – orange, apple and banana; with them, too, were muscatel grapes, which I did not hesitate to burst against my palate. But the business man was now undoing the buttons of his boots and I felt that the time had come to remove myself, first complying with the Company's request to passengers to see that their bills are written out in their presence and to pay no money without one.

PIERCE SYNNOTT,
Wine and Food, 18

What of the Night

About nine Betsey brought the supper-tray, and Jorrocks would treat Pigg to a glass of brandy and water. One glass led to another, and they had a strong talk about hunting. They drank each other's healths, then the healths of the hounds.

"I'll give you old Priestess's good 'ealth!" exclaimed Mr Jorrocks, holding up his glass. "Fine old bitch, with her tan eyebrows – thinks I never saw a better 'ound – wise as a Christian!" Pigg proposed Manager. Mr Jorrocks gave Rummager. Pigg gave Dexterous; and they drank Mercury, and Affable, and Crowner, and Lousey, and Mountebank, and Milliner – almost all the pack in short.

The fire began to hiss, and Mr Jorrocks felt confident his prophecy was about to be fulfilled.

Mr Jorrocks and Pigg drink "Fox-hunting".

"Look out of the winder, James, and see wot sort of a night it is", said he to Pigg, giving the log a stir to ascertain that the hiss didn't proceed from any dampness in the wood.

James staggered up, and after a momentary grope about the room – for they were sitting without candles – exclaimed "Hellish dark and smells of cheese!"

"*Smells o' cheese!*" repeated Mr Jorrocks, looking round; "vy man, you've got your nob in the cupboard – this be the vinder"; going to the other corner, and opening some shutters painted like the cupboard door, and throwing up the sash.

ROBERT SMITH SURTEES,
Handley Cross

A Supper with the Poachers

My horse being lamed with a stone in his foot, I was under the necessity of putting up at a small alehouse, with a stable and a yard behind it. The man received me very civilly, but when I inquired if he could accommodate me all night, he answered that he had no room. I requested him to put something to my horse's foot, and I would sit up all night. He was silent. The good wife was more rude, and insisted upon her husband's bringing my horse out instantly; but putting a crown into her hand, and promising another in the morning, she became more accommodating. She then told me that there was a small bed upstairs, upon which she would lay a pair of clean sheets, and added that she supposed I was more of a gentleman than to take any notice of what I saw passing there. This created in me much uneasiness, and I concluded that I had fallen into a den of highwaymen; that I would not only be robbed, but have my throat cut; necessity, however, constrained me to submit.

It was now dark, and I heard three or four men dismount from their horses, lead them into the yard, and as they were coming into the room I heard the landlord say, "Indeed, brother, you need not be uneasy, I am positive the gentleman is a man of honour." Another said, "What good could our death do to a stranger? The gentleman will be happy of our company. Hang fear! I'll lead the way." So said and so done; in came five, so effectually disguised, that unless it were in the same disguise, I should not be able to distinguish any one of them. Down they sat, and their captain accosted me with great civility, and requested me to honour them with my company at supper. Supposing that my landlord would not permit either a robbery or a murder in his house, I gradually became composed.

About ten I heard the noise of a number of horses arriving, and the feet of men stamping in an upper room. In a little time the landlord came to inform me that supper was upon the table. Upon this we all went upstairs, and the captain ,with a ridiculous kind of ceremony, introduced me to a man more disguised than the rest, sitting at the head of the table; at the same time adding that he hoped I would have no objections to pay my respects to Prince Oronooko, King of the Blacks. Then I began to perceive what kind of persons they were, and was astonished that the hurry and agitation I was in had prevented me from discovering sooner.

The supper consisted of eighteen dishes of venison in various shapes – roasted, boiled with broth, hashed collops, pasties, umble pies, and a large haunch in the centre, larded. The table we sat at was large, and twenty-one sat down to supper. Each had a bottle of claret, and the man and woman of the house sat at the lower end of the table. A few of them had good musical voices, and the evening was spent with a great jollity as by the rakes at King's Arms or the city apprentices at Sadler's Wells. About two the company broke up, all of them assuring me that, upon any Thursday evening, they would be happy to see me at supper.

CAPTAIN JOHNSON,
Lives of the Highwaymen

"I forgot the salt."

AT DEATH'S DOOR. A party of undertakers make merry
at the Falcon Inn, kept by Robert Death. The motto *virtus
post funera vivit* (virtue lives on after death) was translated by
an eighteenth-century clergyman as *virtus*, a parish clerk,
vivit, lives well, *post funera*, at funeral feasts.

Diversions at Dinner

At the banquet the choice wines were brought forth, and the table was
covered with pastry and sweetmeats, of which our forefathers at this
period [early seventeenth century] appear to have been extremely fond.

A usual article at the banquet was marchpanes, or biscuits made of sugar and almonds, in different fanciful forms, such as men, animals, houses, etc. There was generally one at least in the form of a castle, which the ladies and gentlemen were to batter to pieces in frolic, by attacking it with sugar-plums. Taylor, the water-poet, calls them –

> Castles for ladies, and for carpet knights,
> Unmercifully spoil'd at feasting fights,
> Where battering bullets are fine sugared plums.

THOMAS WRIGHT,
Homes of Other Days (1871

A Shortage of Glasses

When the last "natural" had been declared, and the profit and loss account of fish and sixpences adjusted to the satisfaction of all parties, Mr Bob Sawyer rang for supper, and the visitors squeezed themselves into corners while it was getting ready.

It was not so easily got ready as some people may imagine. First of all it was necessary to awaken the girl, who had fallen asleep with her face on the kitchen table; this took a little time, and, even when she did answer the bell, another quarter of an hour was consumed in fruitless endeavours to impart to her a faint and distant glimmering of reason. The man to whom the order for the oysters had been sent had not been told to open them. It is a very difficult thing to open an oyster with a limp knife or a two-pronged fork, and very little was done in this way. Very little of the beef was done either; and the ham (which was also from the German-sausage shop round the corner) was in a similar predicament. However, there was plenty of porter in a tin can; and the cheese went a great way, for it was very strong. So upon the whole, perhaps, the supper was quite as good as such matters usually are.

After supper another jug of punch was put upon the table, together with a paper of cigars and a couple of bottles of spirits. Then there was an awful pause, and this awful pause was occasioned by a very common occurrence in this sort of place, but a very embarrassing one notwithstanding.

The fact is, the girl was washing the glasses. The establishment boasted four; we do not record the circumstance as at all derogatory to Mrs Raddle, for there never was a lodging-house yet that was not short of glasses. The landlady's glasses were little thin blown glass tumblers, and those which had been borrowed from the public-house were great, dropsical, bloated articles, each supported on a huge gouty leg. This would have been in itself sufficient to have possessed the company with the real state of affairs; but the young woman of all work had prevented the possibility of any misconception arising in the mind of any gentleman upon the subject, by forcibly dragging every man's glass away long before he had finished his beer, and audibly stating, despite the winks and interruptions of Mr Bob Sawyer, that it was to be conveyed downstairs and washed forthwith.

CHARLES DICKENS,
Pickwick Papers

EATING IN
FOREIGN PARTS

Innocents Abroad

We are getting foreignized rapidly, and with facility. We are getting reconciled to halls and bed-chambers with unhomelike stone floors, and no carpets – floors that ring to the tread of one's heels with a sharpness that is death to sentimental musing. We are getting used to tidy, noise-less waiters, who glide hither and thither, and hover about your back and your elbows like butterflies, quick to comprehend orders, quick to fill them; thankful for a gratuity without regard to the amount; and always polite – never otherwise than polite. That is the strangest curiosity yet – a really polite hotel waiter who isn't an idiot. We are getting used to driving right into the central court of the hotel, in the midst of a fragrant circle of vines and flowers, and in the midst, also, of parties of gentlemen sitting quietly reading the paper and smoking. We are getting used to ice frozen by artificial process in ordinary bottles – the only kind of ice they have here. We are getting used to all these things; but we are *not* getting used to carrying our own soap. We are sufficiently civilized to carry our own combs and tooth-brushes; but this thing of having to ring for soap every time we wash is new to us, and not pleasant at all. We think of it just after we get our heads and faces thoroughly wet, or just when we think we have been in the bath-tub long enough, and then, of course, an annoying delay follows. These Marseillaises make Marsel-laise hymns, and Marseilles vests, and Marseilles soap for all the world; but they never sing their hymns, or wear their vests, or wash with their soap themselves.

We have learned to go through the lingering routine of the table d'hôte with patience, with serenity, with satisfaction. We take soup;

then wait a few minutes for the fish; a few minutes more and the plates are changed, and the roast beef comes; another change and we take peas; change again and take lentils; change and take snail patties (I prefer grasshoppers); change and take roast chicken and salad; then strawberry pie and ice cream; then green figs, pears, oranges, green almonds etc.; finally coffee. Wine with every course, of course, being in France. With such a cargo on board, digestion is a slow process, and we must sit long in the cool chambers and smoke – and read French newspapers, which have a strange fashion of telling a perfectly straight story till you get to the "nub" of it, and then a word drops in that no man can translate, and that story is ruined. An embankment fell on some Frenchmen yesterday, and the papers are full of it to-day – but whether those sufferers were killed, or crippled, or bruised, or only scared, is more than I can possibly make out, and yet I would just give anything to know.

We were troubled a little at dinner to-day, by the conduct of an American, who talked very loudly and coarsely, and laughed boisterously where all others were so quiet and well-behaved. He ordered wine with a royal flourish, and said: "I never dine without wine, sir," (which was a pitiful falsehood), and looked around upon the company to bask in the admiration he expected to find in their faces. All these airs in a land where they would as soon expect to leave the soup out of the bill of fare as the wine! – in a land where wine is nearly as common among all ranks as water! This fellow said: "I am a free-born sovereign, sir, an American, sir, and I want everybody to know it!" He did not mention that he was a lineal descendant of Balaam's ass; but everybody knew that without his telling it.

MARK TWAIN,
The Innocents Abroad

Forks and their Uses

I observed a custome in all those Italian cities and townes through which I passed, that is not used in any other country that I saw in my travels, neither doe I thinke that any other nation of Christendome doth use in but only Italy. The Italian, and also most strangers that are commorant, in Italy, doe alwaies at their meals use a little forke, when they cut their meate. For while with their knife which they hold in one hande they cut the meat out of the dish, they fasten their forke, which they hold in their other hande, upon the same dish, so that whatsoever he be that sitting in the company of any others at meale, should unadvisedly touch the dish of meate with his fingers, from which all at the table do cut, he will give occasion of offence unto the company, as having transgressed the laws of good manners, insomuch that for his error he shall be at the least browbeaten, if not reprehended in wordes. This forme of feeding I understand is generally used in all places of Italy, their forkes being for the most part made of yron or steele, and some of silver, but those are used only by gentlemen. The reason of this their curiosity is, because the Italian cannot by any means indure to have his dish touched with fingers, seeing all men's fingers are not alike cleane.

THOMAS CORYATE,
Coryate's Crudities hastily gobbled up in Five Month's Travel (1611)

Chopsticks and All

We dined one night with Mr Kao, the Chinese Consul-General, another English couple name of Scott (M.O.I), another Chinaman, Martin, Tony and I. The meal was a *chinoiserie*, chopsticks and all. The house was a European disgrace, full of photographs of Chiang Kai-Shek and scrolls of characters, treated as Titians, not texts. "Whose calligraphy is that, Mr Kao?" I gathered from Tony was the correct question. There was a grog-tray on the terrace, bearing a hundred bottles, many of which are only seen in bars, like Crème de Cacao, de Viollette and Crème besides every known spirit and aperitif. After some adventurous drinks we sat down to a table of Mr Kao's own design. It was round, and the centre of its circle (in diameter about a yard) whizzed round dumb-waiter fashion – very ingenious and well suited to Bognor. Soup first, next a very small spatchcocked sucking-pig with sly unspatched almost-human face and the crackliest of skins, eaten from the centre dish with chopsticks. The host, Mr Kao, handled an extra pair of sticks for passing delicacies to his guests. Then a fish *à la nage* in its own *bouillon*, thin shark's fins swimming in the same, followed by cabbage and mushrooms sweetly blended. Then – East compromising with West – a chicken pie very unlike ours. A delicious dish of sweet-sour something came next, and then little bags of suet containing I don't really know what – a great many eaten by each guest (Duff made a beast of himself) and we *wound up* with a nice delicate duck soup. All very good, eaten out of little Chinese bowls with sticks and all tasting, to my amateur palate, identical. Conversation was restricted to food-subjects with occasional health drinking. If Tony said, "You're a wonderful man, Mr Kao" in a rollicking way, Mr Kao would grin and say, "You think so, Mr Keswick? You think so?" delighted and in part believing it. Mrs Kao, a dear woman, was the fifteen-stone skeleton of the feast, having no English. She all but wept in the ladies' lu when she explained to me in pidgin how fond she was of conversation. The evening broke up in an avalanche of rare gifts – tins of green tea, four scroll-pictures of the seasons by a living though traditional artist (they will greatly ornament our house) and a book by Madame Chiang Kai-Shek. We came home laden like children from a Christmas tree. The two Chinamen trying to translate the poems on the scrolls were so reminiscent of poor Maurice. He, though, was always sure, since his were extempore, whereas they could never agree as to the meaning of the characters, let alone the translation.

DIANA COOPER,
Trumpets from the Steep

Peruvian Meals

Every few days our friend Senor Gomez from the steamship office would lay in our hands a sheaf of pink meal tickets. These stated that the bearer, "Grace Tourist", was good for a meal at any one of various hostelries. Now at our hotel there was a vast table d'hôte dining room on the main floor which was cold, pale, and tardy of service; the food was (if I may be frank) uninspired – except the ever-delicious *palta*, a kind of alligator pear, and the glorious coffee. The roast beef and cabinet pudding and that sort of thing were rather dreary after our exciting meals aboard ship. I believe some sort of waiters' strike was in progress, which may have embarrassed the management; at any rate, our attempts to elicit something as apparently simple as orange juice (*jugo de naranjas*, if you can manage those j's) would have caused laughter in a dinosaur. But downstairs in the basement was a little grillroom, with bright lights, and dancing, and meats turning warmly on a spit. Many times did the waiter explain to us that the pink tickets were no good in the grill, only upstairs. We firmly refused to understand. We gradually made the round of the grill's excellent menu, particularly *corbina* (a delicious fish), *lomo de chancho* (loin of pork), *rinones de cordero* (lamb's kidneys) and *cabrito* (little goat), laid a generous tip beside the pink tickets, murmured the prayer-book rubric "collect for Grace", and left the *mozo* to argue it out with the maitre d'hotel. The pleasures of dealing with an unknown language are impossible to exaggerate. I think the children's favorite word on the menu was *panqueque*, which was not hard to guess among the *postres* (excellent term for dessert). But they were disappointed when they ordered *ciruelas*, which sound so exotic, and found them the homely prune.

CHRISTOPHER MORLEY,
Hasta la Vista

George du Maurier mocks the self-made man:
Sir Gorgius Midas (to his Younger Son). *"There's a glass of
champagne for yer, 'Enry! Down with it, my lad – and thank
'Eaven you're an Englishman, and can afford to drink it!"*

Diplomat's Disappointment

I am disappointed not to find upon this boat the variety of puddings to
which I had looked forward. One of the to me more distressing manifestations of the changing world in which I live, is that the fashion for
puddings has almost wholly faded. As a child, when staying at Clande-
boye or Shanganagh, there were always two different puddings at every
meal. We were offered College Pudding, Bachelor's Pudding, Hasty
Pudding, Tipsy Pudding, Treacle Pudding, Lemon Sponge, Pancakes,
Junket, Coconut Custard, Marmalade Pie, Roly Poly, Suet Pudding,
Toffee Pudding, Almond Sponge, Cherry Whirl, Coffee Honeycomb,

Apple Charlotte, Macaroon Hasties, Meringues, Marshmallows, Smyrna Mould, and all manner of tarts and creams. Moreover, before the first war, a "luncheon cake" was always handed round with the cheese. V. does not herself care for sweet dishes and prefers those sour concoctions which are called "savouries" although they so seldom are. In fact I feel that she regards my passion for puddings as effeminate or perhaps Scottish, or perhaps middle-class. Although at Sissinghurst I am pampered with the best tarts that I have ever known, I am not offered these delicacies at my club. Day after day, luncheon after luncheon, dinner after dinner, does the menu bear the single word "semolina", and although ices are also provided I happen to hate ice. When once I dared to suggest to our secretary (who although a generous man does not enjoy pandering to any form of decadence), that I might have a soufflé for dinner, his face fell abruptly and in contempt. "But that", he said sharply, "would mean getting in another chef". I did not have the courage to pursue the theme.

I had hoped none the less that the *Willem Ruys*, with her long Teutonic tradition of puddings, and considering the lavish variety of fish, meat and game that she provides, would at last give me the pudding opportunity that I have, since the age of fourteen, been denied. I was thus delighted when I saw on the menu such suggestive varieties as "Malakoff Pudding", "Rubane Pudding", "Harlekin Pudding" and "Noga Ijs". But when I called for these delicacies night after night, I discovered that they were in fact what in British restaurant-cars are called "shape", being little dabs the size and form of a child's sand-pie and differing from each other solely owing to the fact that some contained specks of angelica and some bits of orange or ginger. I must therefore resign myself in future to the fact that the puddings of my childhood have, even as four-wheelers, passed from circulation.

SIR HAROLD NICOLSON,
Journey to Java

A Surfeit of Turtle

We lived at Ega, during most part of the year, on turtle. The great fresh-water turtle of the Amazons grows on the upper river to an immense size, a full-grown one measuring nearly three feet in length by two in breadth, and is a load for the strongest Indian. Every house has a little pond called a curral (pen), in the back-yard to hold a stock of the animals through the season of dearth – the wet months; those who have a

Facing: The Gourmet by Picasso (1881-   ). *Chester Dale Collection.*

number of Indians in their employ sending them out for a month when the waters are low, to collect a stock, and those who have not, purchasing their supply; with some difficulty, however, as they are rarely offered for sale. The price of turtles, like that of all other articles of food, has risen greatly with the introduction of steam-vessels. When I arrived in 1850 a middle-sized one could be bought pretty readily for ninepence, but when I left in 1859, they were with difficulty obtained at eight and nine shillings each. The abundance of turtles, or rather the facility with which they can be found and caught, varies with the amount of annual subsidence of the waters. When the river sinks less than the average, they are scarce; but when more, they can be caught in plenty, the bays and shallow lagoons in the forest having then only a small depth of water. The flesh is very tender, palatable and wholesome; but it is very cloying; every one ends, sooner or later, by becoming thoroughly surfeited. I became so sick of turtle in the course of two years that I could not bear the smell of it, although at the same time nothing else was to be had, and I was suffering actual hunger. The native women cook it in various ways. The entrails are chopped up and made into a delicious soup called *sarapatel*, which is generally boiled in the concave upper shell of the animal used as a kettle. The tender flesh of the breast is partially minced with farinha, and the breast shell then roasted over the fire, making a very pleasant dish. Steaks cut from the breast and cooked with the fat form another palatable dish. Large sausages are made of the thick-coated stomach, which is filled with minced meat and boiled. The quarters cooked in a kettle of Tucupi sauce form another variety of food. When surfeited with turtle in all other shapes pieces of the lean part roasted on a spit and moistened only with vinegar make an agreeable change. The smaller kind of turtle, the tracaja, which makes its appearance in the main river, and lays its eggs a month earlier than the large species, is of less utility to the inhabitants although its flesh is superior, on account of the difficulty of keeping it alive; it survives captivity but a very few days...

HENRY WALTER BATES,
The Naturalist on the Amazons (1863)

Epigram on an Academic Visit to the Continent

I went to Frankfort, and got drunk
With that most learn'd professor – Brunck:
I went to Worts, and got more drunken
With that more learn'd professor – Ruhncken.

RICHARD PORSON

Eating in the Far North

Besides fish and flesh the Chukches consume immense quantities of herbs and other substances from the vegetable kingdom. The most important of these are the leaves and young branches of a great many different plants (for instance Salix, Rhodiola, etc.) which are collected and after being cleaned are preserved in seal skin sacks. Intentionally or unintentionally the contents of the sacks sour during the course of the summer. In autumn they freeze together to a lump of the form of the stretched seal-skin. The frozen mass is cut in pieces and used with flesh, much in the same way as we eat bread. Occasionally a vegetable soup is made from the pieces along with water, and is eaten warm. In the same way the contents of the reindeer stomach is used. Algae and different kinds of roots are also eaten, among the latter a kind of wrinkled tubers, which have a very agreeable taste.

In summer the Chukches eat cloud-berries, red bilberries, and other berries, which are said to be found in great abundance in the interior of the country. The quantity of vegetable matter which is collected for food at that season of the year is very considerable, and the natives do not appear to be very particular in their choice, if the leaves are only green, juicy, and free from any bitter taste. The writers who quote the Chukches as an example of a race living exclusively on substances derived from the animal kingdom thus commit a complete mistake. To judge from the Chukches our primitive ancestors by no means so much resembled beasts of prey as they are commonly imagined to have done, and it may, perhaps, have been the case that "bellum omnium inter omnes" was first brought in with the higher culture of the Bronze or Iron Age.

The cooking of the Chukches, like that of most wild races, is very simple. After a successful catch all the dwellers in the tent gormandise on the killed animal, and appear to find a special pleasure in making their faces and hands as bloody as possible. Fish is eaten not only in a raw state, but also frozen so hard that it can be broken in pieces. When opportunity offers the Chukches do not, however, neglect to boil their food, or to roast pieces of flesh over the train-oil lamp – the word *roast* ought, however, in this case to be exchanged for *soot*. At a visit which Lieutenant Hovgaard made to Naitskai, the natives in the tent where he was a guest ate for supper first seal-flesh soup, then boiled fish, and lastly, boiled seal-flesh. They thus observed completely the order of eating approved in Europe. As examples of Chukchi dishes I may further mention, vegetable soup, boiled seal-flesh, boiled fish, blood soup, soup of seal-blood and blubber. To these we may add soup from finely crushed bones, or from seal-flesh, blubber, and bones. The bones which are used for food are finely crushed against a stone anvil or a whale's vertebra, and then boiled with water and blood, before being eaten. The hammer used in crushing bones is of interest as forming one of the stone implements which are most frequently found in graves from the Stone Age. That the hammer was mainly intended for kitchen purposes appears from the circumstance that the women alone had it at their disposal and were consulted when it was parted with. Along with such hammers there was to be found in every tent an anvil, consisting of a whale's vertebra or a large round stone with a bowl-formed depression worn or cut out in the middle of it.

Spirits, to which they are exceedingly addicted, they call, as has been already stated, in conversation with Europeans, "ram", the utterance of the word being often accompanied by a hawking noise, a happy expression, and a distinctive gesture, which consisted in carrying the open right hand from the mouth to the waist, or in counterfeiting the unintelligible talk of a drunken man. Among themselves they call it firewater (*akmimil*). The promise of it was the most efficient means of getting an obstinate Chukchi to comply with one's wishes. That drunkenness, not the satisfying of the taste, was the main object, is shown by the circumstance that they often fixed, as price for the articles they saw we were anxious to have, such a quantity of brandy as would make them completely intoxicated. When on one occasion I appeared very desirous of purchasing a fire-drill, which was found in a tent inhabited by a newly-wedded pair, the young and very pretty housewife undertook the negotiation, and immediately began by declaring that her husband could not part with the fire-producing implement unless I gave him the means of getting quite drunk, for which, according to her statement, which was illustrated by lively gesticulations representing the different degrees of intoxication, eight glasses were required. Under the influence of liquor they are cheerful, merry, and friendly, but troublesome by their excessive caressing. Even the women readily took a glass, though evidently less addicted to intoxicants than the men. They, however, got their share, as did even the youngest of the children.

A. E. NORDENSKIÖLD,
The Voyage of the Vega Round Asia and Europe (1883)

The destiny of nations depends on the manner in which they are fed.

BRILLAT-SAVARIN

Upon what meat doth this our Caeser feed, that he is grown so great?

WILLIAM SHAKESPEARE
Julius Caesar

A South Sea Feast

The whole population of the valley seemed to be gathered within the precincts of the grove. In the distance could be seen the long front of the Ti, its immense piazza swarming with men, arrayed in every variety of fantastic costume, and all vociferating with animated gestures; while the whole interval between it and the place where I stood was enlivened by groups of females fancifully decorated, dancing, capering, and uttering wild exclamations. As soon as they descried me they set up a shout of welcome; and a band of them came dancing towards me chanting as they approached some wild recitative. The change in my garb seemed to transport them with delight, and clustering about me on all sides, they accompanied me towards the Ti. When, however, we drew near it, these joyous nymphs paused in their career, and parting on either side, permitted me to pass on to the new densely thronged building.

So soon as I mounted to the pi-pi I saw at a glance that the revels were fairly under way.

What lavish plenty reigned around! – Warwick feasting his retainers with beef and ale was a niggard to the noble Mehevi! – All along the piazza of the Ti were arranged elaborately carved canoe-shaped vessels, some twenty feet in length, filled with newly made poee-poee, and sheltered from the sun by the broad leaves of the banana. At intervals were heaps of green bread-fruit, raised in pyramidical stacks, resembling the regular piles of heavy shot to be seen in the yard of an arsenal. Inserted into the interstices of the huge stones which formed the pi-pi were large boughs of trees; hanging from the branches of which, and screened from the sun by their foliage, were innumerable little packages with leafy coverings, containing the meat of the numerous hogs which had been slain, done up in this manner to make it more accessible to the crowd. Leaning against the railing of the piazza were an immense number of long, heavy bamboos, plugged at the lower end, and with their projecting muzzles stuffed with a wad of leaves. These were filled with water from the stream, and each of them might hold from four to five gallons.

The banquet being thus spread, nought remained but for every one to help himself at his pleasure. Accordingly not a moment passed but the transplanted boughs I have mentioned were rifled by the throng of the fruit they certainly had never borne before. Calabashes of poee-poee were continually being replenished from the extensive receptacle in which that article was stored, and multitudes of little fires were kindled about the Ti for the purpose of roasting the bread-fruit.

Within the building itself was presented a most extraordinary scene. The immense lounge of mats lying between the parallel rows of the trunks of cocoa-nut trees, and extending the entire length of the house, at least two hundred feet, was covered by the reclining forms of a host of chiefs and warriors, who were eating at a great rate, or soothing the cares of Polynesian life in the sedative fumes of tobacco. The smoke was inhaled from large pipes, the bowls of which, made out of small cocoa-nut shells, were curiously carved in strange heathenish devices. These were passed from mouth to mouth by the recumbent smokers, who, taking two or three prodigious whiffs, handed the pipe to his neighbour; sometimes for that purpose stretching indolently across the body of some dozing individual whose exertions at the dinner-table had already induced sleep.

The tobacco used among the Typees was of a very mild and pleasing flavour, and as I always saw it in leaves, and the natives appeared pretty well supplied with it, I was led to believe that it must have been the growth of the valley. Indeed Kory-Kory gave me to understand that this was the case; but I never saw a single plant growing on the island. At Nukuheva, and I believe, in all the other valleys, the weed is very scarce, being only obtained in small quantities from foreigners, and smoking is consequently with the inhabitants of these places a very great luxury. How it was that the Typees were so well furnished with it I cannot divine. I should think them too indolent to devote any attention to its culture; and, indeed, as far as my observation extended, not a single atom of the soil was under any other cultivation than that of shower and sunshine. The tobacco-plant, however, like the sugar-cane, may grow wild in some remote part of the vale.

There were many in the Ti for whom the tobacco did not furnish a sufficient stimulus, and who accordingly had recourse to "arva", as a more powerful agent in producing the desired effect.

"Arva" is a root very generally dispersed over the South Seas, and from it is extracted a juice, the effects of which upon the system are at first stimulating in a moderate degree; but it soon relaxes the muscles, and exerting a narcotic influence produces a luxurious sleep. In the valley this beverage was universally prepared in the following way: – Some half-dozen young boys seated themselves in a circle around an empty wooden vessel, each one of them being supplied with a certain quantity of the roots of the "arva" broken into small bits and laid by his side. A cocoa-nut goblet of water was passed around the juvenile company, who rinsing their mouths with its contents, proceeded to the business before them. This merely consisted in thoroughly masticating the "arva" and throwing it mouthful after mouthful into the receptacle provided. When a sufficient quantity had been thus obtained water was poured upon the mass, and being stirred about with the forefinger of the right-hand, the preparation was soon in readiness for use. The "arva" has medicinal qualities.

Upon the Sandwich Islands it has been employed with no small success in the treatment of scrofulous affections, and in combating the ravages of a disease for whose frightful inroads the ill-starred inhabitants of that group are indebted to their foreign benefactors. But the tenants of the Typee valley, as yet exempt from these inflictions, generally employ "arva" as a minister to social enjoyment, and a calabash of the liquid circulates among them as the bottle with us.

Mehevi, who was greatly delighted with the change in my costume, gave me a cordial welcome. He had reserved for me a most delectable mess of "kokoo", well knowing my partiality for that dish; and had likewise selected three or four young cocoa-nuts, several roasted bread-fruit and a magnificent bunch of bananas for my especial comfort and gratification. These various matters were at once placed before me; but Kory-Kory deemed the banquet entirely insufficient for my wants until he had supplied me with one of the leafy packages of pork, which, notwithstanding the somewhat hasty manner in which it had been prepared, possessed a most excellent flavour, and was surprisingly sweet and tender.

HERMAN MELVILLE,
Typee

Sardines in Sand

By this time we felt that our own little effort to draw a new red line across a survey map was very small and insignificant and that we should certainly be able to walk to Jaghabub carrying a fanatis and a tin of corned beef if necessary! We were much less confident of it next morning, however, when all the camels turned up their noses at the date food offered them and deliberately ran away. There was nowhere for them to run to among the dunes, so we got them back after a laborious half-hour, but felt that the word "agal" and not Kufara would be written across my heart in future! There was no fire that morning, and uncooked soaked rice is not appetizing. I remember I was tying the remains of my stocking round my feet when I heard a gloomy voice say: "We ate the last box of sardines last night because you lost the beef-tin-opener in the sand and the rice is coal black. I wish you would not be so miserly with the fanatis water!" I didn't pay much attention as I hadn't any more stockings. Evidently the primrose and scarlet boots which I had bought for four mejidies (sixteen shillings) at Jof were not suited for walking, for I had been wearing two pairs of woollen stockings one over the other and now they all hung in shreds round my feet. However, I did look up when the plaintive tones continued. "I've found one sardine. He must have fallen out when you upset the canteen in the sand." With horror I saw a soddened, dark mass and on the top of it a minute yellow block shaped like a fish, but I did not like to be discouraging. "Are you sure that there is a sardine inside that sand?" I asked diffidently. Hassanein was offended. "Will you carve him or shall I?" he asked majestically.

ROSITA FORBES,
The Secret of the Sahara: Kufara

Saharan Food

When we returned from our matutinal walks we had enough appetite to cope with Sidi Saleh's prodigious hospitality. Every morning on the stroke of nine a light tap came on my green and yellow door and there was Durur, with smiling ebony face, ready to lead us by sandy path and intricate court and passage to the wide, carpeted loggia, where waited our kindly host to wave us into the long, dark chamber redolent of roses and cinnamon. After we had gravely washed our hands in the Damascus basin, we crouched cross-legged beside the immense brass tray and there was a moment of thrilled expectation while another slave lifted the lids of a dozen dishes. Sometimes there was a small carved tray, inlaid with silver, on which stood half a score of bowls of sweetmeats, stiff blanc-manges of all colours adorned with almonds, very sweet pastes something like Yorkshire pudding, junket made of the milk of newly lambing sheep, all sorts of date concoctions, couss-couss made with raisins and sugar, a white, sticky cream, flavoured with mint. Always there were bowls of sweet hot milk and piles of thin, crisp, heavy bread fried with butter and eaten hot with sugar, called in Egypt "bread of the judge". Arab custom ordains that a guest must be entertained for three days and three nights, but the generous kaimakaan would not hear of our getting anything for ourselves. The story of Jedabia was repeated over again. Once we protested about the mighty meals provided in the house of Sidi el Abed, and the next day, as a reminder that the hospitality of the East is unbounded and must be accepted with the simplicity with which it is offered, the number of dishes was doubled and there were no fewer than twenty loaves ranged round the tray, while the centre *plat* was no longer a bowl, it was literally a bath of mellow, golden rice in which lay the buttery fragments of a whole sheep. Two hours each morning were spent in that quiet room going through the various ceremonies dependent on "breakfasting". When the highly-spiced and peppered coffee was finished there were always the three glasses of green tea, hot and strong, with dignified slow conversation, punctuated by many pauses, while the brazier smoke made little hypnotic spirals, and through the open door a splash of sunlight crept over the castellated wall and lingered on the purple and rose of the carpets between the great arches of the loggia.

About eleven o'clock, scented and very replete, we took ceremonious leave of our host and departed slowly.

Ibid.

Monkey Business

The Rest House was perched on the edge of the precipice with a view of the gorge and was available for picnics and most popular, being only a dozen miles from Jubbulpore, where my battalion was then stationed. On the occasion I refer to, I and two companions had arranged a party of six on a hot weather night *au clair de lune*, and had taken out with us a sumptuous meal. This was laid on a table just outside the bungalow some ten yards from the veranda, where the party of six was sitting. The servants were just announcing that everything was ready when there was a terrible commotion – a mob of fifty or sixty langoors, the big grey and white and black Indian monkey – came leaping up from the rocks, overran the plateau, upset the table, scattered the glasses and bottles and cutlery, and disappeared as quickly as they had come with every morsel of our beautiful dinner. All that remained was to drive home twelve miles and scratch up some beer and sandwiches.

SIR FRANCIS COLCHESTER-WEMYSS,
Wine and Food, 29

A Meal in Abyssinia

Another smiling pause. At last supper arrived; first a basket containing half-a-dozen great rounds of native bread, a tough, clammy substance closely resembling crepe rubber in appearance; then two earthenware jugs, one of water, the other of *talla* – a kind of thin, bitter beer; then two horns of honey, but not of honey as it is understood at Thame; this was the product of wild bees, scraped straight from the tree; it was a greyish colour, full of bits of stick and mud, bird dung, dead bees, and grubs. Everything was first carried to the abuna for his approval, then to us. We expressed our delight with nods and more extravagant smiles.

The food was laid before us and the bearers retired. At this moment the Armenian shamelessly deserted us, saying that he must go and see after his boy.

The three of us were left alone, smiling over our food in the half darkness.

In the corner lay our hamper packed with Irene's European delicacies. We clearly could not approach them until our host left us. Gradually the frightful truth became evident that he was proposing to dine with us.

I tore off a little rag of bread and attempted to eat it. "This is a very difficult situation," said the professor; "I think, perhaps, it would be well to simulate ill-health", and, holding his hands to his forehead, he began to rock gently from side to side, emitting painfully subdued moans. It was admirably done; the abuna watched him with the greatest concern; presently the professor held his stomach and retched a little; then he lay on his back, breathing heavily with closed eyes; then he sat up on his elbow and explained in eloquent dumb show that he wished to rest. The abuna understood perfectly, and, with every gesture of sympathy, rose to his feet and left us.

In five minutes, when I had opened a tinned grouse and a bottle of lager and the professor was happily mumbling a handful of ripe olives, the Armenian returned. With a comprehensive wink, he picked up the jug of native beer, threw back his head, and, without pausing to breathe, drank a quart or two. He then spread out two rounds of bread, emptied a large quantity of honey into each of them, wrapped them together, and put them in his pocket. "Moi, je puis manger comme abyssin", he remarked cheerfully, winked at the grouse, wished us good night, and left us.

EVELYN WAUGH,
When the Going was Good

Food in the Gobi Desert

The melon merchant always claims a big space for his wares on the *bazar* floor. He sits on a mat, surrounded by melons of every kind. The largest and most showy is the heavy water-melon, weighing over twenty pounds, with a glossy myrtle-green rind and a centre of juicy rose-madder flesh, flecked with shining black seeds. These seeds will be collected, salted and dried by fire-heat, after which they have a good sale, for the Chinese love to lighten a social hour by splitting the crisp husks with their teeth and nibbling the thin tasty seeds as they talk. The seller can supply many varieties of firm-fleshed cantaloups, and his customers test them with infinite care in order to select the very best. The degree of ripeness is known by pressure of the finger, but a melon is really chosen by the tone it emits when rapped with a jerk of the forefinger, for there is a reverberation from the perfect flesh which is lacking in any inferior fruit. There is great art in choosing melons, for appearances are deceptive and what looks a tempting fruit may prove tasteless. Even the most skilful buyer cannot be finally certain of the flavour, but if the customer will buy a whole melon, the merchant will scoop a square chunk from the centre and allow it to be sampled. Some of the melons are smooth and others rough-skinned, and the flesh is white, greenish, pinkish or an atractive peach shade, according to the variety. There is one kind in which the pulp is mushy even when the fruit is not over-ripe, and has a perfumed flavour which needs an acquired taste. Some are cut open that passers-by may throw down a coin, seize a slice and walk away eating it as they go, tossing the rind into the gutter, but the more fastidious refuse the piece on which the flies have feasted, though the merchant constantly waves a switch made from a horse's tail to and fro over his wares.

The Turki is a burly man and a voracious eater, and there is always a crowd in that part of the *bazar* where food is sold. One group of men, squatting on their heels, surround the cook, who sells snippets of meat and kidney speared on an iron skewer and grilled over a portable charcoal fire. This grilled meat is very tasty, though generally tough. Another man, who wheels a large barrow covered with a white cloth, offers slices of cold boiled mutton and boiled liver, and not far off is the soup vendor, who sells the broth made from the boiled meat at a copper a bowl. From the bee-hive oven of the Moslem baker come cakes of delicious bread of varying shapes and sizes. This oven is heated with wood, and the unbaked cakes, moistened with a little water, are stuck round the inside wall, where they bake very quickly, so that each customer can carry away bread which is hotter than his hands can comfortably hold.

The favourite dish of the Turki, however, is *pilau*, which is made in a large cauldron from the fattest of the mutton, cut small and cooked with rice, chopped carrots and seedless raisins. There is always a seller of *pilau* in the market, he generally has his stand at the door of a restaurant and is the centre of a buzzing crowd of customers.

MILDRED CABLE with FRANCESCA FRENCH,
The Gobi Desert

Nothing helps scenery like ham and eggs.

MARK TWAIN

Natives of Virginia at their meal; after John White's drawing, 1586.

Tell Me What You Eat

When we arrived at any village, the women all turned out to lulliloo their chief. Their shrill voices, to which they give a tremulous sound by a quick motion of the tongue, peal forth "Great lion!" "Great Chief!" "Sleep my lord!" etc. The men utter similar salutations; and Sekeletu receives all with becoming indifference. After a few minutes conversation and telling the news, the head man of the village, who is almost always a Makololo, rises and brings forth a number of large pots of beer. Calabashes, being used as drinking-cups, are handed round, and as many as can partake of the beverage do so, grasping the vessels so eagerly that they are in danger of being broken.

They bring forth also large pots and bowls of thick milk; some contain six or eight gallons; and each of these, as well as of the beer is given to a particular person, who has the power to divide it with whom he pleases. The head man of any section of the tribe is generally selected for this office. Spoons not being generally in fashion, the milk is conveyed to the mouth with the hand. I often presented my friends with iron spoons, and it was curious to observe how the habit of hand-eating prevailed, though they were delighted with the spoons. They lifted out a little with the utensil, then put it on the left hand, and ate it out of that.

As the Makololo have great abundance of cattle, and the chief is expected to feed all who accompany him, he either selects an ox or two of his own from the numerous cattle stations that he possesses at different spots all over the country, or is presented by the headmen of the villages he visits with as many as he needs by way of tribute. The animals are killed by a thrust from a small javelin in the region of the heart, the wound being purposely small in order to avoid any loss of blood, which, with the internal parts, are the perquisites of the men who perform the work of the butcher; hence all are eager to render service in that line. Each tribe has its own way of cutting up and distributing an animal. Among the Makololo the hump and ribs belong to the chief; among the Bakwains the breast is his perquisite. After the oxen are cut up, the differerent joints are placed before Sekeletu and he apportions them among the gentlemen of the party. The whole is rapidly divided by their attendants, cut into long strips, and so many of these are thrown into the fires at once that they are nearly put out. Half broiled and burning hot the meat is quickly handed round; everyone gets a mouthful, but no one except the chief has time to masticate. It is not the enjoyment of eating they aim at, but to get as much of the food into the stomach as possible during the short time the others are cramming as well as themselves, for no one can eat more than a mouthful after the others have finished. They are eminently gregarious in their eating; and, as they despise any one who eats alone, I always poured out two cups of coffee at my own meals, so that the chief, or some one of the principal men, might partake along with me. They all soon became very fond of coffee; and, indeed, some of the tribes attribute greater fecundity to the daily use of this beverage. They were all well acquainted with the sugarcane, as they cultivate it in the Barotse country, but knew nothing of the method of extracting the sugar from it. They use the cane only for chewing. Sekeletu, relishing the sweet coffee and biscuits, of which I then had a store, said, "he knew my heart loved him by finding his own heart warming to my food." He had been visited during my absence at the Cape by some traders and Griquas, and "their coffee did not taste half so nice as mine, because they loved his ivory and not himself." This was certainly an original mode of discerning character.

DAVID LIVINGSTONE,
Travels and Researches in South Africa

A Cut off the Joint

They were up long before us, and had breakfast on raw meat cut from a large joint which lay, without regard to cleanliness, among the deposits on the floor of the igloë. Their mode of eating was ingeniously active.

They cut the meat in long strips, introduced one end into the mouth, swallowed it as far as the powers of deglutition would allow, and then, cutting off the protruding portion close to the lips, prepared themselves for a second mouthful. It was really a feat of address: those of us who tried it failed awkwardly; and yet I have seen infants in the mother's hood, not two years old, who managed to perform it without accident.

ELISHA KENT KANE,
Arctic Explorations in Search of Sir John Franklin (1898)

A print from a Japanese book of poems, 1768.

Dinner with the Grand Vizier's Lady

I wrote to you, dear sister, and to all my other English correspondents, by the last ship, and only Heaven can tell when I shall have another opportunity of sending to you; but I cannot forbear to write again, though perhaps my letter may lie upon my hands these two months. To confess the truth, my head is so full of my entertainment yesterday, that 'tis absolutely necessary for my own repose to give it some vent. Without farther preface I will then begin my story.

I was invited to dine with the Grand-Vizier's lady, and it was with a great deal of pleasure I prepared myself for an entertainment which was never before given to any Christian. I thought I should very little satisfy her curiosity (which I did not doubt was a considerable motive to the invitation) by going in a dress she was used to see, and therefore dressed myself in the court habit of Vienna, which is much more magnificent than ours. However, I chose to go *incognito*, to avoid any disputes about ceremony, and went in a Turkish coach, only attended by my woman that held up my train, and the Greek lady who was my interpretess. I was met at the court door by her black eunuch, who helped me out of the coach with great respect, and conducted me through several rooms, where her she-slaves, finely dressed, were ranged on each side. In the innermost I found the lady sitting on her sofa, in a sable vest. She advanced to meet me, and presented me half a dozen of her friends with great civility. She seemed a very good-looking woman, near fifty years old. I was surprised to observe so little magnificence in her house, the furniture being all very moderate; and, except the habits and numbers of her slaves, nothing about her appeared expensive. She guessed at my thoughts, and told me she was no longer of an age to spend either her time or money in superfluities; that her whole expense was charity, and her whole employment praying to God. There was no affectation in this speech; both she and her husband are entirely given up to devotion. He never looks upon any other woman; and, what is much more extraordinary, touches no bribes, notwithstanding the example of all his predecessors. He is so scrupulous on this point, he would not accept Mr Wortley's present, till he had been assured over and over that it was a settled perquisite of his place at the entrance of every ambassador.

She entertained me with all kind of civility till dinner came in, which was served one dish at a time, to a vast number, all finely dressed after their manner, which I don't think so bad as you have perhaps heard it represented. I am a very good judge of their eating, having lived three weeks in the house of an *effendi* at Belgrade, who gave us very magnificent dinners, dressed by his own cooks. The first week they pleased me extremely; but I own I then began to grow weary of their table, and desired our own cook might add a dish or two after our manner. But I attribute this to custom, and am very much inclined to believe that an Indian, who had never tasted of either, would prefer their cookery to ours. Their sauces are very high, all the roast very much done. They use a great deal of very rich spice. The soup is served for the last dish; and they have at least as great a variety of ragouts as we have. I was very sorry I could not eat of as many as the good lady would have had me, who was very earnest in serving me of every thing. The treat concluded with coffee and perfumes, which is a high mark of respect; two slaves kneeling *censed* my hair, clothes, and handkerchief. After this ceremony, she commanded her slaves to play and dance, which they did with their guitars in their hands, and she excused to me their want of skill, saying she took no care to accomplish them in the art.

LADY MARY WORTLEY MONTAGU,
Letter to the Countess of Mar from Adrianople, 18 April, 1717

The Good Food Guide

"If you lose your way and cannot tell what to eat", said the Choco Indian Ailipio, "then you must look for a tree where monkeys are sitting. You will find it most easily by making for the noise. Monkeys are extremely wasteful in their eating. Usually they take only one bite of a fruit, and then drop it to pick another which has caught their eye. For every one they eat, often they take four or five merely to play with and throw away again. These fruits or nuts can be picked up without fear, for you may be sure that what the monkeys like, we can eat too."

PER HØST,
What the World Showed Me

The Eating Houses of Palanka

I will introduce my reader to one of these places. In one corner, on the ground, burns a fierce fire, surrounded by innumerable pots and pans, between which are wooden spits with beef and pork simmering and roasting in the most enticing manner. An ungainly wooden framework, with a long broad plank on it, occupies the middle of the room, and is covered with a cloth whose original colour it would be an impossibility to determine. This is the table at which the guests sit. During the dinner itself the old patriarchal customs are observed with this difference, that not only do *all* the guests eat out of one dish, but that all the eatables are served up in one, and one only. Beans and rice, potatoes and roast beef, Paradise apples and onions, &c., &c., lie quietly side by side, and are devoured in the deepest silence. At the end of the repast, a goblet, filled with wine, or sometimes merely water, is passed from hand to hand, and after this has gone round, the company begin to talk. In the evening dancing is vigorously pursued to the music of a guitar; unfortunately it was Lent during my visit, when all public amusements are prohibited. The people themselves, however, were not so particular, and were only too ready, for a few reaux, to go through the Sammaquecca and Refolosa – the national dances of the country. I had soon seen sufficient; the gestures and movements of the dancers were beyond all description unbecoming and I could but pity the children, whose natural modesty cannot fail to be nipped in the bud by witnessing the performance of these dances.

IDA PFEIFFER,
A Woman's Journey Round the World (1856)

There Were No Table-napkins: a Gastronomic Fantasy

And now for a party in Morocco. The company is more exalted this time. We were the guests of a distinguished sheikh. We sat on exquisite rugs woven in the villages on the foothills of the Atlas. A sort of janissary stood behind the sheikh during the whole meal. He was quite human, but he did not twitch an eyelash. He could give the Horse Guards a lesson in immobility. We were attended by three coal-black negresses, consummate creatures. So silent were these, too, that you might have thought them marionettes, excepting that they did not creak. At the beginning of the meal and between courses, one negress held out a brass basin for us to hold our arms out over it. The second poured scented warm water on our hands from a brass ewer. The third featly wiped our hands. Dish succeeded dish in bewildering opulence, set down between us, in great straw containers usually. There were no forks. We thrust with our hands into odorous hills of *couscous*, or with our fingers stripped delicate ribbons of fish from the bones. But the *chef-d'œuvre* was a dish of mutton and whole onions, stewed in honey. I repeat: stewed in honey. It was celestial. If you are sceptical, go to Morocco for yourself; try it, and you will believe. But remember to be very gracious when your host, the sheikh, explores the hot depths of the stew with his fingers and hands over to you some particularly succulent morsel. And remember there are roast quail to follow, stuffed with raisins and red peppers. Your host in his courtesy and against his principles will offer you beer. But it were pleasanter to join him in a tumbler of sweet tea, one third filled with mint-leaves.

LOUIS GOLDING,
Wine and Food, 4

There was an Old Man of the East,
Who gave all his children a feast;
But they all ate so much,
And their conduct was such,
That it killed that Old Man of the East.

EDWARD LEAR

Headaches and Vapours

At two o'clock we sat down to table *en famille*. I was placed between the the Marchioness and her husband. The dinner was served in plate, and the huge massy dishes brought up by a vast train of gentlemen and chaplains, several of them decorated with the Order of Christ. This attendance had quite a feudal air and transported my imagination to the days of chivalry when great chieftains were waited upon like kings by noble vassals. The Portuguese had need have the stomach of ostriches to digest the loads of greasy victuals with which they cram themselves. Their vegetables, their rice, their poultry are all stewed in the essence of ham, and so strongly seasoned with pepper and spices that a spoonful of pease or a quarter of an onion is sufficient to set one's mouth in a flame. With such a diet and the continual swallowing of sweetmeats, I am not surprised at their complaining continually of headaches and vapours. The rain descending with violence, every window was shut, and the absence of vegetable perfumes from the garden, so delightful after a shower, supplied by a steam of burnt lavender.

The Journal of William Beckford in Portugal and Spain, 1787–88

DESERT ISLAND
DISHES

Eating Alone in the Antarctic

Breakfast didn't count. I rarely took more than tea and a whole-wheat biscuit. Lunch was habitually an out-of-the-can affair, consisting usually of tomato juice, Eskimo biscuits, and frequently a cold meat or fish – either corned beef, tongue, or sardines. These I prepared in masterly fashion. But supper, by rights the high spot in an explorer's day, the hot meal toward which a cold and hungry man looks with mounting anticipation – this meal for a while was a daily fiasco.

I have only to close my eyes to witness again the succession of culinary disasters. Consider what my diary designated as The Corn Meal Incident. Into a boiler I dumped what seemed a moderate quantity of meal, added a little water, and stood it on the stove to boil. That simple formula gave birth to a Hydra-headed monster. The stuff began to swell and dry up, swell and dry up, with fearful blowing and sucking noises. All innocently I added water, more water and still more water. Whereupon the boiler erupted like Vesuvius. All the pots and pans within reach couldn't begin to contain the corn meal that overflowed. It oozed over the stove. It spattered the ceiling. It covered me from head to foot. If I hadn't acted resolutely, I might have been drowned in corn meal. Seizing the container in my mittened hands, I rushed it to the door and hurled it far into the food tunnel. There it continued to give off deadly golden lava until the cold finally stilled the crater.

There were other disasters of the same order. There was the Dried Lima Beans Incident of April 10th ("It's amazing", the diary reports soberly, "how much water lima beans can absorb, and how long it takes

245

them to cook. At supper time I had enough half-cooked lima beans to feed a ship's company.") My first jelly dessert bounded like a rubber ball under my knife; the flapjacks had to be scraped from the pan with a chisel. ("And you, the man who sat at a thousand banquets", goes the accusing entry of April 12th.) I dreaded banquets before I went to Advance Base; and I have come to dread them since. But in April's dark hours I ransacked my memory, trying to remember what they were like. All that I could recall was *filet mignon* spiced and darkened to the colour of an old cavalry boot; or lobster thermidor; or squabs perched on triangles of toast; or chicken salad heaped on billowing lettuce. All these were far beyond the simple foods in my larder. When I did experiment the results filled the shack with pungent burning smells and coated the skillets with awful gummy residues. But in spite of the missing cook book, the record was not one of unmitigated failure. Resolved to make a last stand, I took the surviving chicken, hung it for two days from a nail over the stove to thaw, boiled it all one day, seasoned it with salt and pepper, and served. The soup, which was an unexpected by-product, was delicious; that night I broached a bottle of cider and drank a toast to Escoffier.

ADMIRAL RICHARD BYRD
Alone

A Meal on Mont Blanc

Our porters left us: a baton was stretched across the room over the stove, and our wet socks and leggings were thrown across it to dry; our boots were placed around the fire, and we set about preparing our evening meal. A pan was placed upon the fire and filled with snow, which in due time melted and boiled; I ground some chocolate and placed it in the pan, and afterwards ladled the beverage into the vessels we possessed, which consisted of two earthen dishes and the metal cases of our brandy flasks. After supper Simond went out to inspect the glacier, and was observed by Huxley, as twilight fell, in a state of deep contemplation beside a crevasse.

Gradually the stars appeared, but as yet no moon. Before lying down we went out to look at the firmament, and I noticed what I suppose has been observed to some extent by everybody, that the stars near the horizon twinkled busily, while those near the zenith shone with a steady light. One large star in particular excited our admiration; it flashed intensely, and changed colour incessantly, sometimes blushing like a ruby, and again gleaming like an emerald. A determinate colour would sometimes remain constant for a sensible time, but usually the flashes followed each other in very quick succession. Three planks were now placed across the room near the stove, and upon these, with their rugs folded round them, Huxley and Hirst stretched themselves, while I nestled on the boards at the most distant end of the room. We rose at eleven o'clock, renewed the fire and warmed ourselves, after which we lay down again. I at length observed a patch of pale light upon the wooden wall of the cabin, which had entered through a hole in the end of the edifice, and rising found that it was past one o'clock. The cloudless moon was shining over the wastes of snow, and the scene outside was at once wild, grand and beautiful.

Breakfast was soon prepared, though not without difficulty; we had no candles, they had been forgotten; but I fortunately possessed a box of wax matches, of which Huxley took charge, patiently igniting them in succession and thus giving us a tolerably continuous light. We had some tea, which had been made at the Montanvert, and carried to the Grands Mulets in a bottle. My memory of that tea is not pleasant; it had been left a whole night in contact with its leaves, and smacked strongly of tannin. The snow-water, moreover, with which we diluted it was not pure, but left a black residuum at the bottom of the dishes in which the beverage was served. The few provisions deemed necessary being placed in Simond's knapsack, at twenty minutes past two o'clock we scrambled down the rocks, leaving Huxley behind us.

JOHN TYNDALL,
The Glaciers of the Alps (1860)

Seal Steaks and Soot

Seal meat is coarse and black and sometimes it has a sickeningly oily taste which catches you suddenly unawares and which I think is quite loathsome. Penguin meat is much the same but it plays a straighter game. It does not catch you unexpectedly with a revolting mouthful. In the *Discovery II* we often killed seals towards the end of the season when the meat supplies were running low. We hung the black carcases in the rigging. "Seal steak, sir?" but nearly always I and several others either delicately left ours on our plates or found ourselves suddenly with an unpleasant mouthful and were compelled, much less delicately, to eject it. But somehow, under the pram upon our wind-swept beach, we lost our sense of taste. Manna from heaven could not have seemed more delicious than lumps of seal or penguin meat made into a hash with a handful of oatmeal. We had two meals a day, two plates of stew each, cooked by old Jock Matheson in the huge, faithful and satisfying sauce-pan, sooty and heavy and broad-based for an old-fashioned kitchen range. The saucepan sat somewhat precariously upon an iron brazier which the guardian angel of one or other of us had left in the after peak of the *Rapid*. George found it there, lying upon its side under buckets and coils of rope, and brought it ashore. It stood proudly on three legs in an iron tray. We started the fire in the brazier with slivers of wood damped with paraffin, and then hung little squares of seal blubber over the embers on a frame of twisted wire. The blubber melted and dripped with a crackle on to the embers below. The drips burnt with a bright smoky flame that stank and sent up a hovering cloud of little black smuts. As Matheson stirred his cooking pot over this smelly greasy little altar he lifted it from time to time so that one of us, sitting nearby, could drop on to the fire a chunk of blubber with our hands or with a sharp splint of wood. Sometimes the chunk of blubber missed the wire frame on which we meant to drop it and fell into the brazier. When that hap-pened it was liable to put the fire out and we would have to light it again. This was at first just a nuisance but later it became a continually recurring disaster, for we began to run short of paraffin and matches. When, as always seemed to be the case, it happened while I was tending the fire I used to resort to subterfuge to keep the knowledge of the calamity from Walker and, if I could, from Matheson. But it was not easy. When a voice said, from the dark interior of the shelter, "For God's sake go easy on the paraffin there!" I knew that I had been caught out. When old Matheson cooked the seal hash over the fire the smoke rose and filled his beard and hair with black smuts. It filled ours, too, when we tended it. They hung from our eyebrows and eyelids and we brushed them away, smearing the soot in streaks across our faces.

We kept the fire going all day and all night with chunks of blubber, keeping watches to tend it. Our hands became covered in grease which we wiped off on our clothes. The bitter smoke stung our eyes and blackened our faces. At night we placed the brazier in the entrance to our shelter and warmed ourselves at its flickering smoky flames as much as we could, sitting over it in turns. It filled the inside of our house with acrid fumes and covered the roof with soot, but its light, dancing on the over-arching timbers of the boat, was a friendly and reassuring thing. It cheered us as we lay with our arms around each other in our quad-ruple sleeping bag, shivering and fearing to fall asleep because of the horror of waking.

F. D. OMMANNEY,
South Latitude

Opening Oysters

While we were thus talking, Jack had been vainly endeavouring to open an oyster with his large knife. "Here is a simpler way", said I, placing an oyster on the fire; it immediately opened. "Now", I continued, "who will try this delicacy?" All at first hesitated to partake of them, so unattractive did they appear. Jack, however, tightly closing his eyes and making a face as though about to take medicine, gulped one down. We followed his example, one after the other, each doing so rather to provide himself with a spoon than with any hope of cultivating a taste for oysters.

Our spoons were now ready, and gathering round the pot we dipped them in, not, however, without sundry scalded fingers. Ernest then drew from his pocket the large shell he had procured for his own use, and scooping up a good quantity of soup he put it down to cool, smiling at his own foresight.

JOHANN RUDOLF WYSS,
The Swiss Family Robinson

Antarctic Meals

At first the meals, consisting mostly of seal meat with one hot drink per day, were cooked on a stove in the open. The snow and wind, besides making it very unpleasant for the cook, filled all the cooking-pots with sand and grit, so during the winter the cooking was done inside the hut.

A little Cerebos salt had been saved, and this was issued out at the rate of three-quarters of an ounce per man per week. Some of the packets containing the salt had broken, so that all did not get the full ration. On the other hand, one man dropped his week's ration on the floor of the hut, amongst the stones and dirt. It was quickly collected, and he found to his delight that he had enough now to last him for three weeks. Of course, it was not *all* salt. The hot drink consisted at first of milk made from milk-powder up to about one-quarter of its proper strength. This was later on diluted still more, and sometimes replaced by a drink made from a pea-soup-like packing from the Bovril sledging rations. For midwinter's day celebrations, a mixture of one teaspoonful of methylated spirit in a pint of hot water, flavoured with a little ginger and sugar, served to remind some of cocktails and *Veuve Cliquot*.

At breakfast each had a piece of seal or half a penguin breast. Luncheon consisted of one biscuit on three days a week, nutfood on Thursday, bits of blubber, from which most of the oil had been extracted for the lamps, on two days a week, and nothing on the remaining day. On this day breakfast consisted of a half-strength sledging ration. Supper was almost invariably seal and penguin, cut up very finely and fried with a little seal blubber.

There were occasionally very welcome variations from this menu. Some paddies – a little white bird not unlike a pigeon – were snared with a loop of string, and fried, with one water-sodden biscuit, for lunch. Enough barley and peas for one meal all round of each had been saved, and when this was issued it was a day of great celebration. Sometimes, by general consent, the luncheon biscuit would be saved, and, with the next serving of biscuit, was crushed in a canvas bag into a powder and boiled with a little sugar, making a very satisfying pudding. When blubber was fairly plentiful there was always a saucepan of cold water, made from melting down the pieces of ice which had broken off from the glacier, fallen into the sea, and been washed ashore, for them to quench their thirst in. As the experience of Arctic explorers tended to show that sea-water produced a form of dysentery, Wild was rather diffident about using it. Penguin carcasses boiled in one part of sea-water to four of fresh were a great success though, and no ill-effects were felt by anybody.

The ringed penguins migrated north the day after we landed at Cape Wild, and though every effort was made to secure as large a stock of meat and blubber as possible, by the end of the month the supply was so low that only one hot meal a day could be served. Twice the usual number of penguin steaks were cooked at breakfast, and the ones intended for supper were kept hot in the pots by wrapping up in coats, etc. "Clark put our saucepan in his sleeping-bag to keep it hot, and it really was a great success in spite of the extra helping of reindeer hairs that it contained. In this way we can make ten penguin skins do for one day."

Some who were fortunate enough to catch penguins with fairly large undigested fish in their gullets used to warm these up in tins hung on bits of wire round the stove.

"All the meat intended for hooshes is cut up inside the hut, as it is too cold outside. As the boards which we use for the purpose are also used for cutting up tobacco, when we still have it, a definite flavour is sometimes imparted to the hoosh, which, if anything, improves it."

Their diet was now practically all meat, and not too much of that, and all the diaries bear witness to their craving for carbo-hydrates, such as flour, oatmeal, etc. One man longingly speaks of the cabbages which grow on Kerguelen Island. By June 18 there were only 900 lumps of sugar left, i.e. just over forty pieces each. Even my readers know what shortage of sugar means at this very date, but from a different cause. Under these circumstances it is not surprising that all their thoughts and conversation should turn to food, past and future banquets, and second helpings that had been once refused.

A census was taken, each man being asked to state just what he would like to eat at that moment if he were allowed to have anything he wanted. All, with but one exception, desired a suet pudding of some sort – the "duff" beloved of sailors. Macklin asked for many returns of scrambled eggs on hot buttered toast. Several voted for "a prodigious Devonshire dumpling," while Wild wished for "any old dumpling so long as it was a large one." The craving for carbo-hydrates, such as flour and sugar, and for fats was very real. Marston had with him a small penny cookery book. From this he would read out one recipe each night, so as to make them last. This would be discussed very seriously, and alterations and improvements suggested, and then they would turn into their bags to dream of wonderful meals that they could never reach. The following conversation was recorded in one diary:

Wild: "Do you like doughnuts?"

McIlroy: "Rather!"

Wild: "Very easily made too. I like them cold with a little jam."

McIlroy: "Not bad; but how about a huge omelette?"

Wild: "Fine!" (with a deep sigh).

Overhead, two of the sailors are discussing some extraordinary mixture of hash, apple-sauce, beer, and cheese, Marston is in his hammock reading from his penny cookery book. Farther down, someone eulogizes Scotch shortbread. Several of the sailors are talking of spotted dog, sea-pie, and Lockhart's with great feeling. Someone mentions nut-food, whereat the conversation becomes general, and we all decide to buy one pound's worth of it as soon as we get to civilization, and retire to a country house to eat it undisturbed. At present we really mean it, too!

Midwinter's day, the great Polar festival, was duly observed. A "magnificent breakfast" of sledging ration hoosh, full strength and well boiled to thicken it, with hot milk was served. Luncheon consisted of a wonderful pudding, invented by Wild, made of powdered biscuit boiled with twelve pieces of mouldy nut-food. Supper was a very finely cut seal hoosh flavoured with sugar.

After supper they had a concert, accompanied by Hussey on his "indispensable banjo". This banjo was the last thing to be saved off the ship before she sank, and I took it with us as a mental tonic. It was carried all the way through with us, and landed on Elephant Island practically unharmed, and did much to keep the men cheerful. Nearly every Saturday night such a concert was held, when each one sang a song about some other member of the party. If that other one objected to some of the remarks, a worse one was written for the next week.

The cook, who had carried on so well and for so long, was given a rest on August 9, and each man took it in turns to be cook for one week. As the cook and his "mate" had the privilege of scraping out the saucepans, there was some anxiety to secure the job, especially amongst those with the larger appetites. The last of the methylated spirit was drunk on August 12, and from then onwards the King's health, "sweethearts and wives" and "the Boss and crew of the *Caird*", were drunk in hot water and ginger every Saturday night.

The penguins and seals which had migrated north at the beginning of winter had not yet returned, or else the ice-foot, which surrounded the spit to a thickness of six feet, prevented them from coming ashore, so that food was getting short. Old seal-bones, that had been used once for a meal and then thrown away, were dug up and stewed down with sea-water. Penguin carcasses were treated likewise. Limpets were gathered from the pools disclosed between the rocks below high tide, after the pack-ice had been driven away. It was a cold job gathering these little shell-fish, as for each one the whole hand and arm had to be plunged into the icy water, and many score of these small creatures had to be collected to make anything of a meal. Seaweed boiled in sea-water was used to eke out the rapidly diminishing stock of seal and penguin meat. This did not agree with some of the party. Though it was acknowledged to be very tasty it only served to increase their appetite – a serious thing when there was nothing to satisfy it with! One man remarked in his diary: "We had a sumptuous meal to-day – nearly five ounces of solid food each."

SIR ERNEST SHACKLETON,
South

Food for the Gods

The ridge continued as before. Giant cornices on the right, steep rock slopes on the left. I went on cutting steps on the narrow strip of snow. The ridge curved away to the right and we had no idea where the top was. As I cut around the back of one hump, another higher one would swing into view. Time was passing and the ridge seemed never-ending. In one place, where the angle of the ridge had eased off, I tried cramponing without cutting steps, hoping this would save time, but I quickly realized that our margin of safety on these steep slopes at this altitude was too small, so I went on step-cutting. I was beginning to tire a little now. I had been cutting steps continuously for two hours, and Tenzing, too, was moving very slowly. As I chipped steps around still another corner, I wondered rather dully just how long we could keep it up. Our original zest had now quite gone and it was turning more into a grim struggle. I then realized that the ridge ahead, instead of still monotonously rising, now dropped sharply away, and far below I could see the North Col and the Rongbuk glacier. I looked upwards to see a narrow snow ridge running up to a snowy summit. A few more whacks of the ice-axe in the firm snow and we stood on top.

My initial feelings were of relief – relief that there were no more steps to cut – no more ridges to traverse and no more humps to tantalize us with hopes of success. I looked at Tenzing and in spite of the balaclava, goggles and oxygen mask all encrusted with long icicles that concealed his face, there was no disguising his infectious grin of pure delight as he looked all around him. We shook hands and then Tenzing threw his arm around my shoulders and we thumped each other on the back until we were almost breathless. It was 11.30 a.m. The ridge had taken us two and a half hours, but it seemed like a lifetime. I turned off the oxygen and removed my set. I had carried my camera, loaded with colour film, inside my shirt to keep it warm, so I now produced it and got Tenzing to pose on top for me, waving his axe on which was a string of flags – United Nations, British, Nepalese and Indian. Then I turned my attention to the great stretch of country lying below us in every direction.

To the east was our giant neighbour Makalu, unexplored and unclimbed, and even on top of Everest the mountaineering instinct was sufficiently strong to cause me to spend some moments conjecturing as to whether a route up that mountain might not exist. Far away across the clouds the great bulk of Kanchenjunga loomed on the horizon. To the west, Cho Oyu, our old adversary from 1952, dominated the scene and we could see the great unexplored ranges of Nepal stretching off into the distance. The most important photograph, I felt, was a shot down the North ridge, showing the North Col and the old route which had been made famous by the struggles of those great climbers of the 1920's and 1930's. I had little hope of the results being particularly successful, as I had a lot of difficulty in holding the camera steady in my clumsy gloves, but I felt that they would at least serve as a record. After some ten minutes of this, I realized that I was becoming rather clumsy-fingered and slow-moving, so I quickly replaced my oxygen set and experienced once more the stimulating effect of even a few litres of oxygen. Meanwhile, Tenzing had made a little hole in the snow and in it he placed various small articles of food – a bar of chocolate, a packet of biscuits and a handful of lollies. Small offerings, indeed, but at least a token gift to the Gods that all devout Buddhists believe have their home on this lofty summit. While we were together on the South Col two days before, Hunt had given me a small crucifix which he had asked me to take to the top. I, too, made a hole in the snow and placed the crucifix beside Tenzing's gifts.

SIR EDMUND HILLARY,
"The Summit" in *The Ascent of Everest* by Sir John Hunt

Five Months Solitary

More than a year has passed since the incidents occurred which are the subject of this chapter. During that time much of the detail has faded from my memory, the impressions have become blurred, and the ideas which then formed themselves in my mind are now forgotten. Yet it may be that a few notes on that time spent on the Greenland Ice Cap will be of some use to travellers who, in the future, may be faced with a similar problem. If I, by these notes, can do something to dispel the strange ideas of danger and risk in leaving a man in such a situation, I shall feel justified. There are many men, trappers and the like, who live by themselves for most of the year. An accident is very rare among these men, nor are their minds usually deranged.

The following is a bare outline, from memory, and from an irregular diary, of my five months alone at the Ice Cap Station.

The total provisions at the Station at this time were, including the supplies brought by our party:

6 ration boxes   2 bottles concentrated lemon juice
26 gallons paraffin   1 bottle cod-liver oil

. . . The food situation was also becoming interesting about this time (March). When I first took over the Station I had, of course, to decide on the scale of rations of food and fuel I was going to keep to, and for this purpose it was necessary to estimate a date of relief. One way would be to choose the latest possible date, which would allow a very small ration indeed, with the probability of a large amount of supplies being left over. This would have been the safest course, but for various reasons I did not take it. In the first place I did not like rationing. I prefer, in fact, to eat my cake rather than have it. "*Carpe Diem*" was a tag which served as an excuse whenever I felt hungry. Another reason was that I needed a large amount of fuel to begin with for drying clothes and for reading. I therefore assumed March 15th as the date of relief, and scaled my rations to last till then, leaving a small amount of the less palatable necessities, and a bare allowance of fuel for cooking after that.

It was, therefore, all according to plan when stores began to run out. The paraffin supply especially got short, owing to leakage. This was very tiresome, since I had to spend more and more time in the dark and the house got considerably colder without the lamp to give heat. The food problem solved itself, since one's appetite becomes very small if one takes no exercise, and an allowance of half a pound a day proved ample towards the latter part of my stay.

. . . By the middle of April there was no more light, luxuries had run out, and the comfort of the house was much reduced. Tobacco was completely exhausted, so tea was used as a substitute. Food consisted of a little oatmeal, just warmed up for breakfast, and thereafter, uncooked pemmican, biscuit and margarine. The most unpleasant part was the frozen condensed moisture which covered the whole inside of the tent, and, hanging down in long icicles from the roof, used to drop off in one's face. It also condensed inside my sleeping-bag, and so froze up any part of it that I was not in contact with. I tried various substitutes for light; paper, string, ski-wax, etc. None of them was satisfactory, though a lamp made of string in a tin of ski-wax was the best, and would last a few minutes if carefully tended.

. . . On May 5th the primus gave its last gasp. A few minutes later an extraordinary scraping and scratching sound was heard overhead, which turned out to be the relief party.

AUGUST COURTAULD,
"Five Months at the Ice Cap Station" in *Northern Lights — The Official Account of the British Arctic Air-Route Expedition, 1930-1*

High Living Alone

July 28 was exceptionally fine. The wind from the north-west was light and the air balmy. I overhauled my wardrobe, and bent on a white shirt against nearing some coasting-packet with genteel folk on board. I also did some washing to get the salt out of my clothes. After it all I was hungry, so I made a fire and very cautiously stewed a dish of pears and set them carefully aside, till I had made a pot of delicious coffee, for both of which I could afford sugar and cream. But the crowning dish of all was a fish-hash, and there was enough of it for two. I was in good health again, and my appetite was simply ravenous. While I was dining I had a large onion over the double lamp stewing for a luncheon later in the day. High living to-day!

JOSHUA SLOCUM,
Sailing Alone Round the World

MEALS TO FORGET

A La Fortune Du Pot

I am going to write about the worst meals I can remember. And when I have finished, in an ecstasy of gratitude, I am going to describe the best. To be dreamy and reminiscent over one's worst meals is a sort of negative form of self-indulgence. Running parallel with your misery, your contempt, your passionate protest that such should enter by your mouth without the Heavens falling, is a divine knowledge that every bad meal has, so to speak, its savoury opposite in space; and that by-and-by you will wring compensation out of space because the more you apprehend badness the more you will strive for perfection.

So I will begin with what I hope will be a moving account of a lunch I had at a Railway Hotel in the West of England. There is no need to identify this railway hotel: similar hotels with similar meals are to be found also in the East, in the Midlands, in the nor'west, in the nor'east, and, in fact, wherever that extraordinary Puritan streak of British character has decreed that it is refined and godly not to notice what is put before you, but to eat it up without complaint. I feel sure that whoever reads about my lunch at the Railway Hotel will notice a sense of growing familiarity, till finally they will start up and cry: "But this was *my* lunch!" "And *my* lunch!" A very multiplication of lunches fit for heroes.

We had two hours to wait, and nothing much to do with them except eat. The little town was blank of interest; ugly and unshaded in the dull pale sunshine. The hour was ten minutes past one; you might have said a reasonable hour in which to order lunch at a place which professes to supply nourishment to travellers; but the look of resentful, sullen astonishment on the face of the maid who came laggingly out into the hall to answer our summons might have suggested that we were asking for lunch at a stocking manufacturer's. We sat for a long time at a table with a dingy cloth, an unhallowed plant, a cruet-stand which was so manifestly neither for use nor for decoration that it could only have had some symbolic meaning unknown to us; and the usual steel engraving on the wall, of General Gordon going forth to meet his death.

The English love to ponder on death over their meals; and yet the association of the two never seems to rouse them to the necessary spirit of homicidal mania. There are five people who should have died over that simple lunch. Firstly, the caterer; secondly, the hotel proprietor; thirdly, the cook; fourthly, the waitress, whose expression dared me not to smile and pay and tip and be satisfied. And fifthly, the victim, myself or you, who should have died twice; once of the meal itself and once for accepting it. There is no more despicable quality than when contentment means the acceptance of what is on the shady side of mediocre.

This, then, was my lunch. The tale is quickly told.

A knobbly lump of cold gristle and fat. I believe they called it ham. Ham. . . . Think for a moment of those tender slices of black Bradenham, or of the peach-fed, corn-fed succulence of a ham from Virginia or Kentucky. To this pallid lump of gristle, two potatoes were added, boiled and very grey. The mind, still creating its rivulet of accompaniment to this meal, thought of little new Jersey potatoes, with mint and butter, of large floury delicious potatoes baked in their skins; of French fried potatoes that include in their flavouring a dash of caraway seed – but what is the good of going on? To the ham gristle and the grey potatoes was added a dark square of vegetable, soggy and yet solid, if you get me, and extremely difficult to masticate. In fairness, let me say that they must have taken a great deal of trouble to cut it so accurately and mathematically into that square. The bred was stale and sour. The beer was slightly warm and poured into a glass that suggested tooth-paste and gargling. The next item on the menu – can you guess it? Yes, dead right. Right every time. Stewed prunes and shape. The prunes were hard and meagre, but the shape wasn't at all bad. Hands up, those who like shape for their lunch! The final effort was a lump of cheddar, aged and discoloured.

How much to pay? Five and sixpence per head, without beer.

The trouble with the Railway Hotel was that, psychologically speaking, it had no burning desire to please. It is sad to think that my next worst meal sprang from a too exuberant desire to do me proud and do me plenty. It was, in fact, a meal of celebration, and probably for my birthday, or for the Saint's day of one of my visitors, or for Garibaldi's march on Rome. I forget, but my Italian cook was a darling and could not bear to let any occasion for celebration pass without pouring forth her very soul ardently and plentifully upon the dining room table. It was a very hot day up at the villa. A fresh salad, and a salad and again a salad would have been what we all fancied. We were a little apprehensive because Vanna had already said "*Che gioia*! To-day is a festa for the signore", with her broadest goblin beam. Vanna, in the ordinary way, was an excellent cook, but not when she tried too hard; she lost all sense of proportion. Also she thought that we enjoyed certain very special native dishes which we simply hated but had not the heart to tell her. For this particular festa she first satiated us with her minestrone; minestrone is, as you doubtless know, supposed to be a soup, but contains everything: the kitchen cat and last year's entire Ligurian yield of artichokes and all the spaghetti there is in all the comestible shops between Marseilles and Rapallo and a few goats and a liver of dissenting toad and cabbages and onions and blue sealing-wax and so forth. It was not at all a bad minestrone, but much too scalding hot: hotter than the day was hot. Then came a huge dish of ravioli: ravioli are little paste envelopes containing chopped meat, also not bad, but filling. And hot. Have I mentioned that this was a fiery day in July on the Italian Riviera? Vanna herself came into the room to watch our delighted reception of her next contribution to festa. An omelette was set before each of us – one omelette to one person. Each omelette could have been divided into eight portions, and each portion would have been enough to divide between three people. When you have worked that out, you will realize that it was a large omelette. And of the solid consistency of bright green flannel. Vanna was a good cook till she came to omelettes. I do not know what pungent-tasting herb she chopped and put into them to make them that lurid colour. This layer after layer of strong green flannel was wrapped round and round an inner treasure of large firm peas. We managed to get rid of Vanna at last, sent her away on a wave of false compliments, and then we buried seven of those eight omelettes in a corner of the garden furthest from the kitchen. The eighth we divided and smeared about our plates, so that when she came in with the zabaglione we could untruthfully, but convincingly, declare that after those superb omelettes, basta and really basta and once again basta, and Vanna was the queen of good cooks.

With this meal we drank, for a special treat provided by our too-devoted staff, some crude local red wine which Vanna's husband proudly declared contained at least one hundred per cent alcohol. It was last October's wine, he said, so should be drunk immediately: "You must not allow wine to get old or it loses its force". . .   G. B. STERN,
Wine and Food, 1

Dinner Was Soon Over

They were walking back very leisurely; Martin arm-in-arm with Mr
Jefferson Brick, and the major and the colonel side-by-side before them;
when, as they came within a house or two of the major's residence, they
heard a bell ringing violently. The instant this sound struck upon their
ears, the colonel and the major darted off, dashed up the steps and in at
the street-door (which stood ajar) like lunatics; while Mr Jefferson Brick,
detaching his arm from Martin's, made a precipitate dive in the same
direction, and vanished also.

"Good Heaven!" thought Martin. "The premises are on fire! It was
an alarm bell!"

But there was no smoke to be seen, nor any flame, nor was there any
smell of fire. As Martin faltered on the pavement, three more gentlemen,
with horror and agitation depicted in their faces, came plunging wildly
round the street corner, jostled each other on the steps; struggled for an
instant; and rushed into the house, a confused heap of arms and legs.
Unable to bear it any longer, Martin followed. Even in his rapid progress he was run down, thrust aside, and passed by two more gentlemen,
stark mad, as it appeared, with fierce excitement.

"Where is it?" cried Martin breathlessly, to a negro whom he en-
countered in the passage.

"In a eatin room sa. Kernell, sa, him kep a seat 'side himself sa."

"A seat!" cried Martin.

"For a dinnar, sa."

Martin stared at him for a moment, and burst into a hearty laugh; to
which the negro, out of his natural good humour and desire to please, so
heartily responded, that his teeth shone like a gleam of light. "You're the
pleasantest fellow I have seen yet", said Martin, clapping him on the
back, "and give me a better appetite than bitters."

With this sentiment he walked into the dining-room and slipped into
a chair next the colonel, which that gentleman (by this time nearly
through his dinner) had turned down in reserve for him, with its back
against the table.

It was a numerous company, eighteen or twenty perhaps. Of these
some five or six were ladies, who sat wedged together in a little phalanx
by themselves. All the knives and forks were working away at a rate that
was quite alarming; very few words were spoken; and everybody
seemed to eat his utmost in self-defence, as if a famine were expected to
set in before breakfast time to-morrow morning, and it had become high
time to assert the first law of nature. The poultry, which may perhaps be

considered to have formed the staple of the entertainment – for there
was a turkey at the top, a pair of ducks at the bottom, and two fowls in
the middle – disappeared as rapidly as if every bird had had the use of its
wings, and had flown in desperation down a human throat. The oysters,
stewed and pickled, leaped from their capacious reservoirs, and slid by
scores into the mouths of the assembly. The sharpest pickles vanished,
whole cucumbers at once, like sugar-plums, and no man winked his eye.
Great heaps of indigestible matter melted away as ice before the sun. It
was a solemn and awful thing to see. Dyspeptic individuals bolted their
food in wedges; feeding, not themselves, but broods of nightmares, who
were continually standing at livery within them. Spare men, with lank
and rigid cheekes, came out unsatisfied from the destruction of heavy
dishes, and glared with watchful eyes upon the pastry. What Mrs Paw-
kins felt each day at dinner-time is hidden from all human knowledge.
But she had one comfort. It was very soon over.

CHARLES DICKENS,
Martin Chuzzlewit

English Cheese

Last summer I was in Cardiff, a city with public buildings which would
do credit to a great metropolis. Having taken advice as to the best eating-
place, I found myself in a beautifully fitted restaurant where, as at
Leicester, the service was performed by waitresses and not by waiters.
A truly excellent and inexpensive luncheon wound up with a local dainty
in the shape of a small bilberry (or blaeberry, or whortleberry, or whinberry) pudding which had been steamed in a basin not much bigger than
a teacup. A bright hope flashed up within me. Within two leagues of
maritime and industrial Cardiff stands the ancient burgh of Caerphilly,
with the ruins of a castle as big as Royal Windsor's: and Caerphilly has
long been renowned for a very pale cheese, made in cakes not much
thicker than the much more modern Italian Bel Paese. It occurred to me
that in a restaurant so laudably regional as to serve bilberry (or blaeberry,
or whortleberry, or whinberry) puddings made from local fruit, I might
expect to find the local cheese. My Hebe, during a long and audible conversation with a sentencious client at the next table, had revealed herself
as an intelligent young woman; but when I asked for Caerphilly cheese
she laughed. She could bring me Cheddar, Camembert, Roquefort,
Gorgonzola, and also little wedges of Gruyère wrapped up in silver
paper; but not Caerphilly. Remembering that she might be a new arrival
in Cardiff from London or Penzance or Southend-on-Sea, I inquired if
she had ever heard of Caerphilly. The damsel replied that she "ought to

have", seeing that her father was born there; but when I said "Surely you know that there is Caerphilly cheese", she answered saucily that she "expected there was plenty of cheese in the Caerphilly shops the same as everywhere else". Thus it dawned upon me that Caerphilly was without honour in its own country, and that this bright young person had never heard of one of the chief glories of her father's native place. I told her that I would be lunching the next day at the same table and that I should look forward to Caerphilly cheese. The morrow came, but not the cheese. Instead a manager was brought to me who admitted the propinquity of Caerphilly, as well as Caerphilly's connection with cheese, but added somewhat reproachfully that nobody ever asked for it and that the last time he bought any most of it went bad.

ERNEST OLDMEADOW,
Wine and Food, 1

A dessert without cheese is like a beautiful woman who has lost an eye.

BRILLAT-SAVARIN

The Invitation

To sup with thee thou didst me home invite;
And mad'st a promise that mine appetite
Sho'd meet and tire, on such lautitious meat,
The like not Heliogabalus did eat:
And richer wine wo'dst give to me, thy guest,
Then Roman Sylla powr'd out at his feast.
I came; tis true, and lookt for fowle of price,
The bastard phenix; bird of paradice;
And for no less then aromatick wine
Of maydens-blush, commixt with jessimine.
Cleane was the herth, the mantle larded jet;
Which wanting lar, and smoke, hung weeping wet;
At last, i'th'noone of winter, did appeare
A ragd-soust-neats-foot with sick vineger:
And in a burnisht flagonet stood by
Beere small as comfort, dead as charity.
At which amaz'd and pondring on the food,
How cold it was, and how it child my blood;
I curst the master; and I damn'd the source;
And swore I'de got the ague of the house.
Well, when to eat thou dost me next desire,
I'le bring a fever; since thou keep'st no fire.

ROBERT HERRICK

The waiter roars it through the hall:
"We don't give bread with one fish-ball!"

GEORGE MARTIN LANE

Bring on the Dancing Girls

We had left all our servants behind at Panjim, and not an iota of our last night's supper had escaped the ravenous maws of the boatmen.

Presently matters began to mend. The old lady recollected that in days of yore she had possessed a pound of tea, and, after much unlocking and rummaging of drawers, she produced a remnant of that luxury. Perseverance accomplished divers other feats, and after about an hour more of half starvation we sat down to a breakfast composed of five eggs, a roll of sour bread, plantains, which tasted exactly like edible cotton dipped in *eau sucrée*, and a "fragrant infusion of the Chinese leaf" whose perfume vividly reminded us of the haystacks in our native land. Such comforts as forks or spoons were unprocurable, the china was a suspicious looking article, and the knives were apparently intended rather for taking away animal life than for ministering to its wants. Sharp appetites, however, removed all our squeamishness, and the board was soon cleared. The sting of hunger blunted, we lighted our "weeds", each mixed a cordial potion in a tea-cup, and called aloud for the nautch, or dance, to begin.

RICHARD F. BURTON,
Goa, and the Blue Mountains (1851)

The Railway Buffet. Dickie Doyle, 1849.

An American Tragedy

The average American probably spends more than the average citizen of any other country in the world upon food and drink, but he certainly is less well nourished than the ordinary peasant class in any part of Europe. To say nothing of the little French bourgeois whose income is half that of a New York elevator boy, and yet feeds far better than a Chicago packing millionaire.

That is indeed a tragedy. To have the opportunity and let it pass. But it can be put right. Not in a day nor even in a generation, but in two or three generations. It cannot be put right, however, until the youths of America are trained to look upon life from a different angle. Their values are mostly wrong. As they speak from the bridge of their noses, probably having never been taught that their chest is their natural sound-box, so they live upon their nerves instead of their food. Their food is the fuel that charges the accumulators; the nerves: and they drive on the accumulators instead of upon the motor, the one source of power, of health and

266

strength: the belly, that is, the stomach-cum-guts, placed by nature amidships, far enough from the navigating room – the brain – to get its orders clearly and near enough from all organs to supply their requirements with a minimum of delay and a maximum of efficiency.

Of course, your belly must not be your god. You should have no false gods. The average American's gods are speed, shows and sugar. They are the first loves of most children; they are desirable in themselves, and in moderation. They are all very well so long as you cannot or do not care to think. There is no exhilaration comparable to that of speed, nor any greater relaxation than a well acted play or even film, no surer way to forget one's worries or one's unsatisfactory self. But if it is good to forget sometimes, it is better to remember and to think: to remember others and to think of so many people and so many things so well worth thinking about. To think of others is what matters most, and that is not done on a doped stomach or closed-up bowels; it is not done on ice water any more than on fire water, "hard liquor". That is what the new generation needs to be taught in America, and maybe elsewhere as well. Food is a very important matter and so is drink. Too few Americans realize it at present. Too many eat what happens to be at hand, good or bad. It is all the same. They have no time to think about it. They drink iced water when they are thirsty and strong spirits when they want to be gay, that is to say, when they want to forget. Wine is too dear to drink when thirsty, and too weak to get drunk on; and who has time to drink wine, anyway? Nobody. It is all wrong. They should drink wine, even if it be poor wine and not appealing to their taste, even if it were merely for the sake of taking more time than they do over their meals, as a cure for that pernicious habit of bolting one's food, a crazy habit which ruins the health of millions of people, people who have no idea of what to do with the spare time on their hands and yet swallow a few sandwiches for lunch in five minutes instead of enjoying a proper meal in a rational manner.

ANDRÉ L. SIMON,
Wine and Food, 5

On Ice

From New York to New Orleans I have eaten delicacies that have been frozen into almost complete tastelessness – strawberries, chicken, asparagus, soft-shelled crabs, all tasting very much the same through too prolonged a sojourn "on the ice". This phrase "on the ice" follows one round the States; it has the same meaning as our "in the larder", which indeed is what the ice-box has become in most American homes.

When, owing to severe illness, I had to cancel on Saturday morning an engagement for a "banquet" on the following Monday night, I was told reproachfully that "the chickens were already on the ice" – on the ice three days, with an outside temperature hovering around zero! I should have been more surprised had I not a short while earlier complained at a famous New York restaurant that my chicken was tough and tasteless through being too long on the ice, and heard the waiter reply, "It's only been on the ice a week." When I told him that normally the chickens I ate had not been on the ice at all, I expect he thought I was a fool.

In Charleston we enjoyed the negro cooking, because negroes like Sussex people and myself, are scared of electrical devices. But I found that American visitors to these places did not share our satisfaction. "I'm disappointed in this negro cookery," a charming New Yorker said to me. "I don't think it's at all what it's cracked up to be. We did very much better at Miami where all the food came down by ice train from New York. You ate it straight off the ice."

SHEILA KAYE-SMITH,
Kitchen Fugue

Avocado, or the Future of Eating

One day not long ago in Los Angeles I found myself, banderillas in hand, facing the horns of a dilemma. I had gone into a Corn Exchange bank to exchange some corn and had fallen into conversation with the manager. He was very affable and insisted I inspect the assets of the branch, which included, among other things, the teeth Bryant Washburn, had used in his film career. Issuing into the hot sunlight of the street, I was dismayed to find that it was time for lunch, and since I had forgotten to bring along a bag of pemmican, I would have to eat in Los Angeles – a fairly exact definition of the term "the kiss of death". I looked around me. On my left I could obtain a duplexburger and a Giant Malted Milk Too Thick For a Straw; on my right the feature was barbecued pork fritters and orangeade. Unnerved, I stopped a passing street Arab and courteously enquired where I might find a cheap but clean eating house. Phil the Fiddler (for it was he) directed my steps to a pharmacy bearing the legend "Best Drug Stores, Inc." Merely for the record I dined off an avocado sandwich on whole wheat and a lime rickey, and flunked my basal-metabolism test later that afternoon. I don't pretend to blame the management for my physical shortcomings; all I want them to do is laugh off their menu, a copy of which I seem to have before me.

In general "Soda Fountain Suggestions" (Best Drug Stores, Inc.) is an attractively printed job in two colours (three if you count the gravy), and though it can hardly hope to rival the success of *Gone with the Wind*, I suppose there is an audience which will welcome it. The salads and three-decker sandwiches are treated with a certain gaiety and quaint charm which recall *Alice of Old Vincennes*. The banana splits and hot-and-cold Ovaltines are handled with a glib humour in the text, which is more than I can say for the way they are handled behind the fountain. The day I was there, a simply appalling oath escaped the lips of one of the dispensers when he dropped some fudge on his shoe. The authors have included a very disarming foreword short enough to quote in its entirety. "It is our earnest desire to fulfil the name that we have chosen for our chain, THE BEST. We can only accomplish this by serving you best. Any criticisms or suggestions will be appreciated by the management." Only a churl would decline so graceful a gambit. *Messieurs en garde!*

Specially, gentlemen, my criticism concerns that cocky little summary of yours at the bottom of the menu. "Best Soda Fountains," you proclaim flatly, "are BEST because: the ice creams contain no 'fillers' (starch, albumen, etc.); the syrups are made from cane sugar and real fruits; the coffee is a special blend made the modern Silex way with a specially filtered water," and so forth. Let some of the younger boys in the troop think the millennium has come to the City of Our Lady, Queen of the Angels, what are the facts?

In the first place, you needn't think you can woo me with any such tinsel as "the ice creams contain no 'fillers' (starch, albumen, etc.)". One thing I'll have in my ice cream or it's no dice – and that's fillers. I don't even insist on ice cream as long as I can stuff myself with fillers. You heap my plate with albumen and starch (any kind, even laundry starch) and stand clear. Call me a piggy if you want to, but I just can't get *enough*. . .

Quite honestly, your statement that the syrups "are made from cane sugar and real fruits" surprised me. If that's a boast, I must say it's a pretty hollow one. It might interest you to know that back in 1917 the Allied High Command specified *beet* sugar and *false* fruits in all syrups purchased by its commissary department. Didn't know that, did you? Probably too busy evading the draft at the time. Well, you just ask any biochemist his recommendation on sugars, as I did recently; you'll get the same terse answer; beet sugar and false fruits. I have this cousin of mine who is a perfect wiz at chemistry – really astonishing marks for a boy of nineteen in high school – and no matter what you ask him, he'll give you the same answers: beet sugar and false fruits. Frankly, the family's getting a little worried about it; they have to keep Benny chained to a ring on the floor most of the time.

Furthermore, it's useless to try to creep into my heart with any blandishments like "the coffee is a special blend made the modern Silex way with a specially filtered water." Filtering Los Angeles water robs it of its many nourishing ingredients, not the least of which is chow mein. It is an interesting fact, known to anybody who has ever been interned in that city or its suburbs, that the water possesses a rich content of subgum almond chow mein, Cantonese style, and one or two cases have even been reported where traces of peanut candy and lichee nuts were found. The assertion of a friend of mine that he once saw an Irish house-boy come out of a water faucet, of course, must be regarded as apocryphal. The Irish are a wiry little people, but they are not as wiry as all that. Nor are they ready as yet for self-government which my distinguished opponents, the gentlemen of the affirmative, claim they should have. And so, honourable judges and ladies and gentlemen, we of the negative conclude that the Irish should not be given independence because (1) we need them for a coaling station, (2) there is a high percentage of illiteracy, and (3) if we do, Ireland will soon be snatching up Guam – or "chewing Guam", so to speak, I thank you.

S. J. PERELMAN,
Crazy Like a Fox

Taking Water With It

There was the sad case of some dehydrated food which was dropped to us at a stage of the winter when we had run very short indeed of ordinary food. It was the first time that any of us had seen dehydrated food, and the pleasure with which we regarded the first sacks of strange dried-up looking flakes, variously labelled "milk", "mutton", "eggs", "carrots", "onions" and "potatoes", but all looking strangely alike, was mingled with curiosity and, to some extent, with misgiving. At any rate, before trying them, we read and carried out meticulously the written directions which accompanied them, of which the principal was to soak them in water for twenty-four hours before cooking and eating them. The result was astonishing. On being soaked, the uninteresting looking flakes swelled up to several times their original size and became lumps of meat or slices of vegetable, as the case might be, and we soon found that a judicious mixture of dehydrated mutton, onions and potatoes properly soaked and then baked in Ginger's mother's oven made a very creditable shepherd's pie, an undreamed-of luxury in our rather strained circumstances. Clearly, dehydrated food was just the thing for us, especially as its light weight made it far more easily transportable than tinned food.

Delighted, we immediately signalled for further supplies in order that we might share with the Partisans the benefit of our new discovery. On their arrival, we handed them over to the Quartermaster's department, being careful to add full instructions for their use. But these they brushed aside light-heartedly. "We know all about that," they said and started to distribute the sacks to various neighbouring units. We had our doubts, but thought it better not to voice them.

It was only afterwards that we heard what had happened. The dehydrated food had not been soaked but gulped down as it was. This was dry work, or so the Partisans thought, and so they washed it down with copious draughts of water from the neighbouring brook. Then, with disconcerting suddenness, the stuff began to swell inside them until it had reached several times its original dimensions. Their ensuing discomfort was considerable, though not so acute as that of another Partisan, who at about this time ate a stick of plastic high-explosive, mashing it up with milk, under the impression that it was some kind of maize porridge.

FITZROY MACLEAN,
Eastern Approaches

There is no love sincerer than the love of food.

BERNARD SHAW

There was an Old Person whose habits
Induced him to feed upon Rabbits;
    When he'd eaten eighteen
    He turned perfectly green,
Upon which he relinquished those habits.

EDWARD LEAR

An Unsatisfactory Vegetable

Time passed slower than ever in our new surroundings and we became painfully aware of hunger and thirst. My friend the Arab seemed the only possible source of refreshment. Once again I made my way over to him, this time rather more cautiously than before, for things were beginning to warm up round us, and opened negotiations. The first thing was to find out where he kept his water supply. It turned out that there was a well in the sand by the side of his allotment. Lying on the sand, with the help of an old leather bucket and a long bit of string, I managed in a short time to pull up enough water to fill two large water-bottles. The slimy, brackish liquid thus produced seemed more delicious than vintage champagne. . .

I next asked him whether he could sell us anything to eat. Always a man of few words, he pointed to a bright green vegetable marrow growing at his feet. "Any eggs?" I said. "No," he said. It was only too clear that the vegetable marrow was all that we were going to get; and eventually it changed hands for a thousand lire note. It was not cheap, but it was the smallest note I had and one could hardly expect change in the circumstances. Carrying it as proudly as if it had won a prize at the Crystal Palace, I started back to the jeeps by a suitably circuitous route. On the way I filled my pockets with unripe dates off the date palms. We had all the makings of a feast.

We had scarcely sat down to breakfast when a fierce controversy broke out over our *plat de résistance*. My own claim that it was a vegetable marrow was brushed scornfully aside by Sandy, who said that he knew that it was a cucumber. On being told that cucumbers did not grow to that size, he said that anyone who knew anything about vegetables could see that it was a tropical cucumber. Nettled by this I retorted rather unjustly that anyone who knew anything at all could see that he was nothing but a city slicker whose knowledge of the country was derived solely from the low suburban race course which he frequented.

Prolonged lack of food and drink is apt to fray the nerves. Our tempers were not at their best, and we both felt by now that we could have cheerfully used up our remaining strength in fighting each other over the identity of the rather sad-looking vegetable which lay between us, cut up into unappetizing green slices already covered with sand and flies. Fortunately a breach of the peace was avoided thanks to Sergeant Seekings, the only real agricultural expert of the party, who drew the fire of both parties by suggesting that the object of our controversy must be a kind of pumpkin, a diagnosis so manifestly outrageous that Sandy and I sank our differences in a united but entirely unsuccessful attempt to persuade Seekings that he was talking nonsense. Not long after eating it, whatever it was, we were all attacked by the most violent stomach ache. Altogether it was an unsatisfactory vegetable.

FITZROY MACLEAN,
Eastern Approaches

Jerusalem Artichoke

These roots are dressed divers wayes, some boile them in water, and after stew them with sacke and butter, adding a little ginger. Others bake them in pies, putting Marrow, Dates, Ginger, Raisons of the sun, Sacke, etc. Others some other way as they are led by their skill in Cookerie. But in my judgement which way soever they be drest and eaten, they are a meat more fit for swine, then men.

JOHN GOODYER,
Gerard's Herbal (1633)

Zuppa di Pesce

"We have a fish soup; *guarracini* and *scorfani* and *aguglie* and *toteri* and . . ."

Take breath, gentle maiden; the while I explain to the patient reader the ingredients of the diabolical preparation known as *"zuppa di pesce"*. The *guarracino*, for instance, is a pitch-black marine monstrosity, one or two *inches* long, a mere blot, with an Old Red Sandstone profile and insufferable manners whose sole recommendation is that its name is derived from *korakimos* (korax = a raven; but who can live on Greek roots?) As to the *scorfano*, its name is unquestionably onomatopoetic, to suggest the spitting-out of bones; the only difference, from a culinary point of view, between the *scorfano* and a toad being that the latter has twice as much meat on it. The *aguglia*, again, is thin as a lead pencil. Who would believe that for this miserable sea-worm with verdigristinted spine, which an ordinary person would thank you for not setting on his table, the inhabitants of Siren land fought like fiends; the blood of their noblest was shed in defence of privileges artfully wheedled out of Anjou and Aragonese kings defining the *ius quoddam pescandi vulgariter dictum sopra le auguglie*; that a certain tract of sea was known as the "aguglie water" and owned up to the days of Murat, by a single family who defended it with guns and man-traps? And everybody knows the *totero* or squid, an animated ink-bag of perverse leanings, which swims backwards because all other creatures go forwards and whose indiarubber flesh might be useful for deluding hunger on desert islands, since, like American gum, you can chew it for months, but never get it down.

These, and such as they, float about in a lukewarm brew of rancid oil and garlic, together with a few of last week's breadcrusts, decaying seashells and onion-peels, to give it an air of consistency.

This is the stuff for which Neapolitans sell their female relatives. But copious libations will do wonders with a *zuppa di pesce*.

"Wine of Marciano, signore."

"Then it must be good. It grows on the mineral."

"Ah, you foreigners know everything."

We do; we know, for example, that nothing short of a new creation of the world will ever put an end to that legend about the "mineral".

How unfavourably this hotch-potch compares with the Marseillese bouillabaisse! But what can be expected, considering its ingredients? Green and golden scales, and dorsal fins embellished with elaborate rococo designs, will satisfy neither a hungry man nor an epicure, and if Neapolitans pay untold sums for the showy Mediterranean sea-spawn, it only proves that they eat with their eyes, like children who prefer tawdry sweets to good ones. They have colour and shape, these fish of the inland sea, but not taste; their flesh is either flabby and slimy and full of bones in unauthorized places, or else they have no flesh at all – heads like Burmese dragons but no bodies attached to them; or bodies of flattened construction on the *magnum in parvo* principle, allowing of barely room for a sheet of paper between their skin and ribs: or a finless serpentine framework, with long-slit eyes that leer at you while you endeavour to scratch a morsel off the reptilian anatomy.

NORMAN DOUGLAS,
Siren Land

Unfortunate Effects
of Cheese and Plums

Since reaching the islands (the Azores) I had lived most luxuriously on fresh bread, butter, vegetables, and fruits of all kinds. Plums seemed the most plentiful on the *Spray*, and these I ate without stint. I had also a Pico white cheese that General Manning, the American consul-general, had given me, which I supposed was to be eaten, and of this I partook with the plums. Alas! by night-time I was doubled up with cramps. The wind, which was already a smart breeze, was increasing somewhat, with a heavy sky to the sou'west. Reefs had been turned out, and I must turn them in again somehow. Between cramps I got the mainsail down, hauled out the earings as best I could, and tied away point by point, in the double reef. There being sea-room, I should, in strict prudence, have made all snug and gone down at once to my cabin. I am a careful man at sea, but this night, in the coming storm, I swayed up my sails, which reefed though they were, were still too much in such heavy weather; and I saw to it that the sheets were securely belayed. In a word, I should have laid to, but did not. I gave her the double-reefed mainsail and whole jib instead and set her on her course. Then I went below, and threw myself upon the cabin floor in great pain. How long I lay there I could not tell, for I became delirious. When I came to, as I thought, from my swoon, I realized that the sloop was plunging into a heavy sea, and looking out of the companionway, to my amazement I saw a tall man at the helm. His rigid hand, grasping the spokes of the wheel, held them as in a vice. One may imagine my astonishment. His rig was that of a foreign sailor, and the large red cap he wore was cockbilled over his left ear, and all was set off with shaggy black whiskers. He would have been taken for a pirate in any part of the world. While I gazed upon his threatening aspect I forgot the storm, and wondered if he had come to cut my throat. This he seemed to divine. "Senor", said he, doffing his cap, "I have come to do you no harm." And a smile, the faintest in the world, but still a smile, played on his face, which seemed not unkind when he spoke. "I have come to do you no harm, I have sailed free", he said, "but was never worse than a *contrabandista*. I am one of Columbus's crew", he continued. "I am the pilot of the *Pinta* come to aid you. Lie quiet, senor captain", he added, "and I will guide your ship to-night. You have a *calentura*, but you will be all right to-morrow." I thought what a very devil he was to carry sail. Again, as if he read my mind he exclaimed: "Yonder is the *Pinta* ahead; we must overtake her. Give her sail; give her sail! *Vale, vale, muy vale!*" Biting off a large quid of black twist, he said, "You did wrong, captain to mix cheese with plums. White cheese is never safe unless you know whence it comes. *Quien sabe*, it may have been from *leche de Capra* and becoming capricious –"

"Avast there!" I cried. "I have no mind for moralizing."

JOSHUA SLOCUM,
Sailing Alone Round the World

Little boy: "*Oh, Lor, Mar, I feel just exactly as if my jacket was buttoned.*"

ANOTHER MAN'S
POISON

Strange Meat

Man has eaten of the earth itself and sampled nearly everything that grows, runs, crawls, flies or swims on, above or below it. Yet the number of deaths caused directly by food poisoning is so small as to be almost negligible in counting up the total causes of human mortality.

The reason is twofold. First, man is equipped with a remarkably versatile digestive outfit. He possesses the molars of a plant eater, a rodent's incisors and canines for the heavy work of mastication. His alimentary system is equipped with a whole battery of chemical solvents and is designed to deal with a large volume of the most diverse fodder. Possibly no other living creature comes to its dining-table with a better equipment for gustatory adventure than man.

The second reason for the comparatively few deaths caused by food poisoning, despite the great variety of food eaten, is that of all the earth's multitudinous forms of animal and vegetable life only a tiny fraction can be classed as inedible and a still smaller proportion as definitely poisonous.

Two authorities may suffice for the latter statement. L. R. Brightwell, after sampling many of the London Zoo's "lamenteds" over a period of thirty years, says: "I incline to the view that few creatures are definitely inedible. Some tropic fish are, of course poisonous at all times." And Frank Buckland, who may literally be said to have eaten his way through the London Zoo, since he sampled *anything* which died at that famous institution, was never poisoned, despite such recklessness.

One of the greatest treats which comes the way of an African Native is an elephant feast. Very few parts of the great beast are left for the scavengers of the forest when the last Native departs from the gargantuan repast. The most profitable part of the meat is said to be the base of the trunk. Other desirable tit-bits are the cheeks and feet, whilst the marrow from the leg-bones eaten raw, constitutes a sovereign remedy for a barren woman or a pain in the belly!

Europeans react differently when faced with a spread of elephant. F. C. Selous, most famous of African big-game hunters, swore by the heart of an elephant roasted on a forked stick over red embers or stewed with rice. An elephant's heart, incidentally, is upwards of five feet in circumference and can weigh over sixty pounds. The meat from the thick part of the trunk and from the cavity above the eyes Selous considered among the least palatable parts of the body and he also did not favour baked foot. He described this once vaunted dish as tasteless, and insipid. David Livingstone, on the other hand, considered broiled elephant's hoof delicious. Theodore Roosevelt enjoyed the soup made from elephant trunk and pronounced it excellent. Writing of elephant meat as a whole, R. J. Smith, another game-eater adventurer, said that except when taken from very young animals, it was like particularly tough beef.

Two other African heavyweights, the rhinoceros and the hippopotamus, have also been eaten and found good. Dr Kolb killed scores of rhinos for food and was particularly fond of the liver. The flesh of the rare white rhino, especially if fat, used to be in great demand among Dutch hunters in South Africa. This rhino meat was said to taste like beef, but it had a characteristic flavour of its own. The hump was the favoured part of the carcase: when cut off whole and roasted in its skin it was considered a rare delicacy by the old school of African hunters.

The meat from a young, healthy hippopotamus has been described by H. A. Bryden as "quite excellent eating; the flesh is dark red in colour and a good deal resembles beef". Bryden adds that the most treasured part of the flesh is that cut from the flank: the foot, after boiling for twenty-four hours, is also very good to eat.

Bryden, who wrote from considerable experience, put the flesh of the springbok first on his list of palatable African venison. In fact, his description of it makes my mouth water! After saying that it is "quite the best game meat to be found in the country, being tender, delicate and possessed of the true game flavour", he goes on to particularize: "Chops from the loin of a springbok in good condition are delicious eating, and the fry of this goodly antelope is also one of the greatest delicacies a hunter can partake of. I once had a very good native boy as cook. When we shot a springbok, he used to cut double chops right across the loin and fry them with tinned tomatoes, and the result always gave great satisfaction to my hunting friends and myself".

Some of the most unlikely creatures have yielded surprisingly palatable meat. Few, I imagine, would willingly sit down to a meal of crocodile flesh. Yet Dr William T. Hornaday, late Director of the New York Zoological Society and a man of great experience in the game-eating realm, declared that crocodile tail "is as tasty and tender as the best roast veal"; and R. H. Bruce Lockhart said of the same fare: "the flesh is rather superior to venison." But it is only fair to add that R. J. Smith, who followed in Hornaday's footsteps, did not agree. "Crocodile, I assure you", he wrote, "is not bad, neither is it good. It still looked like fish when it was brought to table, but it tasted and smelt like meat." However, whilst not professing to be a good judge of the best roast veal I do not think that roast crocodile can be put in the same class. (A quotation from the diary of a guest of Frank Buckland's father is apposite here: "Party at the Deanery: tripe for dinner; don't like crocodile for breakfast.") And as for the eggs of crocodile, Theodore Roosevelt said that when scrambled they are "found good", whilst Bruce Lockhart wrote: "Crocodile's eggs taste like plover's", praise which is praise indeed.

According to David Haig-Thomas, one of the greatest luxuries in the Arctic is narwhal skin. "When fresh", he writes, "the flavour is delicious and reminds one of nuts or mushrooms. It is about half an inch thick and looks rather like linoleum. When one bites it, it has the same consistency as celery. There is no blood whatever in the outer skin. Below it is the tough hide, and then six inches of blubber before one comes to the narwhal itself".

I imagine that very few, if any, Members of the Wine and Food Society, would accept an invitation to a meal of bat flesh, yet in several parts of the world such a dish is quite commonplace. In fact Dr Glover Morrill Allen, in his fine book, *Bats*, devotes a whole chapter to bats as food. Dr Allen points out that there is no reason why some of the larger species of the fruit-eating bats, living as they do upon a diet mostly of fruit juices, buds and flowers, should not be quite suitable for food.

In a famous Australian cookery book there appears the following recipe for the proper cooking of the "Flying Fox" Bats. "Flying Foxes are excellent eating, though anything but agreeable creatures to touch or indeed to have anything to do with on account of the strong, unpleasant smell they have, but once get rid of the wings and skin and you will hardly know the flesh from pork . . . I cut them up, along with an onion, and seasoned with all sorts of herbs, and stewed for a couple of hours, then turned them into a pie-dish and covered with a good paste. Curried you would not know Flying Fox from pork, indeed, the flesh, when they are in season, very much resembles sucking pig. I don't think they are good except in the fruit season, as when there is no fruit they live on scrub berries and leaves, which give them an unpleasant flavour. The

Kanakas told me this, and I afterwards proved it myself, for when there was little or no good fruit, the *Foxes* were thin and tough, indeed quite uneatable."

The gipsies long ago discovered what dainty tit-bits were concealed beneath the hedgehog's spiny coat. The gipsy method of preparing this animal for the table is to kill it and to encase its body in wet clay; they place it then on an open fire until it is cooked, when the spines come away together with the clay covering and the cooked flesh is ready to eat. The best season for hedgehogs, according to the gipsies, is Michaelmas in England, that is when the hedgehogs have had their fill of windfalls, crab apples and other fruits. The flesh is white and tender; it is said to taste very much like that of a young chicken.

Our ancestors appear to have made use of many of the smaller birds as items of food. An English queen is reported to have been particularly fond of bullfinch pie. Much earlier still, the Romans mewed redwings and fieldfares which they fattened on bruised figs and flour. But as near to us as two hundred years ago the mewing of ruffs was an important industry in Lincolnshire. Wheatears, yellowhammers, chaffinches ("fitter for the spit than the cage"), larks, blackbirds, crossbills ("very good meate"), and martins were among the other small birds eaten in the past in these our animal-loving islands.

To explore fully the possibilities of birds' eggs one must, I fear, go to foreign climes. Think, for example, what a boon to egg-short British housewives would be a crate – one can hardly say a basketful – of ostrich eggs! The ostrich egg weighs about three and a half pounds, and from a culinary point of view is equal to about three dozen chicken eggs. It takes forty minutes to boil lightly and four hours to hard boil one of these giant eggs.

In China, where so much that is bizarre in life and living is found, it is possible to order an egg that is not weeks but years old. Yes, and the older it is the more you pay for it. Chinese restaurants supply their customers with an "egg-list" from which the diner can take his choice; should he be in a reckless mood he may order an egg half a century old and it will be brought up for him from its bin in the cellar!

Insects as food have never been favoured in our own country, but they form an important part of the diet of native races in different parts of the world. In Africa, termites are regarded by some of the tribes as such a valuable article of food that fighting breaks out over the disputed ownership of some termites' nest. Termites are said to taste like pineapple; but there is a knack in popping them into the mouth and synchronizing the bite. If the action is bungled the enraged insect may give the tongue a nasty nip.

Ants also supply several different dishes on the menu of some natives. There are lands where ants are eaten like jam; they are made into a paste which is spread upon bread and butter. In India, the green weaver ant of the Orient is also made into a paste but is served, not as a sweetmeat, but as a condiment with curry. The Dyaks of Borneo mix the same ants with their rice, the formic acid, which the ants supply, gives to the rice a pungent flavour which one can evidently be trained to enjoy. The natives of North Queensland, Australia, actually *drink* ants! Green weaver ants are captured and then mashed up in water. The resultant concoction is said to taste exactly like lemon squash.

Winged insects appear to vary considerably in their suitability as human food. The omniverous Frank Buckland once declared that he had found something even less palatable than a mole – the blue-bottle! Some species of flies, on the other hand, are said to taste like bananas and to be a fair source of proteins.

An American traveller in Asia was once given a dish of ground bees which live in the sands at the edge of streams. To prepare them for the table they are plucked and fried in butter. The American who ate them said: "They are extremely crisp, and fairly melt in your mouth. I had never tasted anything more delicious. I ate one hundred and twenty-seven of them. I ate three platters full."

In the insect world civilized man has an almost untapped source of food supply with immense and fascinating possibilities.

FRANK W. LANE,
Wine and Food, 35

Guatemalan Food

But you must now notice especially one flower, that here is bought either for decoration or to be eaten. This is the yucca; large spikes, clustering spires of cup-like blossom, creamy and green, ivory and white. The petals, cool, crisp and aromatic, of these flowers, sprinkled with their golden centres shredded over them, dressed with oil and vinegar and rubbed with garlic, form one of the usual dishes of this country. Texture and flavour are both excellent. The stalk is then cooked and eaten as a vegetable but to me – though I seldom recognized what it was until I enquired – it seemed always rather tasteless and pithy, with a suggestion of soft wood and badly cooked root vegetables. . . . I cannot say whether these yuccas, though they look precisely the same, only larger and more florescent, are identical with those grown in English gardens, and I have not dared to find out empirically.

Passing on, you reach a court devoted to the sale of Guatemalan blankets, and, beyond it, another that displays embroidered shirts for men and shawls and scarves for women. In its turn, this leads into a colossal sunny *plaza* where the native pottery is to be bought, mounds of earthenware pots and jars, their shape, the perfection of their irreproachable line, seeming more Greek than Spanish – a remark even more applicable to the neighbouring collections of flat dishes, made of an earthenware that is almost rose-coloured, which are used for cooking *tortillas*. Indeed, these large, flat, round plates resemble the discs of the *Discobolus*, so suave and stream-lined are they. From the next immense court, over which hangs a mantle of dust, issues that mingled lowing, bleating and squealing which you have already remarked.

Here, among the young pink porkers on string leads, who so resolutely make an inevitably ineffectual dash for freedom upon their short, apparently unjointed legs, here among the tufted calves attempting to escape – and indeed perhaps the cause of the general frantic behaviour of the animal world – sits a woman with a large round linen basket full of the strangest cattle, the greatest living delicacy of the land: iguanas. These giant lizards, three or four feet long, are tied, like whitings upon an English breakfast-table, or the symbol of eternity, mouth to tail. Otherwise they would thresh out with their tails, which are spiked and can inflict formidable injuries. Their jaws, too, are bound together to prevent their snapping at and biting their prospective devourers, already bargaining over their bodies. Incidentally, the customers cannot poke them in the ribs in the same manner in which they prod the calves and small pigs, to see if they are fat, because, even if an iguana possesses ribs – and at this point my knowledge of reptilian anatomy breaks down – the knobs and spikes of its armour would defeat prying fingers. Weight, alone is the criterion.

A clean feeder, the creature lives in the tree-tops of the steaming jungles on sea-level, and subsists on the green leaves round it. The iguana-catcher is trained to net his prey, a difficult profession that needs a long schooling in these swamps and forests; or again, it may be shot – sitting I apprehend – and in these tropical regions "a day's iguana shooting" is a popular sport, comparable to "a day's partridge shooting" here.... Now it may be that the iguana is no pleasant object to look at. Its small eyes, pail-shaped snout and shark-like jaws, lined with a saw's teeth of steel, are, I know, repellent to many. Even the reptile's best friends, indeed, will be obliged to admit that at first sight it presents a somewhat case-hardened exterior, and that its saurian countenance bears an unpleasing expression, both sarcastic and ferocious. But it is good, *very good*, to eat: and its cost does not amount to more than the equivalent of a shilling; two facts which must tell in its favour. The ways of cooking it are many, but the best seemed to me to be roast saddle, cooked with herbs, and served in a circle of its own eggs with a rich brown sauce, flavoured with madeira or port. The saddle is white and tender as the best capon, and the eggs, too, are a suitable, and even delicious, concomitant, once you have grown accustomed to the idea of them.

SIR OSBERT SITWELL,
Sing High! Sing Low!

Explorers' Diet

October 8, [1853] *Sunday.* – "When I was out in the *Advance*, with Captain de Haven, I satisfied myself that it was a vulgar prejudice to regard the liver of the bear as poisonous. I ate of it freely myself, and succeeded in making it a favourite dish with the mess. But I find to my cost that it may sometimes be more savoury than safe. The cub's liver was my supper last night, and to-day I have the symptoms of poison in full measure – vertigo, diarrhoea, and their concomitants."

I may mention, in connection with the fact which I have given from my journal that I repeated the experiment several times afterward, and sometimes, but not always, with the same result. I remember once, near the Great Glacier, all our party sickened after feeding on the liver of a bear that we had killed; and a few weeks afterward, when we were tempted into a similar indulgence, we were forced to undergo the same penance. The animal in both cases was old and fat. The dogs ate to repletion, without injury.

Another article of diet, less inviting at first, but which I found more innocuous, was the rat. We had failed to exterminate this animal by our varied and perilous efforts of the year before, and a well-justified fear forbade our renewing the crusade. It was marvellous, in a region apparently so unfavourable to reproduction, what a perfect warren we soon had on board. Their impudence and address increased with their numbers. It became impossible to stow anything below decks. Furs, woollens, shoes, specimens of natural history, everything we disliked to lose, however little valuable to them, was gnawed into and destroyed. They harboured among the men's bedding in the forecastle, and showed such boldness in fight and such dexterity in dodging missiles, that they were tolerated at last as inevitable nuisances. Before the winter ended I avenged our griefs by decimating them for my private table.

ELISHA KENT KANE,
Arctic Explorations in Search of Sir John Franklin (1898)

Heads were an Extra

My meditations were interrupted by a shout informing the whole camp that dinner was ready. I have sat down to many a barbaric feast among Eskimos in my time, but I have never seen anything to equal this. Only the elders used knives, the younger members of the party simply tore the meat from the bones in the same voracious fashion which we may imagine to have been the custom of our earliest ancestors. Besides the two caribou, a number of heads had been cooked, and one was served out to each member of our party. The heads were an extra, and we were allowed to keep them till after, to eat in our own tent, on condition that none of the leavings should under any circumstances be touched by women or dogs. The muzzle especially was regarded as sacred meat, which must not be defiled.

Then came dessert; but this was literally more than we could swallow. It consisted of the larvae of the caribou fly, great fat maggoty things served up raw just as they had been picked out from the skin of the beasts when shot. They lay squirming on a platter like a tin of huge gentles, and gave a nasty little crunch under the teeth, like crushing a black-beetle.

Ingjugarjuk, ever watchful, noted my embarrassment and observed kindly: "No one will be offended if you do not understand our food; we all have our different customs." But he added a trifle maliciously: "After all, you have just been eating caribou meat; and what are these but a sort of little eggs nourished on the juices of that meat?"

KNUD RASMUSSEN,
Across Arctic America

No Pie For Me, Please

Away back in '54 when commercial telly got cracking, we were kept busy making film visuals for advertisers sharpening their hooks for an eager public.

Ours was a pocket-size affair, and the living room of my house did duty as studio and, later, projection room when the rushes came back from the labs.

One day the room would be bodged up to resemble a doctor's consulting room where a grey-haired physician warned sternly of the dangers of neglected constipation. A few hours later, the whole place had been turned into the forecourt of a garage where the same grey-haired physician (now magically changed into a mechanic) proclaimed the virtues of some viscous looking lubricating oil.

It was all great fun except, perhaps, for my wife and for Granny who lived with us in those distant days. Granny, by the way, although well over eighty, had the appetite of a strapping school girl.

The big day came when Superclient from an advertising agency announced that he was coming along to direct a filmlet boosting Lemon Meringue Pie. Apparently *his* pie had some gimmick that made it irresistible to housewives from Battle to Bootle.

All was bustle at the studio. The garage scene was struck and, in a trice, appeared a tastefully laid table. Everything sparkled; the cloth was snowy-white; the cutlery gleamed; the napery was impeccable. (The Ritz would have been hard pressed to have done as well.)

Meanwhile, in the kitchen, my wife battled with the lemon meringue pie. As this delicacy was to be photographed only, she permitted herself great liberties in its construction. A sodden clag of dough provided the basis of the structure and the formality of cooking was omitted. On top of this she poured grudging froth of an egg-white and browned it lightly in the oven. The whole nonsense was then garnished with slivers of runner-bean in economical *lieu* of angelica.

"How does it look?"

I held to my eye the neutral-density filter from which no ace cameraman is ever parted.

"Lousy!" I barked. "Just lousy! Lacks colour! No tonal values! Won't register on pan stock! *TED!*" (As I only had one assistant, I might just have well shouted for Charlie, Alf, Harry or Joe. It wouldn't have mattered.)

"Listen Ted", I said urgently, "Nip round to the corner shop and get a small tin of brown plastic paint. Tell 'em I'll pay at the week-end without fail. . . ."

We flimped up the anæmic crust of the pie until it looked mouth-wateringly crisp and, suddenly, Superclient arrived bringing with him the groomed young man who was to play the part of the husband sampling his wife's masterpiece.

"It's like this", explained Superclient tersely, "our clients make just that thing that turns the simplest lemon meringue pie into a real smasher. I've brought a jingle with me; think your daughter could help us out?"

(Sorry to bring in so many characters, but I should explain that Ann spent several years at the Guildhall School of Music struggling with the intricacies of Bach, Beethoven, Brahms, Mendelssohn, Schubert and various other fuddy-duddies quite unknown in the world of advertising.)

Ann examined the masterpiece. "H'm. Could do, maybe." She read the words aloud, tapping the rhythm on the lid of the piano. . . .

> "For ting and tang
> Choose lemon-meringue
> All frothy and feathery whi - ite!
>
> It's as light as a dream
> And made with fresh cre - eem . . ."

She rippled her fingers over the keyboard. "How does this sound?" Superclient nodded his head. "Roger! Got it, son?"

The young man nodded confidently. "Yup!" From now on it was all strict filming technique. . . .

"Lights!" Ted switched on our modest selection of bulbs in their tin-basin reflectors.

"Sound!" The tape recorder started to clank away in the corner.

"Roll 'em!"

All was disciplined efficiency. The young man plunged his spoon into the horrible pudding and then waved it in time with the words. Super-client beat the rhythm with a folded newspaper. Ann bashed away at the piano. Ted grabbed a light (on the verge of collapse. . .)

"No, *no*, NO!" shouted Superclient after half a dozen attempts. "It stinks! You're supposed to be *enjoying* the stuff so much that you're singing about it." He glanced at his watch. "Half past twelve, damme, let's go and find a drink and then have some lunch."

And so we left everything just as it was; the elaborately laid table; the camera; the lights on their rickety stands; the pie. Only Granny remained in her quiet sitting room. Fuss and noise, she always said, gave her the jimjams.

Quarter of an hour after chucking-out time we all came trooping back . . . and stood speechless in the doorway leading to the studio.

The table was bare and newly polished. All the photographic junk had been stacked neatly in a corner. By the fire sat Granny and on her face was the expression of a cat who has just had a whole scotch salmon to itself. . . .

"Well, it *was* kind of you young people to lay me such a *lovely* meal . . . you may think me an awfully greedy girl but I just couldn't resist that pie . . . I ate every single mouthful . . ."

The smile of a gourmet spread across her face, "And I've been such a good girl, too. I've done all the washing-up and put all your nasty photo things away in the corner. . . ."

. . . .

I snatched up the telephone and dialled furiously.

"Let me know how she gets on", reassured the voice "but I should imagine that with all that farinaceous matter the slightly toxic qualities of the paint. . . ."

Since that day it has always been biscuits-and-cheese for me. Somehow I just cannot look a lemon-meringue pie in the face.

GORDON CATLING

"Chuck out those – they're harmless."

An Epicurean Treat

All the inhabitants of the valley treated me with great kindness; but as to the household of Marheyo, with whom I was now permanently domiciled, nothing could surpass their efforts to minister to my comfort. To the gratification of my palate they paid the most unwearied attention. They continually invited me to partake of food, and when after eating heartily I declined the viands they continued to offer me, they seemed to think that my appetite stood in need of some piquant stimulant to excite its activity.

In pursuance of this idea, old Marheyo himself would hie him away to the sea-shore by the break of day, for the purpose of collecting various species of rare sea-weed; some of which among these people are considered a great luxury. After a whole day spent in this employment, he would return about nightfall with several cocoa-nut shells filled with different descriptions of kelp. In preparing these for use he manifested all the ostentation of a professed cook, although the chief mystery of the affair appeared to consist in pouring water in judicious quantities upon the slimy contents of his cocoa-nut shells.

The first time he submitted one of these saline salads to my critical attention I naturally thought that anything collected at such pains must possess peculiar merits; but one mouthful was a complete dose; and great was the consternation of the old warrior at the rapidity with which I ejected his Epicurean treat.

How true it is, that the rarity of any particular article enhances its value amazingly. In some part of the valley – I know not where, but probably in the neighbourhood of the sea – the girls were sometimes in the habit of procuring small quantities of salt, a thimble-full or so being the result of the united labours of a party of five or six employed for the greater part of the day. This precious commodity they brought to the house, enveloped in multitudinous folds of leaves; and as a special mark of the esteem in which they held me, would spread an immense leaf on the ground, and dropping one by one a few minute particles of the salt upon it, invite me to taste them.

From the extravagant value placed upon the article, I verily believe, that with a bushel of common Liverpool salt, all the real estate in Typee might have been purchased. With a small pinch of it in one hand, and a quarter section of a bread-fruit in the other, the greatest chief in the valley would have laughed at all the luxuries of a Parisian table.

HERMAN MELVILLE,
Typee

Chinese Dishes

It is true, the Chinese are not too particular in their food; they eat dogs, cats, mice and rats, the intestines of birds and the blood of every animal, and I was even assured that caterpillars and worms formed part of their diet. Their principal dish, however, is rice, which is not only employed by them in the composition of their various dishes, but supplies the place of bread. It is exceedingly cheap; the pekul, which is equal to 124 lbs English avoirdupois, costing from one dollar and three-quarters to two dollars and a half.

IDA PFEIFFER,
A Woman's Journey Round the World (1856)

Musical Jack

After a brief interview, they politely invited me to partake of the supper they had already bespoken, informing me, at the same time, that they considered themselves peculiarly fortunate in having procured an excellent dish, – in fact, a great delicacy – in a place where they expected to meet with but indifferent fare. What this great delicacy was, they did not attempt to explain; and, having without hesitation accepted of their invitation, I felt no inclination to make any further inquiries.

When the hour of supper arrived, the principal dish – and, indeed, almost the only one upon the table – appeared to me to be a dish of good-sized eels fried. I being the guest of my new acquaintances had the honor of being the first served with a plate of what the person who presided called "Musical Jack". "Musical Jack", thought I, is some species of eel peculiar to the Mississippi and its tributary waters; and taking it for granted that it was all right, I forthwith began to ply my knife and fork. "Stop," said the individual that occupied the bottom of the table, before I had swallowed two mouthfuls. "You, sir, have no idea, I presume, what you are eating; and since you are our guest for the time being, I think it but right that you should have no cause hereafter to think yourself imposed upon. The dish before you, which we familiarly call 'Musical Jack', is composed of rattlesnakes, which the hunter who accompanies us in our tour of exploration was so fortunate to procure for us this afternoon. It is far from the first time that we have fared thus; and, although our own hunter skinned, decapitated, and dressed the creatures, it was only through dint of coaxing that our hostess was prevailed upon to lend her frying-pan for so vile a purpose."

Although curiosity had on many occasions prompted me to taste strange and unsavoury dishes, I must confess that never before did I feel such a loathing and disgust as I did towards the victuals before me. I was scarcely able to listen to the conclusion of this short address, ere I found it prudent to hurry out of the room; nor did I return till supper was over, and "Musical Jack" had either been devoured or dismissed their presence.

As far as I recollect the circumstances, there was nothing peculiar or disagreeable in the flavour of the small quantity I ate; and when the subject was calmly discussed on the following day, one of the party assured me he was really partial to the meat of the rattlesnake, although some of the other members of his party had not been fully able to conquer their early-conceived antipathies towards this snake; but that during their long journey they had been occasionally prevailed upon to make trial of a small quantity of the flesh, and were willing to own that had they been ignorant of its nature, they should have pronounced it of a quality passably good.

PETER LUND SIMMONDS,
*The Curiosities of Food or The Dainties and Delicacies of Different Nations
Obtained from the Animal Kingdom* (1859)

There was an Old Person of Ewell,
Who chiefly subsisted on gruel;
But to make it more nice,
He inserted some mice,
Which refreshed that Old Person of Ewell.

EDWARD LEAR

FOOD AND FANTASY

Variations Upon Whitebait

"Oh, yes, the whitebait," rejoined the Sphinx, glad of a subject to hide her emotion. "Now tell me something nice about them, though the poor little things have long since disappeared. Tell me, for instance, how they get their beautiful little silver waterproofs?"

"Electric Light of the World," I said, "it is like this. While they are still quite young and full of dreams, their mother takes them out in picnic parties of a billion or so at a time to where the spring moon is shining, scattering silver from its purse of pearl far over the wide waters, silver, silver, for every little whitebait that cares to swim and pick it up. The mother, who has a contract with some such big restaurateur as ours here, chooses a convenient area of moonlight, and then at a given signal they all turn over on their sides, and bask and bask in the rays, little fin pressed lovingly against little fin – for this is the happiest time in the young whitebait's life: it is at these silvering parties that matches are made and future consignments of whitebait arranged for. Well, night after night, they thus lie in the moonlight, first on one side then on the other, till by degrees, tiny scale by scale, they have become completely lunar-plated. Ah! how sad they are then the end of that happy time has to come."

"And what happens to them after that?" asked the Sphinx.

"One night when the moon is hidden their mother comes to them with treacherous wile, and suggests that they should go off on a holiday again to seek the moon – the moon that for a moment seems captured by the pearl-fishers of the sky. And so off they go merrily, but, alas, no moon appears, and presently they are aware of unwieldy bumping presences upon the surface of the sea, presences as of huge dolphins, and rough voices call across the water, till, scared, the little whitebaits turn home in flight – to find themselves somehow meshed in an invisible prison, a net as fine and strong as air, into which, O agony, they are presently hauled, lovely banks of silver, shining like opened coffers beneath the coarse and ragged flares of yellow torches. The rest is silence."

"What sad little lives! and what a cruel world it is!" said the Sphinx – as she crunched with her knife through the body of a lark, that but yesterday had been singing in the blue sky. Its spirit sang just above our heads as she ate, and the air was thick with the grey ghosts of all the whitebait she had eaten that night.

But there were no longer any tears in her eyes.

RICHARD LE GALLIENNE,
The Yellow Book, *VIII*, *January, 1896*

My Last Meal on Earth

I know little or nothing of judicial procedure, but from my earliest youth I have heard it said that by the law of the land a condemned man may choose what he will eat for his last meal on earth. This last meal, owing to the early hour at which criminals are called upon to face the trap and noose, is customarily breakfast. I fear, however, that coffee and a *brioche*, or even bacon and eggs, would do little to cheer me on that cold and dreadful morning.

No, were I a convicted murderer I would forgo my breakfast; my last meal on earth would be dinner on the night before. Towards the end of spring it would be, for in spite of advancing years the *crime passionel* is the only breach of the peace which appeals to my imagination. With the first crocus comes awakening love; April Fool's Day sees me a cuckold; more in sorrow than in anger my revolver speaks; I admit nothing; I am brought to trial, convicted, and sentenced to death; until the end of May skilly and repentance is my bitter portion.

On the morning of the day before I am to be hanged the Governor sends for me. He explains the nature of the last indulgence allowed to murderers and asks my wishes. I request to be allowed to telephone. Though this is contrary to the rules of the prison I prevail on the Governor to let me have my way. Once connected with a Gerrard number, I explain my sad circumstances to a sympathetic restaurateur. He assures me that I may have complete confidence in him: he will send me to my death fortified and ennobled.

The day passes slowly. Although the lunch is nothing to write home about, I do write home about it, more to pass the weary hours of the afternoon away than for any other reason.

Evening comes, and with it a bustle or preparation along the chill corridors of the prison. Candles are lit and placed in iron sconces about the walls of my cell. The rough trestle table is covered with soft napery and the subdued reflections of fine silver and crystal charm my prisoner's eye. A glass is placed in my hand: it contains old brown sherry, very smooth and comforting; a tonic against care.

Greed is the dominant note of the *hors-d'œuvre* which presently appear. Just as, if we are to believe the novelists, a drowning man reviews his life in a series of rapid pictures, so the sentenced gastronome needs to reassure himself by a cursory nibble at his past favourites. There are two oysters – *Belons*, since this is the end of May – a slice of smoked salmon, the veriest morsel of *Foie gras* enclosed in the base of an artichoke, an olive or two stuffed with pimentos, a few shrimps, and a spoonful of anchovy salad. This is no time for sweet or cheerful wines. Corton, commemorated in the death song of the poet Tancrede Martel, white Corton Charlemagne with a flavour as resounding as its name, accompanies these preliminary snacks.

Wine dictates the next course. Since a delicate Claret, a Château Haut Brion of 1923, is on its way to the table, red mullet with a *Sauce Bordelaise* is the chosen fish. It is fresh and flaky with a flavour of crushed thyme. That first glass of Claret, whose bouquet is as delicate as the ghost of a departed rose, sets the pace of the evening. From now on the shadows deepen into a vinous obscurity.

The door of my cell clangs open and two warders enter, bearing a great silver dish. On this dish, symbolic of slaughtered innocence, reposes a whole sucking pig, its face upturned and wistful. Remorselessly the carving knife shears through the crisp and golden crackling into the tender meat within. A bouquet of Lauris asparagus aids the general effect. I pour another glass of the Haut Brion.

With the next course a new bottle comes to table in its wicker basket. Richebourg, 1919. Perhaps the supreme product of our Western civilization, it forgathers happily with an Eastern delicacy, Chinese ricebirds on savoury toast. As I eat I meditate darkly on these young lives – some dozen of them – that have been yielded up for me, who am so soon to lose my own. It has to be confessed that the moral of it all escapes me, but such sombre reflections on mortality are given a sinister hue by the cheese which presently appears, a strong, full-bodied Roquefort. And meanwhile the Burgundy improves with every glass.

A cup of black coffee nerves me for the great ordeal of the evening, the serving of an extravaganza aptly described on the menu as *Frivolités Désespoir*. A sarcophagus of burnt sugar, strewn with sugar flowers, is reverently placed before me on the table. The lid is propped up to reveal a variety of sweetmeats fashioned into the form of death's heads and such-like pleasing conceits. A decanter of Warre's 1887 Port is disposed at my elbow.

"You may bring the Brandy in half an hour," I intone as the menials withdraw. Alone, I relapse into a solemn peacefulness. The Brandy comes and goes. My head nods and the candles burn ever lower.

I am awakened by a hearty slap on the back. With a radiant expression on his face the Governor stands over me. At first I can hardly take in the sense of what he is telling me. Then, as I catch the phrases "Full pardon" and "Immediate release", black fury boils up in my heart. With uncontrollable indignation I reflect that the imaginative skill and finesse of one of London's leading restaurateurs have been wantonly abused, to say nothing of my own feelings. I throw off my coat. With sleeves rolled back and clenched fists I advance on the terrified Governor.

"Show me that Home Secretary," I shout. "Just show me that Home Secretary."

CHRISTOPHER DILKE, Wine and Food, 20

Death of a Gourmet

He died with the faint odor of shallots on his breath, a Hollandaise spot on his tie, a look of quiet satisfaction on his lips . . . and, a suspicion of gas on his stomach. He went to Heaven in what resembled an ancient tumbril, rolling through fields of sweet corn, leeks, artichokes, and fresh asparagus, divinely all blooming at once, with *fraises de bois* bordering the beds. In the distance, the green-blue outline of grape vines marked the vineyard areas, while the hill just ahead was alive with great grazing herds of Black Angus. The lovely hens of Bresse, and fat, waddling, Strasbourg geese, with livers too big for their breeches, clucked and honked beside the road.

An azure lake, to the left, harbored schools of shad heavy with roe. Brown trout and rainbows broke water after hovering flies, while lobsters and crayfish crawled about the gleaming lake bottom.

Above, the cry of the bob-white would have drawn the eye Heavenward, if one had not been in Heaven already. A flight of woodcock flitted swiftly by to join the covey of mallards and bronze green pheasants, feeding by the lake shore.

The tumbril creaked to a halt before a long canopy. A doorman, clad in a Heavenly blue uniform, helped him down from the wagon, and ushered him to the entrance of the most stupendous dining room he had ever seen. There was no velvet rope, no line-up of waiting guests; the tables were gleaming with sparkling glassware, silver and white, white napery; the male patrons in white tie and tails were toasting their companions in Dom Perignon cuvée, judging by the shape of the champagne bottles. A *smiling* captain, something one seldom sees outside of Paradise, came up and ushered him to a choice table. He placed a menu in his hand.

To start, a choice of fresh Beluga caviar, goose liver, snails *bourguignon*, smoked Scotch salmon, or *Quiche Lorraine*.

Then, *petite* marmite, *boula boula*, or the double *consommé*.

Les poissons included *pompano*, boneless shad, blue trout, channel sole, or terrapin.

For the main course, would it be pheasant with wild rice, or potted partridge, a double *châteaubriand*, the fowl of Bresse, or *brizzola* steak? Then, a mixed field of green salad, chicory and endive with Crème Chantilly. Dessert – perhaps omelette *flambé*, cherries jubilee, or *soufflé* Grand Marnier.

Hard decisions – all of these – but he made them with little hesitation. After all, everyone had said he was a gourmet. Besides, the right hand side of the menu featured only a succession of zeros, where the prices are generally found. This *was* Heaven!

The *sommelier* arrived, his key of office gleaming like the golden flakes in Danziger Goldwasser. The choices here were more difficult because here in Heaven the best wines were not crossed out! He selected a Montrachet of '28 to accompany the *pompano* and a Grands Echézeaux '29 to moisten the *Châteaubriand*.

The Scotch salmon, with just a twirl of the two-foot pepper mill, and wedges of delicate pumpernickel, was out of this world – obviously.

Then the deft waiter served the double *consommé*. He reached for the salt and gave a generous shake into the soup. There was a sudden crackle of lights, a roll as of thunder. The restaurant dissolved before his eyes. His chair became a large bench, his smiling captain, a stern judge.

"You, sir," he began, "are guilty of a heinous offense. You have poured salt into a double *consommé* without so much as a preliminary taste. You have sinned a gourmet sin. You must atone. Have you anything to say in your own defense?"

"Nothing! I have indeed sinned," he said in a low, hardly intelligible voice.

"I hereby sentence you to return to earth, to Hell on earth, until you do a gourmet act of penitence and worth!" And the lightning flashed again, and the thunder rolled, and at once he was back again at his home in New York. No one looked up as he entered. No one paid the slightest attention to him, so he rightly concluded he was but an invisible wraith, aware of his daughters whilst they were not at all conscious of the ex-paternal presence.

But, hold, what were they up to? Mary and her fiancé, Lou, were seated on the floor on one side of the library, while Kathy and her Will, were seated on the other. Between them were cases of his wine, the contents of his long-cherished cellar, the rare bottles he had squirrelled away all his life, to be drunk only by those special people on those special occasions which never came.

Mary was saying, "Why don't you take these six cases and we'll take these six. That seems fair, not that I know what the stuff is. Wish dad had bought gin and vodka and sensible stuff instead of these oddies. What in the world *is* 'Romanée Conti?' Sounds Italian."

· He winced.

"Okay with us," said Kathy and Will, and Kathy added, "And let's divide up these odd bottles. Here, I'll take this – this – it says 'Grand Fine Champagne'. Certainly doesn't *look* like champagne. And you take this – it says something like Tokay Essence."

He winced again, remembering the two bottles – the one a rare vintage *cognac* of 1899 and the other, a genuine Tokay Essence, the very gift Emperor Franz Joseph gave to George V and Mary on their wedding day. So great indeed were they, that the occasion never seemed right to serve them. He died intestate, so to speak, and here were the rarities being traded like so much Moxie.

"Here, Kathy, here's something called Chartreuse. It's marked 'original French bottling'. You take it and I'll take this one. It says, 'Madeira Rainwater'."

The captain had said, "Hell on earth", and this certainly was. That Madeira – from Baltimore, one of the original bottles before the art was lost forever; the Chartreuse, pre-expulsion, unobtainable, fabulous. Always too good to drink – always being saved. And this was the diabolic result. Will, good old Will, he was wrapping the bottles in the Sunday Real Estate Section!

The room dissolved. Suddenly he was in the living room at Mary and Lou's new apartment. There was a party going on. How many weeks or months had gone by since the gruelling scene at his house, he had no means of knowing. That was the Hell of it.

The party looked pretty good. It was already 2 a.m. by the hall clock and no one showed the least sign of going. In fact, two more convivial couples were just coming in. He stepped aside but realized he didn't need to, as one of the new arrivals walked right through him. He saw Mary and Lou whispering together in a corner and sauntered over to eavesdrop.

"I tell you, hon, there isn't another drop of Bourbon in the house. There's about a half bottle of Scotch and no gin or vodka at all. What *can* we do?" And Will mopped his forehead and looked thoroughly miserable. He wasn't acting the bright, sophisticated host at all.

"Now, don't worry, dear, they just stayed too long, that's all. But, hey, how about that stuff of dad's – you know, those odd bottles!"

"Honey, you're a genius – they'll be too lit to know," and Lou raced upstairs. In the closet, on top of the summer shirts, were the Rainwater Madeira and the Tokay Essence. Lou rushed downstairs with them, to the bar, and pulled both corks with a flourish. As the spirit watched, frozen with horror, Lou poured a bit of the Madeira into a highball glass, took a swig, made a face and promptly spit it out. Next, the Tokay. He put a good slug into a highball glass, tasted, and murmured, "Ugh!". He added ice to the glass and reached for the 7-Up. This was too much. All the spirit's hackles rose. Son-in-law or no, this man was a Philistine. He screamed a noiseless scream, stretched out a fleshless arm, and struck the glass from the desecrator's hand!

At once the lights flashed, the thunder rolled, and forthwith he was once again seated in the Elysian restaurant. The captain-judge was smiling. He said, "Indeed, sir, you have atoned a gourmet's atonement. *Bon apétit!*"

The waiter arrived with the Châteaubriand, done *au point*. The Echézaux was perfect; the salad was exquisite; the dressing piquant; the cheese, creamy; the *soufflé*, risen yet moist; the coffee strong. He called the *sommelier* and ordered Tokay Essence!

ROBERT J. MISCH

One Way to Serve a Meal

The few, that would give out themselves, to be
Court and town-stallions, and each-where, belye
Ladies, who are known most innocent, for them;
Those will I beg, to make me Eunuchs of;
And they shall fan me with ten Estrich tailes
A piece, made in a plume to gather wind.
We will be brave, Puffe, now we ha' the Med'cine,
My meat, shall all come in, in Indian shels,
Dishes of Agate, set in gold, and studded,
With Emeralds, Sapphyres, Hiacinths, and Rubies.
The tongues of Carpes, Dormise, and Camels heeles
Boil'd i' the spirit of Sol, and dissolu'd Pearle.

BEN JONSON,
Sir Epicure Mammon in *The Alchemist*

The Dream

Last night I supped on lobster; it nearly drove me mad
For when at last I got to sleep a funny dream I had.

I dreamed the famous Albert Hall was turned into a pub,
And there was held a sort of Philharmonic club.
With poets, painters, politicians, famous statesmen too,
With actors, authors, clergymen, and ladies not a few.

Chorus
For everyone of them had to sing; if anyone said: "I've a cold."
"Sing or settle for drinks all round," they very soon were told.
The Prince of Wales was chairman, and of course he opened the Ball
And sang the chorus of every song at the concert in Albert Hall.

When Princess Beatrice rose to sing, with cheers the building rang,
"I'll never never marry if he's got no cash," she sang.
Then Henry, Prince of Battenburg, got up and made a bow
And sang in sweet harmonic tones: "I'm living with mother now."

Chorus
For everyone of them had to sing; if anyone said: "I've a cold,"
"Sing or settle for drinks all round," they very soon were told.
The Prince of Wales was chairman, and of course he opened the Ball
And sang the chorus of every song at the concert in Albert Hall.

Then Dizzy sang God Save the Queen, but Parnell hissed him down,
And Mr Gladstone tried to sing The Harp without a Crown.
But Chamberlain soon shut him up, for he sang: "Not for Joe;"
While Henry Churchill warbled: "Is it likely? O dear no."

Chorus
For every one of them had to sing; if anyone said "I've a cold,"
"Sing or settle for drinks all round," they very soon were told.
The Prince of Wales was chairman, and of course he opened the Ball
And sang the chorus of every song at the concert in Albert Hall.

Anon.

A drawing by Jean-Ignace Gérard (1803–47).

Anthropophagy

It is a melancholy object to those who walk through this great town [Dublin] or travel in the country, when they see the streets, the roads, and cabin doors, crowded with beggars of the female sex, followed by three, four, or six children, all in rags, and importuning every passenger for an alms. These mothers, instead of being able to work for their honest livelihood, are forced to employ all their time in strolling to beg sustenance for their helpless infants; who, as they grow up, either turn thieves for want of work, or leave their dear native country to fight for the Pretender in Spain, or sell themselves to the Barbados.

I think it is agreed by all parties that this prodigious number of children in the arms, or on the backs, or at the heels, of their mothers and frequently of their fathers, is in the present deplorable state of the kingdom a very great additional grievance; and therefore whoever could find out a fair, cheap, and easy method of making those children sound useful members of the commonwealth, would deserve so well of the public, as to have his statue set up for a preserver of the nation. . . .

. . . . I shall now therefore humbly propose my own thoughts, which I hope will not be liable to the least objection.

I have been assured by a very knowing American of my acquaintance in London, that a young healthy child, well nourished, is at a year old a most delicious, nourishing, and wholesome food, whether stewed, roasted, baked or boiled; and I make no doubt that it will equally serve in a *fricassee* or a *ragout*. . . .

. . . . A child will make two dishes at an entertainment for friends, and when the family dines alone, the fore or hind quarter will make a reasonable dish and, seasoned with a little pepper or salt, will be very good boiled on the fourth day, especially in winter.

I have reckoned upon a medium that a child just born will weigh 12 pounds, and in a solar year, if tolerably nursed, will increase to 28 pounds.

I grant this food will be somewhat dear, and therefore very proper for landlords who, as they have already devoured most of the parents, seem to have the best title to the children.

Infant's flesh will be in season throughout the year, but more plentifully in March, and a little before and after: for we are told by a grave author, an eminent French physician, that fish being a prolific diet, there are more children born in Roman catholic countries about nine months after Lent than at any other season; therefore, reckoning a year after Lent, the markets will be more glutted than usual because the number of Popish infants is at least three to one in this Kingdom; and therefore it will have one other collateral advantage, by lessening the number of Papists among us.

I have already computed the charge of nursing a beggar's child (in which list I reckon all cottagers, labourers, and four-fifths of the farmers) to be about 2*s*. per annum, rags included; and I believe no gentleman would repine to give 10*s*. for the carcase of a good fat child, which as I have said, will make four dishes of excellent nutritive meat, when he has only some particular friend or his own family to dine with him. Thus the squire will learn to be a good landlord, and grow popular among his tenants; the mother will have 8*s*. net profit, and be fit for work till she produces another child.

Those who are more thrifty (as I must confess the times require) may flay the carcase; the skin of which, artificially dressed, will make admirable gloves for ladies, and summer boots for fine gentlemen.

As to our city of Dublin, shambles may be appointed for this purpose in the most convenient parts of it, and butchers, we may be assured, will not be wanting; although I rather recommend buying the children alive, than dressing them hot from the knife as we do our roasting pigs.

A very worthy person, a true lover of his country, and whose virtues I highly esteem, was lately pleased, in discoursing on this matter, to offer a refinement upon my scheme. He said that many gentlemen of this kingdom having of late destroyed their deer, he conceived that the want of venison might be well supplied by the bodies of young lads and maidens, not exceeding 14 years of age, nor under 12; so great a number of both sexes in every country being now ready to starve for want of work and service; and these to be disposed of by their parents if alive, or otherwise by their nearest relations. But, with due deference to so excellent a friend and so deserving a patriot, I cannot be altogether in his sentiments; for as to the males, my American acquaintance assured me, from frequent experience, that their flesh was generally tough and lean, like that of our schoolboys by continual exercise, and their taste disagreeable; and to fatten them would not answer the charge. Then as to the females, it would, I think with humble submission, be a loss to the public, because they soon would become breeders themselves: and besides, it is not improbable that some scrupulous people might be apt to censure such a practice (although indeed very unjustly), as a little bordering upon cruelty; which, I confess, has always been with me the strongest objection against any project, how wellsoever intended.

But, in order to justify my friend, he confessed that this expedient was put into his head by the famous Psalmanazar, a native of the island Formosa, who came thence to London above twenty years ago; and in

conversation told my friend that in his country, when any young person
happened to be put to death, the executioner sold the carcase to persons
of quality as a prime dainty; and that in his time the body of a plump
girl of 15, who was crucified for an attempt to poison the emperor, was
sold to his imperial majesty's prime minister of state, and other great
mandarins of the court, in joints from the gibbet, at 400 crowns. Neither,
indeed, can I deny that if the same use were made of several plump
young girls in this town, who, without one single groat to their fortune
cannot stir abroad without a chair, and appear at playhouse and assemb-
lies in foreign fineries which they never will pay for, the kingdom would
not be the worse.

JONATHAN SWIFT,

*A Modest Proposal for Preventing the Children of Poor People in Ireland from Being a Burden
to their Parents or Country, and for Making them Beneficial to the Public* (1729)

Buttons

There was an old skinflint of Hitching
Had a cook, Mrs Casey, of Cork;
There was nothing but crusts in the kitchen,
While in parlour was sherry and pork.
So at last Mrs Casey, her pangs to assuage,
Having snipped off his buttonses, curried the page;
And now, while that skinflint gulps sherry and pork
In his parlour adjacent to Hitching,
To the tune blithe and merry of knife and of fork,
Anthropophagy reigns in the kitchen.

WALTER DE LA MARE

The Two Old Bachelors

Two old Bachelors were living in one house;
One caught a Muffin, the other caught a Mouse.
Said he who caught the Muffin to him who caught the Mouse,
"This happens just in time, for we've nothing in the house,
Save a tiny slice of lemon and a teaspoonful of honey,
And what to do for dinner, – since we haven't any money?
And what can we expect if we haven't any dinner
But to lose our teeth and eyelashes and keep on growing thinner?"

306

Said he who caught the Mouse to him who caught the Muffin,
"We might cook this little Mouse if we only had some Stuffin'.
If we had but Sage and Onion we could do extremely well,
But how to get that Stuffin' it is difficult to tell."

Those two old Bachelors ran quickly to the town
And asked for Sage and Onion, as they wandered up and down.
They borrowed two large Onions, but no Sage was to be found.
In the Shops or in the Market or in all the Gardens round.

But some one said "A hill there is, a little to the north,
And to its purpledicular top a narrow way leads forth;
And there among the rugged rocks abides an ancient Sage,
An earnest Man, who reads all day a most perplexing page.
Climb up and seize him by the toes, all studious as he sits,
And pull him down, and chop him into endless little bits.
Then mix him with your Onion (cut up likewise into scraps),
And your Stuffin' will be ready, and very good – perhaps."

Those two old Bachelors, without loss of time,
The nearly purpledicular crags at once began to climb;
And at the top among the rocks, all seated in a nook,
They saw that Sage a-reading of a most enormous book.
"You earnest Sage!" aloud they cried,
                    "your book you've read enough in,
We wish to chop you into bits and mix you into Stuffin'."

But that old Sage looked calmly up, and with his awful book
At those two Bachelors' bald heads a certain aim he took;
And over crag and precipice they rolled promiscuous down –
At once they rolled, and never stopped in lane or field or town;
And when they reached their house, they found
                    (besides their want of Stuffin')
The Mouse had fled – and previously had eaten up the Muffin.

They left their home in silence by the once convivial door;
And from that hour those Bachelors were never heard of more.

EDWARD LEAR

Eating Oysters

"O Oysters, come and walk with us!"
    The Walrus did beseech.
"A pleasant walk, a pleasant talk,
    Along the briny beach:
We cannot do with more than four,
    To give a hand to each."

The eldest Oyster looked at him,
    But never a word he said:
The eldest Oyster winked his eye,
    And shook his heavy head –
Meaning to say he did not choose
    To leave the oyster-bed.

But four young Oysters hurried up,
    All eager for the treat:
Their coats were brushed, their faces washed,
    Their shoes were clean and neat –
And this was odd, because, you know,
    They hadn't any feet.

Four other Oysters followed them,
    And yet another four;
And thick and fast they came at last,
    And more, and more, and more –
All hopping through the frothy waves,
    And scrambling to the shore.

The Walrus and the Carpenter
    Walked on a mile or so,
And then they rested on a rock
    Conveniently low:
And all the little Oysters stood
    And waited in a row.

"But not on us!" the Oysters cried,
    Turning a little blue.
"After such kindness, that would be
    A dismal thing to do!"
"The night is fine," the Walrus said.
    "Do you admire the view?

"The time has come," the Walrus said,
    "To talk of many things:
Of shoes – and ships – and sealing-wax –
    Of cabbages – and kings –
And why the sea is boiling hot –
    And whether pigs have wings."

"But, wait a bit," the Oysters cried,
    "Before we have our chat;
For some of us are out of breath,
    And all of us are fat!"
"No hurry!" said the Carpenter.
    They thanked him much for that.

"A loaf of bread," the Walrus said,
    "Is what we chiefly need:
Pepper and vinegar besides
    Are very good indeed –
Now if you're ready, Oysters dear,
    We can begin to feed."

"It was so kind of you to come!
    And you are very nice!"
The Carpenter said nothing but
    "Cut us another slice:
I wish you were not quite so deaf –
    I've had to ask you twice!"

"It seems a shame," the Walrus said,
    "To play them such a trick,
After we've brought them out so far,
    And made them trot so quick!"
The Carpenter said nothing but
    "The butter's spread too thick!"

"I weep for you," the Walrus said:
    "I deeply sympathize."
With sobs and tears he sorted out
    Those of the largest size
Holding his pocket-handkerchief
    Before his streaming eyes.

"O Oysters," said the Carpenter,
    "You've had a pleasant run!
Shall we be trotting home again?"
    But answer came there none –
And this was scarcely odd, because
    They'd eaten every one.

"I like the Walrus best," said Alice: "because, you see, he was a *little* sorry for the poor oysters."

"He ate more than the Carpenter, though," said Tweedledee. "You see, he held his handkerchief in front, so that the Carpenter couldn't count how many he took: contrariwise."

"That was mean!" Alice said indignantly. "Then I like the Carpenter best – if he didn't eat so many as the Walrus."

"But he ate as many as he could get," said Tweedledum.

LEWIS CARROLL,
Through the Looking-Glass

Not Exactly a Square Meal

My dinner was brought, and four persons of quality, whom I remembered to have seen very near the king's person, did me the honour to dine with me. We had two courses, of three dishes each. In the first course, there was a shoulder of mutton, cut into an equilateral triangle, a piece of beef into a rhomboid, and a pudding into a cycloid. The second course was two ducks trussed up into the form of fiddles; sausages and puddings resembling flutes and hautboys, and a breast of veal in the shape of a harp. The servants cut bread into cones, cylinders, parallelograms and several other mathematical figures.

JONATHAN SWIFT,
Gulliver's Travels

Moonshine

The stones of their grapes are exactly like hail; and I am perfectly satisfied that when a storm or high wind in the Moon shakes their vines, and breaks the grapes from the stalks, the stones fall down and form our hail showers. I would advise those who are of my opinion to save a quantity of these stones when it hails next, and make Lunarian wine. It is common beverage at St Luke's. Some material circumstances I had nearly omitted. They put their bellies to the same use as we do a sack, and throw whatever they have occasion for into it, for they can shut and open it again when they please, as they do their stomachs; they are not troubled with bowels, liver, heart, or any other intestines; neither are they encumbered with clothes, nor is there any part of their bodies unseemly or indecent to exhibit.

Original Travels and Surprising Adventures of Baron Munchausen (1785)

Ferdinando and Elvira

or

The Gentle Pieman

I

At a pleasant evening party I had taken down to supper
One whom I will call Elvira, and we talked of love and Tupper,
Mr Tupper and the poets, very lightly with them dealing,
For I've always been distinguished for a strong poetic feeling.
Then we let off paper crackers, each of which contained a motto,
And she listened while I read them, till her mother told her not to.
Then she whispered, "To the ball-room we had better, dear, be walking;
If we stop down here much longer, really people will be talking."
There were noblemen in coronets, and military cousins,
There were captains by the hundred, there were baronets by dozens.
Yet she heeded not their offers, but dismissed them with a blessing;
Then she let down all her back hair which had taken long in dressing.
Then she had convulsive sobbings in her agitated throttle,
Then she wiped her pretty eyes and smelt her pretty smelling-bottle.
So I whispered, "Dear Elvira, say – what can the matter be with you?
Does anything you've eaten, darling Popsy, disagree with you?"
But in spite of all I said, her sobs grew more and more distressing,
And she tore her pretty back hair, which had taken long in dressing.
Then she gazed upon the carpet, at the ceiling then above me,
And she whispered, "Ferdinando, do you really *really* love me?"
"Love you?" said I, then I sighed and then I gazed upon her sweetly –
For I think I do this sort of thing particularly neatly –
"Send me to the Arctic regions, or illimitable azure,
On a scientific goose-chase, with my Coxwell or my Glaisher.
"Tell me whither I may hie me, tell me, dear one, that I *may* know –
Is it up the highest Andes? down a horrible volcano?"
But she said, "It isn't polar bears, or hot volcanic grottoes,
Only find out who it is that writes those lovely cracker mottoes!"

II

"Tell me Henry Wadsworth, Alfred, Poet Close, or Mister Tupper,
Do you write the bonbon mottoes my Elvira pulls at supper?"
But Henry Wadsworth smiled, and said he had not had that honour;
And Alfred, too, disclaimed the words that told so much upon her.
"Mister Martin Tupper, Poet Close, I beg of you inform us,"
But my question seemed to throw them both into a rage enormous.
Mister Close expressed a wish that he could only get anigh to me.
And Mister Martin Tupper sent the following reply to me: –
"A fool is bent upon a twig, but wise men dread a bandit."
Which I think must have been clever, for I didn't understand it.
Seven weary years I wandered – Patagonia, China, Norway,
Till at last I sank exhausted at a pastrycook his doorway.
There were fuchsias and geraniums, and daffodils and myrtle,
So I entered, and I ordered half a basin of mock turtle.
He was plump and he was chubby, he was smooth and he was rosy,
And his little wife was pretty, and particularly cosy.
And he chirped and sang, and skipped about,
                                       and laughed with laughter hearty –
He was wonderfully active for so very stout a party.
And I said, "Oh, gentle pieman, why so very, very merry?
Is it purity of conscience, or your one-and-seven sherry?"
But he answered, "I'm so happy – no profession could be dearer –
If I am not humming 'Tra! la! la!' I'm singing, 'Tirer, lirer!'
"First I go and make the patties, and the puddings and the jellies,
Then I make a sugar birdcage, which upon a table swell is;
Then I polish all the silver, which a supper-table lacquers;
Then I write the pretty mottoes which you find inside the crackers" –
"Found at last!" I madly shouted. "Gentle pieman, you astound me!"
Then I waved the turtle soup enthusiastically round me.
And I shouted and I danced until he'd quite a crowd around him –
And I rushed away exclaiming, "I have found him! I have found him!"
And I heard the gentle pieman in the road behind me trilling,
" 'Tira! lira!' stop him, stop him! 'Tra! la! la!' the soup's a shilling!"
But until I reached Elvira's house, I never, never waited,
And Elvira to her Ferdinand's irrevocably mated!

W. S. GILBERT,
The Bab Ballads

Lunch with Aunt Jobiska

The Pobble who has no toes
    Was placed in a friendly Bark,
And they rowed him back, and carried him up
    To his Aunt Jobiska's Park.
And she made him a feast at his earnest wish
Of eggs and buttercups fried with fish; –
And she said, – "It's a fact the whole world knows,
"That Pobbles are happier without their toes."

EDWARD LEAR,
"The Pobble who has no Toes"

A Nightmare Lunch

An epic lunch – partaken in a dream –
With André Simon and Mr Neame
(Maurice Healy of legal fame
And A. J. Symons also came)
Wines and meats and little fishes
Combined to make delicious dishes
To put before these famous men –
Appended is a list of them.

Birds' nest soup and hot *hors-d'œuvre*,
Accompanied by Clicquot (Veuve):
The blending sounds a trifle curious,
Only one guest found it injurious:
Indeed he was so indisposed,
He murmured with his eyes fast closed,
"A this year's bird in last year's nest" –
Then died upon his neighbour's breast.

The chopped-up tails of mountain goats
Pounded with mint and quaker oats,
Proved a very favourite dish
('Twas handed round before the fish).
The trout was cooked in Corton Blanc –
At least one guest burst into song –
Then oysters from the Apennines
Served with a novel blend of wines

For fear the wine should not go round –
The reasoning was very sound –
A 1919 Montrachet
Was wedded to a "vin du pays".
From childhood's days we've learnt to know
Rough with the smooth must always go,
The only comment made was "Reely!"
It came from Mr Maurice Healy.

Sausages (Swiss) with cream and spice,
Garnished with snips of edelweiss.
Crocodiles' livers, a dainty rare,
Carefully packed and sent "by air".
Caviare served with the port,
Oh, surely an unusual thought
Proclaimed a genius was the host,
The subject of a special toast.

Epilogue
The guests retired with thankful hearts,
And even fuller other parts.
They were not seen for many days,
Alas! the gourmet always pays.

BETTY P. METCALFE,
Wine and Food, 2

Mélange

They sailed to the Western Sea, they did,
  To a land all covered with trees,
And they bought an Owl, and a useful Cart,
And a pound of Rice, and a Cranberry Tart,
  And a hive of silvery Bees.
And they bought a Pig, and some green Jack-daws,
And a lovely Monkey with lollipop paws,
  And forty bottles of Ring-Bo-Ree,
    And no end of Stilton Cheese.
      Far and few, far and few,
        Are the lands where the Jumblies live;
      Their heads are green, and their hands are blue,
        And they went to sea in a Sieve.

And in twenty years they all came back,
  In twenty years or more,
And every one said, "How tall they've grown!
For they've been to the Lakes, and the Terrible Zone,
  And the hills of the Chankley Bore";
And they drank their health, and gave them a feast
Of dumplings made of beautiful yeast;
And every one said, "If we only live,
We too will go to sea in a Sieve –
  To the hills of the Chankly Bore!"
    Far and few, far and few,
      Are the lands where the Jumblies live;
    Their heads are green, and their hands are blue,
      And they went to sea in a Sieve.

EDWARD LEAR,
"The Jumblies"

subtle wit

it is not the booze itself
that i regret so
much said the old brown
roach it is the
golden companionship of
the tavern myself
and my ancestors have been
chop house and tavern
roaches for hundreds of years
countless generations back
one of my elizabethan
forebears was plucked from
a can of ale in the
mermaid tavern by
will shakespeare and
put down kit marlowe s back
what subtle wits they were in
those days said i yes
he said and later
another one of my
ancestors was
introduced into a larded
hare that addison
was eating by dicky steele
my ancestor came
skurrying forth dicky
said is that your own
hare joe or a wig a
thing which addison
never forgave . . . .

DON MARQUIS,
archy and mehitabel

Index